SCHULMAN · CEREMONIAL EXECUTION

ORBIS BIBLICUS ET ORIENTALIS

Published by the Biblical Institute of the University
of Fribourg Switzerland
the Seminar für Biblische Zeitgeschichte
of the University of Münster i.W. Federal Republic of Germany
and the Schweizerische Gesellschaft
für orientalische Altertumswissenschaft
Editor: Othmar Keel
Coeditors: Erich Zenger and Albert de Pury

The Author:

Alan Richard Schulman was born in Brooklyn on 14.1.1930. He was
educated at the City College of New York (BA in Classical Languages
and Ancient History, 1952), the Oriental Institute of the University of
Chicago (MA in Egyptology, 1958), and the University of Pennsylvania
(PhD in Egyptology, 1962). He works as an Assistant in the Egyptian
Section of the University Museum from 1958–1962; taught Egyptology
as a Visiting Associate Professor at both Dropsie University and Tel
Aviv University, was an Instructor in History at Columbia University
and is currently Professor of Ancient and Military History at Queens
College and the Graduate Center of City University of New York. He
has participated in excavations in Egypt and Israel, is the author of
Military Rank, Title, and Organization in the Egyptian New Kingdom
(Berlin: 1964) and has contributed over seventy articles and numerous
book reviews to various scholarly periodicals including *The Journal of the
American Research Center in Egypt, The Journal of the Society for the Study
of Egyptian Antiquities, Toronto, Chronique d'Egypte, Israel Exploration
Journal, Tel Aviv, 'Atiqot, Zeitschrift für Ägyptische Sprache und Alter-
tumskunde, Bibliotheca Orientalis, The Journal of Near Eastern Studies,
The Bulletin of the Egyptological Seminar, Natural History,* and *Bollettino
del Centro Camuno di Studi Preistorici.*

ALAN R. SCHULMAN

CEREMONIAL EXECUTION AND PUBLIC REWARDS

Some Historical Scenes on New Kingdom Private Stelae

UNIVERSITÄTSVERLAG FREIBURG SCHWEIZ
VANDENHOECK & RUPRECHT GÖTTINGEN
1988

CIP-Kurztitelaufnahme der Deutschen Bibliothek

Alan R. Schulman:
Ceremonial Execution and Public Rewards. Some Historical
Scenes on New Kingdom Private Stelae / Alan R. Schulman.
– Freiburg, Schweiz: Universitätsverlag; Göttingen: Van-
denhoeck und Ruprecht, 1988.

(Orbis biblicus et orientalis; 75)
ISBN 3-525-53704-2 (Vandenhoeck und Ruprecht)
ISBN 3-7278-0548-X (Univ.-Verl.)
NE: GT

Publication subsidized
by the Swiss Academy of Humanities

ISBN 3-7278-0548-X (Universitätsverlag)
ISBN 3-525-53704-2 (Vandenhoeck & Ruprecht)

To the Memories of
Hilda Schulman, 1904-1986
Rudolf Anthes, 1896-1985

Table of Contents

Preface

My teacher and dear friend, the late Rudolf Anthes, was
fond of telling the following story about one of his colleagues
in Berlin. I think it was Spiegelberg. It seemed that whenever
a student would come up with a clearly absurd translation of a
text, or an ingenious solution to an Egyptological problem,
Spiegelberg would look at him squarely in the eye, muse for a
moment, and then say: "Yes...that _is_ possible. ... With God anything is possible". Even this book, but it would not have possible without the kindness and helpfulness of a number of friends
and colleagues who read the manuscript, discussed its contents
with me, provided me with both the photographs and the permissi-
ons to publish them in the plates, collated texts for me when it
was necessary and possible, and, in general, endured the barrages
of questions with which I assaulted them with the patience of the
Saints. Consequently it gives me great satisfaction to acknowledge here their thoughtfulness, kindness, and assistance, though
I, of course, am solely responsible for any flaws, faults, or er-
rors which may be present: Richard Fazzini, Jim Romano, and Diane
Gutzman of the Department of Egyptian and Classical Art and the
Wilbour Library of the Brooklyn Museum, Henry Fischer, Christine
Lilyquist, Ann Russman of the Department of Egyptian Art of the
Metropolitan Museum of Art, Herman de Meulenaere and C. de Wit of
the Egyptian Department of Musées Royaux d'Art et d'Histoire,
Brussels, the late Labib Habachi, Klaus Baer, and John A. Larsen
of the Oriental Institute of the University of Chicago, Louise
Berge and Maebetty Langdon of the Art Institute of Chicago, Susan
H. Auth of the Newark Museum, Wolfgang Müller and Karl-Heinz
Priese of the Aegyptisches Museum Berlin, DDR, Peter and Irmgard

Munro of the Kestner Museum, Hannover, Jaromir Málek and Helen
Murray of the Griffith Institute of the Ashmolean Museum, Oxford,
and Geoffrey T. Martin of University College, London. And, finally to my wife, Dalia and my children, 'Anath and Magen, without
whose patience and forbearance this book could never have been
written. To all of the above, individually and collectively I
tender my sincerest and deepest thanks.

Basically I am a historian. My training is essentially
Egyptological. What I am not is an artist or draftsman. The
line drawings which illustrate the individual stelae discussed
and catalogued in the text are not and do not pretend to be fac-
similies of the various monuments, but they do show everything
of the latter which I could see. In most cases I worked from a
combination of studying the original monument, my own photograph
of it, and the published photographs of it, but in some cases I
had to depend only on the published photograph or line drawing.
In such instances, however, this has been noted in the text. In
most instances my line drawings show both the scene and the text
of the individual stelae, but in a few instances I have shown
only the scene. In all cases of the published monuments, the
publications in which they appear are easily accessible and are
given as fully as possible. In the case of the unpublished documents I have included a photograph.

New York and Tel Aviv, 1986

Abbreviations

ARE	J.H. Breasted, Ancient Records of Egypt.
ASAE	Annales du service des antiquités de l'Égypte.
Atlas	W.Wreszinski, Atlas zur altägyptischen Kulturgeschichte.
BIFAO	Bulletin de l'Institut Français d'Archéologie Orientale.
CAH	Cambridge Ancient History. 3rd edition.
CdÉ	Chronique d'Égypte.
CRIPEL	Cahier de Recherches de l'Institut de Papyrologie et d'Égyptologie de Lille.
GM	Göttinger Miszellen.
JAOS	Journal of the American Oriental Society.
JARCE	Journal of the American Research Center in Egypt.
JEA	Journal of Egyptian Archaeology.
JNES	Journal of Near Eastern Studies.
KRI	K.A. Kitchen, Ramesside Inscriptions, Historical and Biographical.
LD	C.R. Lepsius, Denkmäler aus Aegypten und Aethiopien.
LdAe	Lexikon der Aegyptologie.
MDAIK	Mitteilungen des Deutschen Archäologischen Instituts Abteilung Kairo.
MIO	Mitteilungen des Instituts für Orientforschung.
PM	B. Porter, R. Moss, E.W. Birney, and J. Málek, Topographical Bibliography of Ancient Egyptian Hieroglyphic Texts, Reliefs, and Paintings.
PN	H. Ranke, Die ägyptische Personennamen.
PSBA	Proceedings of the Society of Biblical Archaeology.
Rec. trav.	Recueil de travaux relatifs à la philologie et à l'archéologie égyptiennes et assyriennes.
Rev. d'Egy.	Revue d'Égyptologie.

Bibliography

Aimé-Giron, N. "Adversaria Semitica (III)", ASAE 40 (1941) 433–460, pls. 30-42.

Aldred, C. Jewels of the Pharaohs. abridged ed. (New York: 1979).

Allam, S. Hieratische Ostraka und Papyri aus der Ramessidenzeit. (Tübingen: 1973).

Allen, T.G. Egyptian Stelae in the Field Museum of Natural History. (Chicago: 1936).

_____. A Handbook of the Egyptian Collection. (Chicago: 1923).

Aly, M., F. Abdel-Hamid, and M. Dewachter, Le temple d'Amada IV. (Cairo: 1967).

Arkell, A.J. A History of the Sudan from the Earliest Times to 1821. 2nd ed. (London: 1961).

Arnold, D. Wandrelief und Raumfunktion in ägyptischen Tempeln des Neuen Reiches. (Berlin: 1962).

Avdiev, V.I. "Religionznoje opravdanie vojny v drevneegipetskom iskusstuie, Sceny triumfa", VDI 4 (9) 1939, 103-117.

Badawy, A. A History of Egyptian Architecture. The Empire (the New Kingdom). From the Eighteenth Dynasty to the End of the Twentieth. 1580-1085 B.C. (Berkeley: 1968).

_____. "A Monumental Gateway for a Temple of King Sety I, An Ancient Model Restored", Miscellanea Wilbouriana 1 (1972) 1-20.

Barguet, P. "Au sujet d'une représentation du ka royal", ASAE 51 (1951) 98-101.

Barta, W. "Zwei ramessidische Stelen aus dem Wadi Sannûr", MDAIK 20 (1965) 98-101.

Bass, G. Cape Gelidonya: A Bronze Age Shipwreck. (Philadelphia: 1967).

Berend, W. Principaux monuments de Musée égyptien de Florence. (Paris: 1882).

Blackman, A.M. The Temple of Derr. (Cairo: 1913).

Blok, H. "Remarques sur quelques stèles dites 'à oreilles'", Kemi 1 (1928) 123-135.

Boeser, P. Denkmäler des Neuen Reiches: Dritte Abteilung. Stelen. (Leiden: 1913).

Bogoslovskaya, I.V. "The Dress of Ethnic Groups Settled in Canaan as Depicted in Egyptian Art of the Sixteenth to Twelfth Centuries B.C." (Russian), VDI 3 (153) 1980, 117-141.

Bonnet, H. Die Waffen der Völker des Alten Orients. (Leipzig: 1913).

Borchardt, L. Das Grabdenkmal des Königs Sahu-Re'. II (Leipzig: 1913).

Boreux, Ch. Musée nationale du Louvre: Départment des antiquités égyptiennes: guide-catalogue sommaire. I (Paris: 1932).

Bosticco, S. Museo Archeologico di Firenze. Le stele egiziane. 3 vols. (Florence: 1965-1972).

Bouriant, U., G. Legrain, and G. Jequier, Monuments pour servir à l'étude du culte d'Atonou en Égypte. (Cairo: 1913).

Botti, G. and P. Romanelli, Le Sculture del Museo Gregoriano Egizio. (Vatican City: 1951).

Breasted, J.H. Ancient Records of Egypt. 5 vols. (Chicago: 1906).

British Museum, A Guide to the Fourth, Fifth and Sixth Egyptian Rooms and the Coptic Room. (London: 1922).

_____. Hieroglyphic texts from Egyptian stelae, etc. in the British Museum. 10 vols. (London: 1911-   ).

Brunner-Traut, E. Die altägyptischen Scherbenbilder (Bildostraka) der Deutscher Museen und Sammlungen. (Wiesbaden: 1956).

_____. Egyptian Artists' Sketches. (Leiden: 1979).

Bruyère, B. Deir el Médineh Année 1926. Sondage au temple funéraire de Thòtmes II (Hat Ankh Shepset). Cairo: 1952.

_____. "Quelques stèles trouvées par M. É. Baraize à Deir
el Médineh", ASAE 25 (1925) 76-96.

_____. Rapport sur les fouilles de Deir el Médineh (1934-
1935): troisième parte. (Cairo: 1939).

_____. Rapport sur les fouilles de Deir el Médineh (1935-
1940). (Cairo: 1940).

Bryan, B.M. The Reign of Tuthmosis IV. (unpublished Yale Ph. D.
dissertation. New Haven: 1980).

Budge, E.A.W. A Guide to the Egyptian Galleries (Sculpture).
(London: 1909).

Caminos, R.A. The Shrines and Rock-Inscriptions of Ibrim. (London: 1968).

Capart, J. "Ostraca illustrant des textes littéraires", CdE 16
(1941) 190-195.

_____. "Stèles égyptiennes", Bulletin des Musées Royaux des
arts décoratifs et industriels 4 (1913) 49-51.

Carter, H. The Tomb of Tut.ankh.Amen, Discovered by the Late Earl
of Carnarvon and Howard Carter. III (London: 1933).

Černý, J. A Community of Workmen at Thebes in the Ramesside Period. (Cairo: 1973).

_____. "Egypt from the Death of Ramesses III to the End of
the Twenty-First Dynasty", CAH 3rd ed. II chapter 35.

_____. "Egyptian Oracles" in R.A. Parker, A Saite Oracle Pa-
pyrus in the Brooklyn Museum. (Providence: 1962) 35-48.

_____. Egyptian Stelae in the Bankes Collection. (Oxford:
1958).

_____. "Le culte d'Amenophis Ier chez les ouvriers de la

nécropole thébaine", BIFAO 27 (1927) 159-203.

_____. Le temple d'Amada. Cahier V. Les inscriptions histor-
iques. (Cairo: 1967).

_____. Review of W. Helck, Zur Verwaltung des Mittleren und
Neuen Reiches in Bibliotheca Orientalis 19 (1962) 140-144.

_____, A.H. Gardiner, and T.E.Peet, The Inscriptions of Sin-
ai. 2nd ed. (London: 1952).

Chevrier, H. "Rapport sur les travaux de Karnak (1952-1953)",
ASAE 53 (1955) 7-19.

Cooney, J.D. Amarna Reliefs from Hermopolis in American Collections. (Brooklyn: 1965).

Daressy, G. "Tombeaux et stèles-limites de Hagi-Qandil", Rec.
trav. 15 (1893) 36-62.

David, A.R. Religious Ritual at Abydos. (Warminster: 1973).

Davies, N.D.G. "Akhenaton at Thebes", JEA 9 (1923) 132-152.

_____, "The Graphic Work of the Expedition" in "The Egyptian
Expedition 1928-1929", Bulletin of the Metropolitan Museum
of Art (November 1929) 35-49.

_____. "The Work of the Graphic Branch of the Expedition" in
"The Egyptian Expedition 1929-1930", ibid. (December 1930)
29-42.

_____. The Rock Tombs of El Amarna. 6 vols. (London: 1903-
1908).

_____. The Tomb of Ken-Amun at Thebes. (New York: 1930).

_____. The Tomb of Nefer-Hotep at Thebes. (New York: 1933).

_____. The Tomb of Two Sculptors at Thebes. (New York: 1925).

_____. The Tomb of the Vizier Ramose. (London: 1941).

_____. The Tombs of Two Officials of Tuthmosis the Fourth
(nos. 75 and 90). (London: 1923).

_____. Two Ramesside Tombs at Thebes. (New York: 1927).

De Morgan, J. Catalogue des monuments et inscriptions de l'Égypte antique. I (Cairo: 1894).

Dewachter, M. "Remarques à propos d'huisseries en pierre retrouvées au temple Nord de Ouadi es-Séboua", CRIPEL 7 (1985) 23-37.

Drioton, E. "Recueil de cryptographie monumentale", ASAE 40 (1940) 305-429.

Dunham, D. "Four New Kingdom Monuments in the Museum of Fine Arts, Boston", JEA 21 (1935) 147-151.

Edgerton, W.F. and J.A. Wilson, Historical Records of Ramses III. (Chicago: 1936).

Epigraphic Survey, The Battle Reliefs of King Sety I. (Chicago: 1986).

_____. Medinet Habu I. The Earlier Historical Records of Ramesses III. (Chicago: 1930).

_____. Medinet Habu II. The Later Historical Records of Ramesses III. (Chicago: 1932).

Erman, A. "Denksteine aus der thebanische Gräberstadt", Sitzungberichte der preussischen Akademie der Wissenschaften zu Berlin, phil.-hist. Kl. (Berlin: 1911) 1086-1110.

_____. Neuägyptische Grammatik. 2nd ed. (Leipzig: 1933).

_____. Die Religion der Aegypter. (Berlin: 1934).

_____. "Zwei Weihgeschenke aus der thebanischen Nekropole", Amtliche Berichte aus den Königl. Kunstsammlungen 33 (1911-1912) 15-20.

_____. and H. Grapow, eds. Wörterbuch der ägyptischen Sprache im Auftrage der deutschen Akademien. new unchanged impression. (Berlin: 1955).

Ertman, E. "The Gold of Honor in Royal Representation", Newsletter of the American Research Center in Egypt 83 (Oct. 1972)

26-27.

Fairman, H.W. The Triumph of Horus: An Ancient Egyptian Sacred Drama. (London: 1974).

Fakhry, A. "A Note on the Tomb of Kheruef at Thebes", ASAE 42 (1943) 447-508.

Faulkner, R.O. "Egypt from the Inception of the Nineteenth Dynasty to the Death of Ramesses III", CAH 3rd ed. (1976) II chapter 23.

_____. "The Wars of Sethos I", JEA 33 (1947) 34-39.

Federn, W. "Ḥtp (r)dj(w) (n) ꞽInpw: zum Verständnis der vor-osirianischen Opferformel", MDAIK 16 (1958) 120-130.

_____. "Roi ou statue royale?", CdÉ 34 (1959) 214.

Feucht, E. Die königlichen Pektorale. (Dissertation Munich: 1967).

Fischer, H.G. "The Nubian Mercenaries of Gebelein", Kush 9 (1961) 44-80.

_____. "Redundant Determinatives in the Old Kingdom", The Metropolitan Museum of Art Journal 8 (1975) 7-24.

Gaballa, G.A. Narrative in Egyptian Art. (Mainz am Rhein: 1976).

_____. "Some Nineteenth Dynasty Monuments in the Cairo Museum", BIFAO 71 (1972) 129-137.

Gabra, S. Les conseils de fonctionnaires dans l'Égypte pharaoniques. Scenes de recompenses royales aux fonctionnaires. (Cairo: 1929).

Gardiner, A.H. Ancient Egyptian Onomastica. 2 vols. (Oxford: 1947).

_____. Egypt of the Pharaohs. (Oxford: 1961).

_____. Egyptian Grammar. 3rd ed. (Oxford: 1957).

_____. "Tuthmosis III Returns Thanks to Amun", JEA 38 (1952) 6-23.

Gauthier, H. Dictionnaire des noms géographiques contenus dans les textes hiéroglyphiques. 6 vols. (Cairo: 1925-1929).

_____. "Les 'Fils Royaux de Kouch' et le personnel adminis-
tratif de l'Éthiopie", Rec. trav. 39 (1921) 179-238.

Giveon, R. "Tuthmosis IV and Asia", JNES 28 (1969) 54-59.

Goyon, J.C. Rituels funéraires de l'ancienne Égypte. (Cairo: 1972).

Grdseloff, B. Les debuts du culte de Rechef en Égypte. (Cairo:
1942).

Habachi, L. Features of the Deification of Ramesses II. (Glückstadt: 1969).

_____. "The Graffiti and Work of the Viceroys of Kush in the
Region of Aswan", Kush 5 (1957) 13-36.

_____. "Khataʿna-Qantir: Importance", ASAE 52 (1954) 443-562.

_____. "King Amenmesse and Viziers Amenmose and Khaʿemtore:
Their Monuments and Place in History", MDAIK 34 (1978) 57-
67.

_____. "The Military Posts of Ramesses II on the Coastal Road
and the Western Part of the Delta", BIFAO 80 (1980) 13-20.

_____. "The Qantir Stela of the Vizier Rahotep and the Statue
Ruler-of-Rulers", Festgabe für Dr. Walter Will Ehrensenator
der Universität München. (Köln: 1966) 67-77.

Hall, E.S. "The Pharaoh Slays his Foes" (unpublished manuscript in
the Brooklyn Museum).

Hall, H.R. A Catalogue of Egyptian Scarabs, etc. in the British
Museum. I (London: 1913).

Hassan, S. The Great Sphinx and Its Secrets. (Cairo: 1953).

Hayes, W.C. The Scepter of Egypt. II (New York: 1959).

Helck, W. "Abgeschnitten Hände als Siegeszeichen", GM 18 (1975)
23-24.

_____. "Das Dekret des Königs Haremheb", ZAeS 80 (1955) 109-
136.

_____. "Die Inschrift über die Belohnung des Hohenpriesters ʿImn-ḥtp", MIO 4 (1956) 161-178.

_____. Historische-Biographische Texte der 2. Zwischenzeit und Neue Texte der 18. Dynastie. (Wiesbaden: 1975).

_____. Urkunden der 18. Dynastie. Uebersetzung zur den Heften 17-22. (Berlin: 1961).

_____. "Zum Kult am Königsstatuen", JNES 25 (1966) 32-41.

_____. Zur Verwaltung des Mittleren und Neuen Reiches. (Leiden: 1958).

_____, and E. Otto, Kleines Wörterbuch der Aegyptologie. (Wiesbaden: 1956).

_____, ed. Lexikon der Aegyptologie. (Wiesbaden: 1975-   ).

Hermann, A. "Jubel bei Audienz. Zur Gebardensprache in der Kunst des Neuen Reiches", ZAeS 90 (1963) 49-66.

_____. "Das Motiv der Ente mit zurückgewendeten Kopfe im ägyptischen Kunstgewerbe", ZAeS 68 (1932) 86-105.

Hintze, F. "Die Felsenstele Sethos I bei Qasr Ibrim", ZAeS 87 (1962) 31-40.

Hölscher, U. The Mortuary Temple of Ramesses III. II (Chicago: 1951).

Ippel, A. and G. Roeder, Die Denkmäler des Pelizaeus-Museums zu Hildesheim. (Hildesheim: 1921).

Jequier, G. Le monument funéraire de Pépi II. (Cairo: 1938).

Kamal, A. "Rapport sur les fouilles du Comte du Galarza", ASAE 10 (1910) 117-118.

Kayser, H. Die ägyptische Altertümer im Roemer-Pelizaeus Museum in Hildesheim. (Hildesheim: 1973).

_____. "Söhne des Sonnengottes", Zeitschrift des Museums zu Hildesheim. NF 23 (1971) 43-44.

Kees, H. "Bemerkungen zum Tieropfer der Aegypter und seiner Symbolik", <u>Nachrichten der Akademie der Wissenschaften zu Göttingen. Phil.-Hist. Kl.</u> (1942) nr. 2, 71-88.

Kemp, B.J. "The Window of Appearance at El-Amarna and the Basic Structure of the City", <u>JEA</u> 62 (1976) 81-99.

Kitchen, K.A. "Historical Observations on Ramesside Nubia" in E. Endeselder et ali. eds. <u>Aegypten und Kusch</u>. (Berlin: 1977) 40-48.

_____. <u>Ramesside Inscriptions, Historical and Biographical</u>. 7 vols. (Oxford: 1969-   ).

_____ and G.A.Gaballa, "Ramesside Varia II", <u>ZAeS</u> 96 (1969) 14-28.

Koefoed-Petersen, O. <u>Les stèles égyptiennes</u>. (Copenhagen: 1948).

_____. Recueil des inscriptions hiéroglyphiques de la Glyptothek <u>Ny Carlsberg</u>. (Brussels: 1936).

Königliche Museen zu Berlin, <u>Ausführliches Verzeichnis der ägyptischen Altertümer und Gipsabgüsse</u>. 2nd ed. (Berlin: 1929).

Lacau, P. <u>Les stèles du Nouvelle Empire</u>. (Cairo: 1909-1957).

Leclant, J. "La 'famille libyenne' au temple haut de Pépi Ier", <u>Livre du centenaire</u> (Cairo: 1980) 49-54.

_____. "Fouilles et travaux en Égypte 1952-1953", <u>Orientalia</u> 23 (1954) 64-79.

_____. "La 'Mascarade' des boeufs gras et le triomphe de l'Égypte", <u>MDAIK</u> 14 (1956) 129-145.

Ledrain, E. <u>La stèle du Collier d'or</u>. (Paris: 1876).

_____. Les monuments égyptiennes de la Bibliothèque Nationale. (Paris: 1879-1891).

Lefebvre, G. <u>Inscriptions concernant les grandes prêtres d'Amon Romê-Roy et Amenhotep</u>. (Paris: 1929).

Leiblein, J. <u>Dictionnaire des noms hiéroglyphiques en ordre généalogique et alphabetique</u>. I (Christiana: 1871).

Lepsius, C.R. Denkmäler aus Aegypten und Aethiopien. 12 vols. (Berlin: 1849-1859).

Lesko, L.H. "The Wars of Ramses III", Serapis 6 (1980) 83-86.

Liebowitz, H.A. "Horses in New Kingdom Art and the Date of an Ivory from Megiddo", JARCE 6 (1967) 129-134.

Loat, W.L.S. Gurob. (London: 1905).

Lutz, H.F. Egyptian tomb steles and offering stones of the Museum of Anthropology and Ethnology of the University of California. (Berkeley: 1927).

Macadam, M.F.L. The Temples of Kawa. II. History and Archaeology of the Site. (Oxford: 1955).

Mariette, A. Monuments divers recueilles en Égypte et en Nubie. (Paris: 1879).

Matiegka, L. "Individual Characteristics of Figures on the Egyptian Stelae", Archiv Orientální 20 (1952) 15-27.

Meulenaere, H. de. Le règne du Soleil. Akhenaton et Néfertiti. (Brussels: 1975).

Mogensen, M. "A Stela of the XVIIIth or XIXth Dynasty with a Hymn to Ptah and Sekhmet", PSBA 35 (1913) 37-40.

Mohammed, M. Abdul-Kader, "The Administration of Syro-Palestine during the New Kingdom", ASAE 56 (1959) 105-137.

_____. The Development of the Funerary Beliefs and Practices Displayed in the Private Tombs of the New Kingdom at Thebes. (Cairo: 1966).

Moret, A. Catalogue du Musée Guimet, Galerie Égyptienne, stèles, bas-reliefs, monuments divers. (Paris: 1901).

Munro, P. "Untersuchungen zur altägyptischen Bildmetrik", Städel-Jahrbuch NF 3 (1971) 7-42.

Murnane, W.J. Ancient Egyptian Coregencies. (Chicago: 1977).

Muscarella, O.W. "Ziwye and Ziwye: the Forgery of a Provenience",

Journal of Field Archaeology 4 nr. 2 (1977) 197-218.

Noblecourt, C.D., S. Donadoni, and E. Edel, *Grand temple d.'Abou Simbel: la bataille de Qadech*. (Cairo: 1971).

Otto, E. *Die ägyptische Mundöffnungsritual*. (Wiesbaden:1960).

Petersen, B.J. "Aegyptische Stelen und Stelenfragmente aus Stockholmer Sammlungen", *Opuscula Atheniensia* 9 (1969) 95-123.

_____. *Zeichnungen aus einer Totenstadt*. (**Stockholm**: 1973).

Petrie, W.M.F. *Gizeh and Rifeh*. (London: 1907).

_____. Hyksos and Israelite Cities. (London: 1906).

_____. *Memphis I*. (London: 1909).

_____. *Riqqeh and Memphis VI*. (London: 1915.

Pflüger, K. "The Edict of King Haremhab", *JNES* 5 (1946) 260-276.

_____. "The Private Funerary Stelae of the Middle Kingdom and their Importance for the Study of Ancient Egyptian History", *JAOS* 67 (1947) 127-135.

Pierret, P. *Recueil d'inscriptions inédités du Musée du Louvre*. II (Paris: 1878).

Pijoan, J. *Summa Artis. Historia General del Arte. 3. El arte egipcio hasta la conquesta romana*. 2nd ed. (Madrid: 1945).

Platt, A.F.R. "Notes on the Stela of Sekhmetmer", *PSBA* 35 (1914) 129-132.

Porter, B., R. Moss, and E.W. Birney, *Topographical Bibliography of Ancient Egyptian Hieroglyphic Texts, Reliefs and Paintings*. 7 vols. (Oxford: 1927-   ).

Pörtner, B. *Aegyptische Grabsteine und Denksteine aus Athen und Konstantinopel*. (Strassburg: 1908).

Posener, G. ed. *Dictionary of Egyptian Civilization*. (New York: 1959).

Pritchard, J.B. ed. *Ancient Near Eastern Pictures Relating to the Old Testament*. (Princeton: 1954).

_____. "Syrians as Pictured in the Paintings of the Theban Tombs", <u>Bulletin of the American Schools of Oriental Research</u> 122 (1951) 36-41.

Ramond, P. <u>Les stèles égyptiennes du Musée G. Labit à Toulouse</u>. (Cairo: 1977).

Ranke, H. <u>Die ägyptischen Personennamen</u>. 2 vols. (Glückstadt: 1935-1952).

_____. <u>The Egyptian Collections of the University Museum</u>. (Philadelphia: 1950).

Redford, D.B. "The Chronology of the Egyptian Eighteenth Dynasty", <u>JNES</u> 25 (1960) 113-124.

Ricke, H., G.R. Hughes, and E.F.Wente, <u>The Beit el-Wali Temple of Ramesses II</u>. (Chicago: 1967).

Riefstahl, E. "An Egyptian Portrait of an Old Man", <u>JNES</u> 10 (1951) 65-73.

Rijksmuseum van Oudheden, Leiden. <u>Kunst voor de Eeuwigheid</u>. (Leiden: 1960).

Roeder, G. <u>Der Felsentempel von Bet el-Wali</u>. (Cairo: 1935).

_____. <u>Hermopolis 1929-1939</u>. (Hildesheim: 1959).

_____. "Ramses II als Gott", <u>ZÄeS</u> 61 (1926) 57-67.

_____. "Der Schmuckwert der ägyptischen Hieroglyphen", <u>Buch und Schrift</u> 3 (1928) 83-88.

_____, ed. <u>Aegyptische Inschriften aus den Königlichen Museen zu Berlin</u>. II (Berlin: 1914).

Rosellini, I. <u>Oggetti di antichita egiziane riportati dalla spezione letteraria Toscana in Egitto e in Nubia</u>. (Florence: 1830).

Rowe, A. <u>A Catalogue of Egyptian Scarabs, Scaraboids, Seals, and Amulets in the Palestine Archaeological Museum</u>. (Cairo: 1936).

_____. The Topography and History of Beth-Shan. (Philadelphia: 1930).

Saleh, J.M. Les antiquités égyptiennes de Zagreb. (Paris: 1970).

Sandman, M. Texts from the Time of Akhenaton. (Brussels: 1938).

Sandman-Holmberg, M. The God Ptah. (Lund: 1948).

Säve-Söderbergh, T. Aegypten und Nubien. (Lund: 1941).

El-Sayed, R. "Stèles des particuliers relatives au culte rendu au statues royales de la XVIIIe dynastie à la XXe dynastie", BIFAO 79 (1979) 155-166.

Schäfer, H. "Aus einem ägyptischen Kriegslager", Amtliche Berichte aus den preussischen Kunstsammlungen 40 (1919) 157-158.

_____. "Das Niederschlagen der Feinde. Zur Geschichte eines ägyptischen Sinnbildes", WZKM 54 (1957) 168-176.

_____. "Der König im Fenster. Ein Beitrag zum Nachleben der Kunst von Tell El-Amarna", Amtliche Berichte aus den preussichen Kunstsammlungen 49 nr. 9 (1928) 34-40.

Schott, S. "Ein ungewohnliches Symbol des Triumphes über Feinde Aegyptens", JNES 14 (1955) 96-98.

Schmidt, J.D. Ramesses III: A Chronological Structure for His Reign. (Baltimore: 1973).

Schulman, A.R. "'Ankhesenamūn, Nofretity, and the Amka Affair", JARCE 15 (1978) 43-48.

_____. "Aspects of Ramesside Diplomacy: The Treaty of Year 21", The SSEA Journal 8 (1977-1978) 112-130.

_____. "Beyond the Fringe: Sources for Old Kingdom Foreign Affairs", The SSEA Journal 9 (1979) 79-104.

_____. "A Cult of Ramesses III at Memphis", JNES 22 (1963) 177-184.

_____. "The Iconographic Theme: 'Opening of the Mouth' on Stelae", JARCE 21 (1984) 169-196.

_____. "A Memphite Stela, the Bark of Ptah, and Some Icono-
graphic Comments", Bulletin of the Egyptological Seminar 2
(1980) 83-109.

_____. The Military Establishment of the Egyptian Empire.
(unpublished MA thesis, Chicago: 1958).

_____. Military Rank, Title, and Organization in the Egypt-
ian New Kingdom. (Berlin: 1964).

_____. "The Nubian War of Akhenaton", in L'Égyptologie en
1979: axes prioritaires des recherches. II (Paris: 1982)
299-316.

_____. "A Private Triumph in Brooklyn, Hildesheim and Ber-
lin", JARCE 7 (1968) 27-35.

_____. "Reshep Times Two", in W.K.Simpson and W.M.Davis, eds.
Studies in Ancient Egypt, the Aegean, and the Sudan. Essays
in honor of Dows Dunham on the occasion of his 90th birthday, June 1, 1980. (Boston: 1980) 157-166.

_____. "The Royal Butler Ramessesemperre'", JARCE 13 (1970)
117-130.

_____. "The Royal Butler Ramessessami'on", CdE 61 (1986 in
press).

_____. "Setau at Memphis", The SSEA Journal 8 (1977-1978)
42-44.

_____. "Siege Warfare in Pharaonic Egypt", Natural History
78 (March 1964) 12-21.

_____. "Two Unrecognized Monuments of Shedsunefertem", JNES
39 (1980) 303-311.

_____. "The Winged Reshep", JARCE 16 (1981) 157-166.

Seton, D.R. The king of Egypt annihilating his enemies: a study
in the symbolism of ancient monarchy. (Unpublished MA thesis, Birmingham: 1971-1972).

Sharpe, S. Egyptian Inscriptions from the British Museum and Other Sources. 2nd series. (London: 1841).

Simpson, W.K. The Terrace of the Great God at Abydos: the Offering Chapels of Dynasties 12 and 13. (New Haven: 1974).

Śliwa, J. "Some Remarks Concerning Victorious Ruler Representations", Forschungen und Berichte 16 (1974) 97-117.

_____. "Zagadnienie przedstawieńzwycięskiego władcy w sztuce egipskiej" (The Problem of the Representations of the Victorious Ruler in the Egyptian Art), Zeszyty Naukowe Uniwersytetu Jagiellońskiego 330 (1973) 7-22.

Smith, H.S. The Fortress of Buhen: The Inscriptions. (London: 1970).

Smith, R.W., and D.B.Redford, The Akhenaton Temple Project I. Initial Discoveries. (Warminister: 1976).

Spalinger, A.J. "A Fragmentary Biography", The SSEA Journal 10 (1979-1980) 215-228.

_____. "The Northern Wars of Seti I: An Integrative Study", JARCE 16 (1979) 29-47.

_____. "Traces of the Early Career of Ramesses II", JNES 38 (1979) 276-281.

Speelers, L. Recueil des inscriptions égyptiennes des Musées Royaux du Cinquantenaire à Bruxelles. (Brussels: 1923).

Spiegelberg, W. Aegyptische und Andere Graffiti (Inschriften und Zeichnungen) aus den thebanischen Nekropolis. (Heidelberg: 1921).

_____, B.Pörtner, and K.Dryoff, Aegyptische Grabsteine und Denksteine aus süddeutschen Sammlungen. 3 vols. (Strassburg: 1902-1906).

Staatliche Museen Preussischer Kulturbesitz. Aegyptische Museum Berlin. (Berlin: 1967).

Stadelmann, R. "Tempelpalast und Erscheinungsfenster in der the-banischen Totentempeln", MDAIK 29 (1973) 221-242.

Steindorff, G. "Vier Grabstelen aus der Zeit Amenophis IV", ZAeS 34 (1896) 63-69.

Szafranski, Z.M. "Problematyka stel 2 drugiego okreu przejściowe-go pochodzących z Edfu w zbiorach Muzeum Narodowego w Wars-zawie" (Problems of Stelae of the Second Intermediate Peri-od Originating from Edfu in the Collection of the National Museum of Warsaw), Rocznik Muzeum Narodowego w Warszawie 24 (1980) 7-62.

Tosi, R. and A. Roccati, Stele e altere epigraffi di Deir el Me-dina. (Turin: 1972).

Trigger, B.G. "The Narmer Palette in Cross-Cultural Perspective", in M. Görg and E. Pusch, eds. Festschrift Elmar Edel 12 März 1979. (Bamberg: 1979) 409-419.

Tylor, J.J. and F.L. Griffith, The Tomb of Paheri at El Kab. (London: 1894).

Urkunden des ägyptischen Altertums. IV. Urkunden der 18. Dynastie. (Leipzig and Berlin: 1927-1957).

Vandier, J. Manuel d'archéologie égyptienne. II-IV (Paris: 1954-1964).

Vandier d'Abbadie, J. Catalogue des ostraca figurés de Deir el Médineh (nos. 2256 a 2722) (Cairo: 1937).

_____. Catalogue des ostraca figurés de Deir el Médineh (nos. 2734 a 3053). (Cairo: 1959).

Vercoutter, J. "Une campagne militaire de Seti I en Haute Nubie", Rev. d'Eg. 24 (1972) 201-208.

Von Deines, H. "Das Gold der Tapferkeit: eine militärisch Aus-zeichnung oder eine Belohnung?", ZAeS 79 (1954) 83-86.

Wente, E.F. "Shekelesh or Shasu?", JNES 22 (1963) 167-172.

Wiedemann, A. "On Some Egyptian Inscriptions in the Musee Guimet
     at Paris", PSBA 14 (1892) 332-335.

Wildung, D. Die Rolle ägyptische Könige im Bewusstsein ihrer
     Nachwelt. I (Berlin: 1969).

_____. Egyptian Saints: Deification in Pharaonic Egypt. (New
     York: 1977).

Wilkinson, A. Ancient Egyptian Jewellery. (London: 1971).

Wilkinson, J.G. The Manners and Customs of the Ancient Egyptians.
     3 vols. new edition, revised by S. Birch. (New York: 1878).

Williams, C.L.R. Gold and silver jewelry and related objects.
     (New York Historical Society: Catalogue of the Egyptian
     antiquities. Numbers 1-160). (New York: 1924).

Wilson, J.A. "The Royal Myth in Ancient Egypt", Proceedings of
     the American Philosophical Society 100 nr. 5 (1956) 439-442.

Wreszinski, W. Atlas zur altägyptischen Kulturgeschichte. I-II
     (Leipzig: 1914-1935).

Woldering, I. Ausgewählte Werke der ägyptischen Sammlung. 2nd
     ed. (Hannover: 1958).

Yadin, Y. The Art of Warfare in Biblical Lands in the Light of
     Archaeological Study. 2 vols. (New York: 1963).

Youssef, A. Abd-El-Hamid, "Merneptah's fourth year Text at Amada",
     ASAE 58 (1964) 273-280.

Yoyotte, J. "Les stèles de Ramses II á Tanis. Ier partie". Kemi
     10 (1949) 60-74.

Žaba, Z. Les maximes de Ptahhotep. (Prague: 1956).

Zibelius, K. Afrikanischer Orts- und Völkernamen in hieroglyph-
     ischen und hieratischen Texten. (Wiesbaden: 1972).

Zivie, C.M. Giza au deuxième millénaire. (Cairo: 1976).

Introduction

To tell the truth, while there have been some hundreds of studies of individual stelae and collections of monuments of this kind, these have usually been made from a single viewpoint, artistic, philological, historical, or religious, and have concerned themselves mainly, if not solely, with the particular stelae which were their subjects. There have been but very few investigations in depth on the subject of stelae in general, on their meaning and function, on their historical, psychological, or sociological perspectives and significance.[1] These considerations are usually dealt with only in short lexicon and dictionary articles[2] Part of the problem and of the rationale for this is, undoubtedly, to be found in the attitude of Egyptological scholarship which has, traditionally, approached the material in the same way, considering it a conventional and commonplace feature of Ancient Egypt, primarily as an element and item in the mortuary cult of the deceased, in the case of private stelae, or as a vehicle for both the propagation and the recording of the king's acta and dicta, in the case of the royal ones.[3] However, in spite of the stereotyped pictorial and textual material found over and over again on the vast bulk of them, particularly on the private stelae, there are enough departures from the standard repertoire of their scenes, chiefly and most noticeably on the New Kingdom, non-royal stelae dating from the later part of the 18th Dynasty until the end of the 20th. There is even enough diversity in the treatment of individual details of those stelae whose scenes are taken directly from the stock repertoire so that we may well consider, in retrospect, if we should not be asking new and different questions.

It is generally accepted that there are three basic clas-
ses or types of stela, funerary, votive, and commemorative-hist-
orical, each probably originally envisioned for a different
function and purpose. The mortuary stela usually contained a
representation of its deceased owner, normally seated before an
offering table, often being worshipped by members of his family.
A second, very common, pictorial motif showed the dead person
adoring one or another of the gods. On virtually all funerary
stelae, when a text was appended, it frequently included, among
other things, the ḥtp-di-nswt invocation for offerings and the
well-being of the deceased in the Afterworld. The commemorative-
historical stela was, basically, of royal origin and in its
scene pictured the king engaged in some activity, usually religious in nature. Its text, often lengthy, recounted an achievement of the king, contained an encomium of him, or the like. The
votive stelae was, in its purest form, an expression of faith on
the part of the worshipper toward a god, and its text indicated
this faith in one way or another, as did also its scene. However,
these three types of stelae frequently overlapped one another in
the way that they were used. Often stelae which clearly are not
funerary, but votive, commemorate an incident. At the same time,
by virtue of their having been found in the tomb, or by virtue
of the occasional pious wishes inscribed on them for the well-
being of the ka of their owner (which, one assumes, were to be
fulfilled in the Afterworld), it would appear that they, then,
were also funerary to some extent.

It is a commonplace Egyptological truism that an essent-
ial feature of the ancient Egyptian's concept of the Afterworld

contained, for those who were fortunate enough to achieve life
in it for Eternity, a repetitive continuation of their existence
in this world, of their lives, deeds, benefits, rewards, and hon-
ours. Certainly, this is reflected, if not borne out, by the
biographical (as opposed to the purely religious) scenes which
decorated the walls of their tombs. And, indeed, one such scene,
the mortuary repast, is, without question, also the most frequent
scene found on funerary stelae. Others, however, on what are
seemingly funerary stelae are not really tomb scenes, for they
show the king, not the stela's owner, as the principal personage,
usually in an act of worship or performing some ritual before one
or more deities.[4] One may well ask why such a scene appears on a
private mortuary or votive stela? By private stelae, I mean
those which were commissioned by or dedicated to an individual
other than the king, and for his own purposes, whatever these may
have been. Such monuments, and these include rock-cut as well as
free-standing stelae, are recognizable either from their texts,
which often include the statement that the monument was "made by"
so-and-so, and by the representation of their instigator, alone,
or with members of his family, as part of the pictorial element.
The main thrust of the present study will attempt to demonstrate
that, in such cases where the pictorial element of a private
stela seems to bear no relation to its text, the basic intent of
the monument in question was neither funerary nor votive, but
commemorative, and that the primarily royal scene (which usually
has a counterpart somewhere on a wall in the temple) pictures,
when it occurs on a private stela, a ceremony in which the king
participated and one which the owner of the stela either witnessed in person, if it was a public affair, or else was among the

throng of spectators outside in the courtyard, if the ceremony
was taking place inside the temple proper, in a part of it where
the lay public was not admitted. In other words, such scenes
recorded actual physical events which took place at specific
points in time and which may, under certain circumstances, be
utilized as reliable historical documents.

That private individuals could and did erect stelae
which remembered specific events in their own lives is unquestioned. Elsewhere I have dealt with two, very clear, examples of
this. The first of these is furnished by those stelae whose
scene shows the processional bark of a deity, carried by its
bearer-priests, being approached by the stela's owner in order
to consult the oracle of the god, while the accompanying text,
beginning with the exact date of the event, verbally narrates
the incident.[5] The second instance illustrates one of the most
important, if not the most important, part of the funeral ceremony, that in which the mummy of the deceased is undergoing the
the ritual which will animate it and revivify the deceased in
the Afterworld, the ritual of Opening-of-the-Mouth.[5a] In the
chapters which follow, I shall deal with two other real situations, ceremonies in which the king figures, which are commemorated on private stelae. In some instances, the obvious indications and criteria for labelling certain of the stelae to be
discussed as private stelae are lacking[6] and, at first glance,
these would appear to be royal monuments. However, on careful
analysis, it can be shown that they, too, are probably of a
private origin. Of the two historical situations which will be
studied, the first is concerned with what surely was a public
holiday, the occasion and ceremony during which the Egyptian

king ritually executed captive enemy rulers in the presence of a god. The second event is more of a personal matter and commemorates the public honouring to the owners of the stelae by the king's own hand.

6

Footnotes:

1. The only studies known to me which even begin to tackle
stelae from these aspects are K. Pflüger, "The Private Funerary Stelae of the Middle Kingdom and their Importance for
the Study of Ancient Egyptian History", JAOS 67 (1947) 127-
135, L. Matiegka, "Individual Characteristics of Figures on
Egyptian Stelae", Archiv Orientální 20 (1952) 15-27, W.K.
Simpson, The Terrace of the Great God at Abydos: the Offering Chapels of Dynasties 12 and 13. (New Haven: 1974), Z.E.
Szafranski, "Problematyka stel 2 drugiego okresu przejścio-
wego pochodzących z Edfu w zbiorach Muzeum Narodowego w Warszawie", Rocznik Muzeum Narodowego w Warszawie 24 (1980) 7-
62 with summaries on 60-62. Of these, only the study of
Matiegka deals with stelae from periods other than the Middle Kingdom.

2. E.g. LdAe VI (1985) 1-6, H.W. Helck and E. Otto, Kleines
Wörterbuch der Aegyptologie (Wiesbaden: 1956) 357; J. Vandier, Manuel d'archéologie égyptienne. II (Paris: 1954) 389-
534, J. Yoyotte apud G. Posener, ed., Dictionary of Egyptian
Civilization. (New York: 1959) 271-272.

3. See, e.g. Yoyotte, loc. cit.

4. Which is not to say that the king does not appear in private
tomb scenes, because he does, but in those situations which
pertain to a personal relationship with the tomb owner:
scenes of audience, reward, promotion, and the like. He
does not, however, to my knowledge, appear in scenes which
show him as the chief participant in a ceremonial rite in
the temple, unless it be at Amarna. And even here the visit
of the king to the temple of the Aton can be explained in

terms of its relationship to the duties of the tomb owners where it occurs.

5. See my "A Memphite Stela, the Bark of Ptah, and Some Iconographic Comments", <u>Bulletin of the Egyptological Seminar</u> 2 (1980) 83-109 and especially 96-97 nn. 34-36, 103, and the stelae cited there.

5a. See my "The Iconographic Theme: 'Opening of the Mouth' on Stelae", <u>JARCE</u> 21 (1984) 169-196 and especially 175-177.

6. See below, chapter 1, Section B, stelae nrs. 2, 5, 7, 10, 12, and 13.

Chapter 1. The Pharaoh Slays His Enemies

A

The familiar motif of the victorious king slaughtering
a vanquished enemy chief, usually in the presence of one or another of the gods, is attested in Egyptian art since the beginning of the 1st Dynasty, if not earlier.[7] An integral part of
the royal myth and persona,[8] it recurs on the walls of the
temples and palaces, on their gateways and pylons, columns and
pillars.[9] It is carved on the sides of the cliffs of the border
marches of Egypt and beyond, wherever Egyptian armies campaigned
against the Asiatic and the Nubian, as a stark reminder of the
power of Egypt and of the fate to be expected by the rebel.[10]
Nor is it restricted to royal and monumental art. It is also
found on a plethora of different kinds of lesser objects, royal
and non-royal alike, ranging from scarabs, pectorals, and other
types of jewelry, to weapons, artists' sketches, and stelae.[11]
Its presence on royal stelae, both rock-cut and free-standing,
is obvious and needs no further comment or discussion.[12]

On private stelae the occurence of the motif of the
triumphant pharaoh in the act of killing an enemy seems to be
restricted to the later 18th Dynasty through the early 20th. At
least, no epigraphically datable examples prior to the reign of
Thutmose IV or later than that of Ramesses III are known to me.
To date 19 instances of this genre of scene on private free-
standing and rock-cut stelae, 5 of them unpublished, have been
forthcoming (see below, Sections B-C), although, undoubtedly,
there are still others, both published and unpublished, which I
have either inadvertently overlooked, or the existence of which
I am unaware.[13] Still, the 19 examples already collected, which

may be taken as a fair random sampling of the private stelae
bearing this scene, provide, when studied as a group, sufficient
material to allow us to draw a number of insights into their
historical, artistic, and art-historical contexts, as well as to
raise and possibly answer a number of previously unasked questions concerning their raison d'être. It should be noted, however, that this chapter will not address itself to the symbolic,
religious, or philosophic concepts associated with or inherent
in the motif. These aspects have already been dealt with previously by other scholars and are, to my knowledge, even the
subject of yet to be published studies.[14]

In the treatment of the individual stelae which follows
in Sections B and C, they have been arranged as far as it is
possible in chronological sequence, with those whose date is not
firmly assured by the presence of a royal name, being placed at
the end, although, typologically, a somewhat different order
could have been followed. No distinction has been made between
those which are, patently, private stelae and those which probably are. The dimensions of most of those listed in Section B
are relatively small, but one does approach a nearly monumental
size.[15] Approximately half of them have the conventional round-
topped shape.[16] The others are rectangular, with the scene
framed by what is certainly a doorway or a gateway.[17] The scene
itself is essentially the same for all 19 stelae and the general
description of it which follows will not be repeated in the discussion of any of the individual pieces, even in the case of the
5 previously unpublished ones, save to note any variations.

On all of the stelae the king is pictured in the act of
slaying an enemy captive, or group of captives,[18] in the presence

of one of the Egyptian gods, usually Ptah.[19] Striding and half-
leaning forward, he grasps the prostrate victims, presumably defeated enemy rulers, by their hair with one hand, in order to
steady their heads for the death blow which he is about to de-
liver with crushing force from the smiting weapon held in his
other hand, this usually, either the maceaxe or the ḫpš-sword.[20]
In most cases the king wears a headdress consisting of the short
Nubian wig,[21] surmounted by a double-plumed disk which rests
upon a pair of ram's horns, from which a disk-crowned uraeus
rears up.[22] This headdress has, on occasion and probably wrongly, been interpreted or described as the atef-crown.[23] Not infrequently, the wig to which the uraeus has been affixed, is
bound by a fillet, the end or ends of which hang down behind the
wig like streamers.[24] The remaineder of the king's dress usually comprises a short, knee-length kilt with apron or flap, held
in place by a belt, and a broad collar around his neck.[25] The
intended victim, whose nationality differs from stela to stela,
is usually shown sunk down on one knee. His face is sometimes
turned towards the king, sometimes away from him and toward the
god. At least one of his hands is raised, either in a gesture
of supplication for mercy, or else in a piteous and futile attempt to ward off his imminent fate.

B

1. Stela Brussels E 4499, from Memphis. Limestone, with no
traces of colour. 27 x 17 cm., texts and figures incised. Bibliography: W.M.F. Petrie, Memphis I (London: 1909) 7 and pls. 7
(photograph) and 8 nr. 4 (line drawing); L. Speelers, Recueil
des inscriptions égyptiennes des Musées Royaux du Cinquantenaire
à Bruxelles (Brussels: 1923) 37 and 134 (text only). Part of

the text also published in Urk. IV, 1563. See also B.M. Bryan,
The Reign of Tuthmosis IV (unpublished Yale PhD dissertation:
1980) 205 n. 61. (Fig. 1).

Rectangular in shape, the stela actually takes the form
of an open portal. The doorway itself is recessed, its jambs
and lintel projecting forward, while a cavetto cornice, now mostly broken away, caps the lintel.[26] Incised squarely in the
center of the lintel is a pair of vertical cartouches, each surmounted by a pair of feathers and horns,[27] that on the left containing the prenomen "Menkheprure'", that on the right the nomen
"Thutmose".[28] Both jambs bear a vertical line of indifferently-
carved hieroglyphs, each facing towards the opening of the doorway and each set within a rectangular frame which runs to the
height of the jamb. The text on the left reads:

"The Horus, the Mighty Bull, the Son of Atum, the king
of Upper and Lower Egypt,[29] the lord of the Two Lands,
Menkheprure', beloved of Amūn the king of the gods".

The text of the corresponding right jamb reads:

"The Horus, the Mighty Bull,[30] the Son of Re', the
lord of Diadems, Thutmose, [beloved of] Ptah the lord
of Ma'at, the king of the Two Lands".

The smiting scene, which takes place in the presence of Ptah, is
set within the aperture of the doorframe. The god is identified
by a vertical line of text as "Ptah, the Great One, the lord of
Ma'at". He is in a mummiform guise and, clutching a w3s-scepter,
stands facing to the left, on a ma'at-shaped pedestal. At the
left, facing him, is the king. His kilt is calf-length and a
lion's tail is attached to the back of his belt. His weapon is
the maceaxe. The enemy whom he is about to slay, a Libyan, to

judge from his phallic sheath, faces the god, but has turned his
head towards the king, to whom he raises up his left arm in a
useless gesture of supplication. All three figures stand on a
ground line. The top of the scene has been set off by a double
border line, so that a wide empty space intervenes between the
top of the scene and the soffit of the lintel. Likewise, there
is an even wider empty space between the ground line and the single horizontal line of text which runs between the jambs at the
bottom of the stela and which is marked off by a border line.
The text itself is damaged and only partly legible. It is clear,
however, that it contained the title and name of the stela's dedicator:

"[Made by] the scribe?[31] in the house of gold?,[32]
Ramose,[33] granted life".

2. Stela Petrie, Riqqeh and Memphis VI (London: 1915) pl. 55
nr. 12, from Memphis, present location unknown. Limestone, with
no traces of colour. Dimensions unknown, texts incised, figures
in raised relief. Bibliography: Petrie, loc. cit. with a brief
mention ibid. 33. See also Bryan, loc. cit. n. 60. (Fig. 2).

Rectangular in shape, the stela shows a portal, the lintel of which is capped by a cavetto cornice with the torus molding clearly preserved. The scene is set within the recessed
aperture. At the left, Ptah, mummiform, stands in a naos which
is set upon a ma'at-shaped pedestal and whose front side is suggested by the lower part of the combination w3s-'nḫ-ḏd-scepter
which the god clutches. In the field within the naos, over the
god's head, a short horizontal line of hieroglyphs names him
"Ptah,[34] the lord of Ma'at". To the left of the shrine and facing it is the sacrificial scene. The lion's tail is attached to

the back of the king's belt. Along with the hair of the semi-
supine captive, the king also holds a bow with his left hand.
The victim, even more clumsily rendered than the other figures,
faces the god, but his head is turned towards the king. One of
his hands grasps the king's left arm as if to restrain it, and
the other is raised helplessly. The only indication of his nationality is his beard which suggests that he is either a Libyan
or an Asiatic. On a raised vertical panel in the field between
the naos and the king's head is a cartouche, surmounted by the
plumed, horned, sundisk and containing the prenomen "Menkhepru-
reᶜ, granted life". In the field behind the king's back a short
vertical line of raised hieroglyphs contains part of an apotropaic statement "all life and stability".[35] The entire tableau
is set off by a raised rectangular border, which abuts the inner
reveals of the jambs, but which is separated from the soffit of
the lintel and from the bottom edge of the stela by a very broad,
empty, field. Exactly how broad the lower of this pair of
fields was, cannot be determined since the bottom of the stela
is lost.

3. Stela Kestner Museum, Hannover, 1935.200.230, provenance
unknown. Limestone, with minimal traces of red colour preserved.
21 x 14.5 cm. texts and scene incised. Bibliography: P. Munro,
"Untersuchungen zur altägyptischen Bildmetrik", Städel-Jahrbuch
N.F. 3 (1971) 35 fig. 32. (Fig. 3 and Pl. 1).

Both registers of this round-topped stela are framed by
a border paralleling its outline. The sacrificial tableau fills
the upper register. The king's weaponry consists of a ḫpš-sword
with which he is delivering the fatal blow, and a bow which he
holds together with the hair of the two prostrate captives, a

Nubian and an Asiatic, who face him. The Asiatic raises one
hand in a plea for mercy. The Nubian's two arms hang down at
his sides, in resignation to his doom. The god in whose presence the execution is being carried out is "Ptah, the lord of
Ma'at". He stands in a naos, the base of which is a ma'at-shaped pedestal, and the open front of which is indicated by the
artist's simply not having continued the carving of its front
wall from the level of the god's stomach up to the cornice just
beneath its top.[36] In the field between the naos and the king's
plumed, horned headdress, is a vertical cartouche reading "the
good god, Menkheprure'". Behind his back is a vertical line
reading: "Horus, powerful of arm".[37] A broad, double line separates the two registers, its upper edge simultaneously serving
as the ground line for the figures in the upper one. In the lower register, facing right, a man, two women, and a second man,
kneel in adoration to the ceremony depicted in the register above them. The first man offers a lighted brazier with one hand,
the second man and the first woman each hold a single lotus
flower in one hand. All three raise the other, and the second
woman both, hands in the gesture of adoration. The first man
wears a shoulder-length wig, the second is shaven-headed. Both
are clad in long kilts. The left arm of the second man, the
hand of which is holding the flower, is shown in front of his
upward-bent left leg. Each of the two women wears an ankle-
length dress, that of the second woman being somewhat more loose-
ly-flowing. The surface of the stela in both of the registers
is marred by scratches. In addition, it has been cracked by salt
action, especially in the lower register, so that the short,
sometimes deeply-incised, vertical inscriptions over the heads of

the four worshippers are obscured and somewhat difficult to read.
Over the head of the first man and slightly in front of it is
"Made by the ḥry-wr-priest".[38] His name, which is continued over
the head of the first woman is damaged because of the scratches
and the salt action, but appears to by "Iry".[39] The name and
title of the first female seem to be written in the field between
her left arm and abdomen. With difficulty the title can be read
as "lady of the house", but the name is completely illegible.
Over the head of the second woman is a clear "his sister" and in
the field between her and the second man is her title, followed
by her name. The title, damaged but legible, is "the lady of his
house",[40] and the name appears to be "Tia",[41] with the determinative, for lack of space, written underneath the upraised arm of
the second male. Finally, over this man's head is a clear "his
sister" (sic!), followed by the common masculine name Ptaḥmose"[42]
which, however, seems to have a feminine determinative written
behind the nape of his neck.[43]

4. Stela Chicago Art Institute 1893.75,[44] provenance unknown.[45] Limestone, with no traces of colour. 14.4 x 23.8 cm.
text and scene incised. Bibliography: Briefly described, but not
illustrated in T.G. Allen, A Handbook of the Egyptian Collection
(Chicago: 1923) 41, and mentioned by Bryan, op. cit. 251. (Fig.
4 and Pl. 2).

In the shape of a gateway with the cavetto cornice and
torus molding in raised relief, the stela is comprised of two registers which are deeply recessed within the gate's aperture. The
upper left corner of the lintel is lost. The surface of the upper
right corner is chipped away. In addition, the left corner of
the soffit is chipped away with slight damage to the beginning of

the text of the left jamb. In the center of the lintel, beneath
the torus molding and facing to the right, are two vertical cartouches containing, respectively, the prenomen "Menkheprure⸢⸣"
and the nomen "Thutmose". The vertical column of text on each
jamb faces inward, towards the aperture. That on the right
reads:

> "The good god, the lord of the Two Lands, Menkheprure⸢,
> the Son of Re⸢, the lord of Diadems, Thutmose, beloved
> of Ptah".

The text of the left jamb is identical, save that it substitutes
the name of "Amūnre' for that of Ptah. The smiting scene is in
the upper of the two registers. The inner ribbing of the
feathers of the king's headdress are indicated. He also wears
a double-stranded broad collar and the ends of his belt are
shown on each side of the wide, triangular apron of his calf-
length kilt. His weapon is the ḫpš-sword. He holds a single
prisoner, an Asiatic who wears a long robe, has long hair, but,
apparently, no beard.[46] The prisoner's head and arms are turned
to the left, towards the king, but his kneeling body faces the
god Ptah who, in his usual mummiform guise, is shown standing
inside a closed naos,[47] this resting on a ma⸢at-shaped pedestal. A side-curtain within the naos is summarily suggested by
a single curved line at the height of the god's chest. Vertically, in the field behind the king's back, is a lotus-headed
fan, the shaft of which terminates in the archaic form of the
cartouche. The entire scene of the upper register is roofed
over by the sky-hieroglyph. This rests upon two supports, that
at the right incorporating the back of the naos.[48] Inside the
shrine, in the field before his head, the name of Ptah is writ-

ten retrograde.[49] In the field between the top of the naos and
the feathers of the king's headdress "Lord of the Two Lands" is
written vertically.[50] Likewise, vertically to the left of the
left support of the sky-hieroglyph there seem to be traces of a
column of text, but this may only be caused by pits on the surface of the stone and by shadows thrown on it by the raised
left jamb.[51] The figures and naos stand on a ground line which
also serves as the register divider. Beneath this, facing to
the right, a woman and a man, respectively, kneel with their
hands raised in adoration to the scene above.[52] The woman
wears a long wig which covers her left shoulder and reaches to
the small of her back. Her sleeved dress is very loose and diaphonous. The man, shaven-headed and bare to the waist, wears
an ankle-length kilt. Two horizontal lines above his navel may
indicate the muscles of his chest. In front of the woman, between her upraised arms and her bent knee, is her name: "Ya".[53]
Behind her head is her title: "lady of the house". Two vertical
lines of text behind the man read:

"Made by the wᶜb-priest of Ptah, Bestu,[54] who will

be revered and justified".

There may be some additional traces after this.[55]

5. Stela Metropolitan Museum of Art, New York, 64.285, provenance unknown. Limestone, with no traces of colour. 5.8 x 7.8
cm., text and scene incised. Bibliography: previously unpublished. (Fig. 5 and Pl. 3).

The original shape of the stela cannot be determined,
inasmuch as part of its left side, running diagonally from approximately just above the upper left corner to the center of
the top is lost, as is also the upper right corner. The design

consists of a scene framed by a gateway or a doorway, but with
the corners of the stela missing, it is impossible to say whether the trace of a horizontal line at the top is merely the top of
the portal's lintel, or whether it is the soffit of an otherwise
missing cornice, although the latter is more likely. Each jamb
rests upon a platform which is bisected at the central axis of
the aperture by a stairway(?) with sidewalls.[56] The top of this
platform projects in a cornicelike overhang, beneath which is an
additional molding. The tops of the ends of the stairway's sidewalls have a similar cornicelike overhang. Only a single step of
the stair itself is shown, since the entire architectural complex
is cut off by a base line. In the tableau which occupies the central axis of the gateway, Ptah, mummiform and holding a w3s-scep-
ter with both hands stands on a m3ʿt-shaped pedestal. The king,
wearing a long kilt with pendant apron faces him and offers the
sacrifice. The break at the left side of the stela has carried
away his upraised right hand along with the shaft of the smiting
weapon which it held. Nevertheless, it is clear from what remains
that the weapon was the ḫpš-sword rather than the maceaxe. A rather deep gouge in the surface of the stone has destroyed the details of the king's right foot and weathering has obliterated the
outline of his left leg, buttocks, and the small of his back.
Both of the pair of enemies whom he is about to sacrifice to Ptah
kneel towards the god, but one of them has swiveled his hips around so that his torso, his head, and his right arm face the king,
with his right hand raised in a vain gesture of supplication. Ev-
en though a pit in the stone slightly obscures the details of his
valanced wig, it is apparent that ethnically he is a Nubian. The
nationality of the second sacrificial victim is equally as clear.

Although the details of his dress are damaged and obscure, his
rather full, pointed, beard marks him out as an Asiatic, and this,
when coupled with what looks to be a shaven head suggests that
his homeland was Mitanni.[57] The entire tableau is enclosed by a
rectangular frame, the bottom of which serves as the ground line
for the humans and also for the pedestal upon which the god
stands. The top of this frame is broken by the plumes of the
king's headdress, the curved blade of his sword, and probably by
his now-lost right hand. In the field beneath the top border
line and the heads of the prisoners a pair of vertical cartouches
contain, respectively, the prenomen "Djeserkheprure'" and a badly mangled form of the nomen "Horemheb".[58] Over the head of the
god is "Ptah, the Lord of Ma'at". Beneath the cartouche with
the royal nomen and facing to the right is a very deeply-incised
"strength". In the field above the top border, between the king's
plumes and the reveal of the right jamb, is the sky-hieroglyph,
elongated and very deeply cut. Above and below the framed scene
are the by-now familiar wide, blank fields, that underneath being
wider than that above.

6. Stela Louvre E 16373, from Deir el-Medineh. Limestone,
with no traces of colour. 32.2 x 34 cm. text and figures incised. Bibliography: B. Bruyère, Rapport sur les fouilles de
Deir el Médineh (1935-1940) (Cairo: 1940) 39 and pl. 38 nr. 1,
62-64 with fig. 4. (Fig. 6).

Round-topped, the stela has two register framed by a
border which parallels its outline. The upper register contains
the sacrificial scene showing the king slaughtering three captives. No god is present. In addition to his usual costume, the
king wears a square, false beard. No lion's tail is attached to

his belt, but a pair of sundisk-crowned uraei adorn the ends of
the pendant apron of his ankle-length kilt. The king's weapon
is a pear-shaped mace. Of the three kneeling enemies, a Nubian,
a Syrian, and another Asiatic,[59] one faces away from him, the
other two toward him, all three with a hand, one with both hands,
raised in a gesture of supplication. In the field over their
heads, framed within a rectangle, the top edge of which has the
shape of the sky-hieroglyph, are two vertical lines of text, facing left and reading:

"the good god, the lord of the Two Lands, Wosimareʿ-
setepenreʿ, granted life".

In the field behind the king's back a single vertical line reads:

"The protection of life, stability, and good fortune
is behind him".

A reed mat which serves as the ground line for the figures of
the upper register also separates it from the lower one. In this,
at the left and facing right, a man kneels with his hands raised
in the gesture of adoration. He wears a long, braided wig, a
multiple-stranded broad collar, a sleeved upper-garment, and a
long kilt with a wide, pleated, triangular apron. Before him is a
text of six vertical lines of well-incised hieroglyphs, reading:

"Giving praise by the scribe in the Place of Eternity,
Ramose,[60] to the lord of the Two Lands, He who lives
on Maʿat, the king of Upper and Lower Egypt, Wosimareʿ-
setepenreʿ, the Son of Reʿ, the lord of Diadems, Ramesses-miʿamūn, granted life, that he may give to me a
beautiful lifetime in the Place of Truth".

7. Stela Florence Museo Archeologico 2587, provenance unknown. Limestone, no traces of colour preserved. 23 x 27 cm.

figures in sunken relief. Bibliography: S. Bosticco, Museo Archeologico di Firenze: Le stele egiziane del Nuovo Regno (Florence: 1965) 57 nr. 49 and pl. 49 nr. 1; I. Rosellini, Oggetti
di antichita egiziane riportati dalla spedizione letteraria toscana in Egitto e in Nubia (Florence: 1830) nr. 58; W. Berend,
Principaux monuments de Musee Egyptien de Florence (Paris: 1882)
84-85 with a fig. on 84. For additional bibliography, see Bosticco, loc. cit. (Fig. 7).

Only the lunette containing the scene of this round-
topped stela is preserved. From the published photograph one
gains the impression that the stela, at some time, had been cut
down and somewhat foreshortened. At the right, facing left, is
the king. Although the details of his coiffure are obliterated,
since he wears the plumed, horned disk, it is most probable that
he also wore the short Nubian wig. A uraeus is faintly visible
on his brow and the texture of the stone behind the back of his
head and immediately beneath his upraised left arm suggests that
a pendant streamer was also affixed to the headdress. His chest
is covered by a short-sleeved jerkin, the crossed ties of which
are visible on his midriff. His short, pleated kilt is of an
archaic pattern and is held in place by an elaborate belt. He
wears the false beard, a pair of armlets and bracelets on his
biceps and wrists, and a double-stranded broad collar. The
kneeling, suppliant prisoner whom he grasps by the hair is a
Libyan, nude save for a decorated belt, a pair of similarly-dec-
orated crossbands over his chest, and a pair of armlets and
bracelets. The god before whom the sacrifice takes place is
Ptah, behind whom is an elaborate bouquet of lotus flowers. No
trace of any inscription is evident today, but according to the

publications, originally there was a line of text identifying
the king as Merneptah.[61] There are some scratches in the field
behind his back which may be the remains of this. Traces of a
reed mat are visible beneath the right foot of the prisoner, the
pedestal of Ptah, and the bouquet of lotus flowers. This served
as a ground line for the tableau and simultaneously separated it
from whatever text and scene might have existed on the now-missing lower part of the stela.

    8. Stela Cairo JE 88879, from Qantir. Sandstone, with no
traces of colour. 90 x 40 cm. scene in sunken relief, text incised. Bibliography: L. Habachi, "Khata'na-Qantir: Importance",
ASAE 52 (1952) 507-514 and pl. 29. (Fig. 8).

    Both the scene above and the text below of this round-
topped stela are framed by a border which parallels the outline
of the stone. In the lunette, over the head of the king, is a
sundisk with a pair of pendant uraei. The king wears the Blue
Crown with uraeus in front and pendant streamers behind. The
lion's tail is affixed to his belt. His weaponry consists of a
ḫpš-sword, which he is wielding with his right hand, and a bow,
which he holds in his left as he grasps the hair of two kneeling,
suppliant prisoners, its lower half concealed by their heads and
bodies. Habachi described these prisoners as Asiatics, with no
further specification.[62] Yet the features of the captive facing
the god seem to me to be clearly Libyan,[63] an impression also
suggested by the traces of what appears to be a band of cloth
running diagonally across his chest from his left side to his
right shoulder.[64] Centered in the field over the heads of the
pair of victims are two vertical cartouches reading:

    "the lord of the Two Lands, Wosimare'-mi'amūn,

the lord of Diadems, Ramesses-hikaon".

The god in whose presence the sacrifice is taking place is represented as an anthropomorphic deity in Asiatic garb. He wears
the tall, conical crown from which a long, tassel hangs down almost to the ground line. His short, striped kilt is fringed at
its hem. In his left hand he holds a w3s-scepter and with his
right he offers a ḫpš-sword to the king. The field above and
in front of his head, where his identifying adscription was, is
damaged and nothing can be read there, so that his identity must
be adduced from his iconography. Habachi was certainly correct
in identifying him as Seth.[65] Below the ground line on which
all of the figures stand and which serves to separate the scene
above from it is a text of 6 horizontal lines of hieroglyphs,
facing to the left and reading:

> "The Horus, the Mighty Bull, Great of Kingship, the
> Embodiment of the Two Ladies, Great of Festivals like
> Tatenen,[66] the king of Upper and Lower Egypt, the
> lord of the Two Lands, Wosimareʿ-miʿamūn, the Son of
> Reʿ, the lord of Diadems, Ramesses-hikaon, granted
> life. Now his majesty commanded that there be given
> fields, 16 arouras,[67] as a reward[68] to the shield-
> bearer, the one from the foreign land, Wosimareʿ-
> nakht,[69] who will be justified, in the district of
> the town of Kheriu,[70] its water-source[71] being the
> Well of Smentowe".[72]

9. Stela Kestner Museum, Hannover, 1935.200.229, from Memphis. Limestone, with no traces of colour. 16 x 11.2 cm. figures in sunken relief, text incised. Bibliography: Petrie,
Memphis I 18-19 and pl. 8 nr. 3;[73] Bryan, loc. cit. n. 61.[74]

(Fig. 9).

Both registers are framed by a border paralleling the
outline of this round-topped stela. The surface has suffered
somewhat because of weathering, with damage to the lower bodies
of the prisoners in the upper register, and to the right arm and
face of the worshipper in the lower. Portions of the stone, at
the upper left side, at the beginning of the curve of the top,
and from the lower left side of the bottom up to about one quart-
er of the height of the upper register, are missing. The sacrificial scene fills the upper register. Over the king's head,
damaged, a falcon deity hovers, its wings protectively outspread.
Vertically, in the field behind the king's back, is the statement
"the protection of all life like Re'" which, coupled with its
physical position, is to be completed ("is behind him"). The
king's weaponry consists of the maceaxe with which he is smiting
the captives, and a bow which he holds in his left hand along
with their hair. The victims are a Nubian and an Asiatic. The
god in whose presence the sacrifice is taking place is Ptah, who
stands in a naos, the base of which is not on the ground, but
rather floats above the outstretched leg of one of the prisoners.
Over their heads, in the field between the protective falcon and
the naos is an unfinished inscription. A rectangular panel which
would have taken a pair of cartouches containing the king's nomen
and prenomen has been left blank. Above it, facing the naos in
two lines, continued by a third below it, is:

    "the good god, the lord of the Two Lands, the Son of

    Re', the lord of Diadems, granted life like Re'".

The lower register shows a man and a woman, facing to the right,
kneeling in adoration. The man, wearing the short "military"

wig[75] and a long, elaborately pleated kilt, has both hands raised. The woman, most of whose body is damaged in back, wears a
pleated garment, a cone of perfumed fat on her fillet-bound wig,
and rattles a sistrum with her left hand.[76] Before the pair is
a text of two vertical lines which fills the height of the register and is continued over their heads in 6 single square high
lines, the last of which is illegible, but which probably contained a determinative. The text reads:

"Giving praise to Ptah and kissing the earth to his ka.[77]
Made by the overseer of weavers, Ramose, (and) his sister,
the lady of the house, Taiat[78] [--]".

10. Stela Kestner Museum, Hannover, 1935.200.204, from
Memphis. Limestone, with no traces of colour. 17 x 9 cm. an-
epigraphic(?), scene in sunken relief. Bibiliography: Petrie,
Memphis I 7 and pl. 8 nr. 2;[79] Bryan, loc. cit. (Fig. 10).

The outline of the stela is that of a rectangular gateway or doorway whose cavetto cornice is actually molded in raised relief. The scene is enclosed by a frame whose upper and
lower borders fill the width of the portal's aperture, but
whose right and left borders are separated from the reveals of
the jambs by a narrow space. A broad, empty field is between
the top of the frame and the soffit of the lintel, and an even
broader, rectangular field, this time containing 4 human ears,[80]
fills the space between the bottom border and the bottom edge
of the stela. The god before whom the king is making the sacrifice is Ptah. Although Petrie's drawing shows no traces of any
inscription, I can barely discern, on my own photograph of the
stela, the surface of which is pitted and weathered here, the
mostly-illegible traces of a short vertical line of hieroglyphs,

the last of which seems to be the nh-bird. If I am correct,
then the line is undoubtedly to be restored "(Ptah, the one who
hears) prayers", the moreso in view of the 4 ears below.[81] Likewise, there may be something in the field between the head of
the god and the head of the king, but the surface of the stone
is so pitted and cracked here, that any attempt to read or restore a text is fruitless. Petrie's drawing also shows the king
smiting a single prisoner with his ḥpš-sword, but, again, a careful examination of my own photograph suggests that there may
have been more. I seem to see 2 bodies facing one another and
at least 3 legs extended outwards in different directions.

11. Stela Brussels E 2386, purchased at Giza and presumably
from the Memphite area. Limestone, with no traces of colour. 18
x 19.3 cm. text incised, figures in sunken relief. Bibliography:
previously unpublished. (Fig. 11 and Pl. 4).

Only the lower part of the stela is preserved, but it
is clear that it originally had the shape of a rectangular portal whose lintel, cornice, most of the left jamb, and part of
the right jamb are now lost. In addition, an almost square
chunk has been chipped off the surface of the lower left corner. The jambs are set on a platform and the aperture of the
portal is reached via a staircase of which only one step is represented and which has no sidewalls. On the outer side of each
jamb is a pillar or flagpole. That on the right rests on a base
and has a streamer wrapped around its lower part. A corresponding base for the left pillar is no longer preserved, but may not
have been as high as that on the right side, since the tip of a
human ear is visible just above the break, with another, fully-
preserved ear above it. If there had been a streamer wrapped

around this pillar to correspond with that on the right, it would have been on a now-lost part of the stela. Standing on the base of the right pillar, his hands raised in adoration towards the the tableau visible within the aperture, is a shaven-headed male worshipper, wearing a long calf-length kilt with a wide flaring triangular apron and, perhaps, some sort of pectoral, of which the right upper corner is visible on his chest, just below the hollow of the throat, the rest being hidden by his left biceps. Above his head, vertically, is part of, if not his complete name: "Ashahebsed".[82] Both the name, his dress and shaven head, as well as the general style of the stela, suggest a Ramesside date. The diagonal fracture of the stone has resulted in, not only the loss of whatever text may have preceded Ashahebsed's name, but also the upper part of the scene, including the upraised arm of the king, the weapon which it wielded, and his headdress, although we may assume that it was the plumed, horned, disk, since the lower part of the short Nubian wig on which this was worn is still visible. Also lost is the face of the king, the upper torso and head of the god, the top of the latter's scepter, and the empty field which separated the scene from the soffit of the lin- tel. The prisoner who is being executed has sunk down on his knees, his head facing the deity, but with his right hand raised in supplication to the king. Although his facial features are indeterminate, his short wig, the band of cloth wrapped over one shoulder, and, particularly, his phallic sheath, indicate that he is a Libyan. The deity, clearly Ptah, stands on the ground line rather than on his usual pedestal. Beneath this ground line and the top of the stair at the bottom of the stela is a broad,empty field.

12. Stela Egyptian Museum, Berlin, DDR, 20912, purchased
in Luxor, provenance unknown. Limestone, with no traces of colour. 23 x 18.5 cm. anepigraphic, scene in sunken relief. Bibliography: previously unpublished. (Fig. 12 and Pl. 5).

No border parallels the outline of this round-topped
stela, but a clearly-preserved doorway runs vertically for almost its entire height, from the bottom to halfway above the
curve of the shoulder, and the torus molding at the top of the
lintel extends horizontally to touch the stela's outer edges.
The cornice, lintel, and jambs are all of equal thickness, as is
the platform on which the jambs stand. This shows no separation
between the bottoms of the jambs and its upper surface, almost
as if it were a threshold. The scene, which is framed by the
doorway, occupies the upper three-fifths of the aperture, the
soffit of the lintel serving as its upper border. The usual
broad empty field is present between the base of the scene and
the top of the platform. The king's knee-length kilt is pleated. His weaponry consists of the maceaxe which he is brandish-
ing and a bow which he holds in the hand which steadies the
heads of two captives. These are an Asiatic, who faces him, and
a Nubian, who faces the god in whose presence the sacrifice is
being performed. This latter, Ptah, is shown in his usual mummiform guise, holding a w3s-scepter and standing on a pedestal.
Unlike the feet of the king and of the prisoners, the pedestal
does not rest on the wide ground line.

13. Stela Victoria and Albert Museum, London, 423.1908,
from Memphis. Limestone, with no traces of colour. 14.6 x 12.4
cm. anepigraphic, scene in sunken relief. Bibliography: Petrie,
Memphis I 7 and pls. 7 and 8 nr. 1. (Fig. 13).

The scene is framed by a border paralleling the outline
of the stela's round top. The king wears the short, valenced
Nubian wig, with a uraeus on his forehead, but not the plumed,
horned disk. His weapon is the ḫpš-sword. The captive being
sacrificed is a Nubian. The deity, Ptah, is shown in his usual
mummiform guise, but without a beard. In the field between the
king and the god, facing the king, a falcon deity hovers with
its wings spread protectively towards the king.

14. Stela Newark Museum 29.1788, provenance unknown, purchased in Cairo. Limestone, with no traces of colour. 18.9 x
14 cm. scene partly in sunken relief, partly incised, text incised. Bibliography: previously unpublished. (Fig. 14 and Pl.
6).

The scene and text of this small stela are set within a
border paralleling its outline, round-topped. Occupying slightly more than half of the left side and running virtually the entire height of the stela is a gateway with cavetto cornice and
torus molding. On the lintel of this gateway, which is very
clearly delineated from the tops of the jambs, very faint traces
of, perhaps, an inscription seem to be visible.[83] The tableau
of the smiting king, framed by a double line at the top and a
single line below, occupies most of the upper half of the aperture of the gate, with only a small, blank field above, and with
the entire bottom half of the opening serving as the empty field
below. The king is at the left, wearing a knee-length kilt with
pendant apron and, as a headdress, what seems to be the plumed,
horned disk, with uraei rearing up from the horns, but these details are quite obscure. His weapon is the ḫpš-sword which he
swings with his upraised right arm, while he grasps the prisoner

by his topknot with his left. The nationality of the latter is
impossible to determine, for the details of his head and face
are not visible. Nor, for that matter, is the position of his
arms clear, although from the position of his legs, bent at the
knees and facing to the right, it is clear that the captive's
body was facing the god. The deity is Ptah, in his usual mummiform guise, holding a w3s-scepter and standing on a pedestal.
The pedestal, the prisoner's outstretched legs and the king's
right leg all rest on the line framing the bottom of the scene,
but the king's somewhat foreshortened left leg looks as if it
were resting on the hollow of the prisoner's left knee. The
field to the right of the gateway contains the figure of a worshipper below and, what at first sight, seems to be 2 vertical
lines of text above. The worshipper, a male, wearing apparently
the so-called "military" wig, cut away in a pronounced vee at
the nape of the neck, kneels with both hands raised in the gesture of adoration to the scene taking place within the aperture
of the gateway. He is obviously wearing a kilt, the waistline
of which is marked off, but its other details are not at all so
visible. His left knee and the toes of his left foot, the sole
of his right foot, and the 2 jambs of the gateway all sit upon a
double ground line which extends in each direction to the side
borders of the stela. This may very well represent a platform.
Although 2 vertical columns had been prepared for a text over
the adorant's head, only the first of these contains an inscription which, however, runs horizontally for a single hieroglyph,
the determinative of the worshipper's name, into the last square
of the second column. A large break has chipped away most of
the surface of the upper part of both columns, but what is not

damaged in the lower portion of the second shows that, with the
exception just noted at the bottom of the column, it never contained an inscription. The text of the first column reads:

"Hail [to y]ou,[84] O Ptah! Made by Hori".[85]

C

Thus far, only free-standing private stelae with the
scene of the king smiting his enemies in the presence of a deity
have been noted. We must now take into consideration those private stelae which are rock-cut which have the same motif. As
before, the criteria used to establish the non-royal origin of
such monuments are the inclusion of a representation of the dedicator and/or a statement to the effect that it was "made by"
him.[86] However, unlike my treatment of the free-standing stelae
in Section B above, I have by no means attempted to deal with
every example of the private rock-cut stelae with this theme
known to me here, although I have included the majority of them.
For those which I have omitted, see the Appendix.[87]

Actually, the distinction which I make between these 2
types of stela is, for the most part, academic. Both had no
mortuary function, but were obviously commemorative in intent.
Both have similar, if not identical, shapes and composition (except that the rock-cut stelae often have almost monumental dimensions). While I have no real explanation as to why some of
the dedicators preferred the rock-cut version over the free-
standing, it might be noted that, in the instances included below, they were officials of a much higher rank than were the
men who commissioned the free-standing stelae. This does suggest that they may have had much more wealth and resources at
their disposal and, consequently, were able to afford the more

lavish variant of the monument.[88]

As in the preceding Section, the rock-cut stelae are or-
dered here in a chronological sequence on the basis of the royal
names which they bear. All are Ramesside, starting with Seti I
and ending with Amenmesse. The scene is that described for the
free-standing stelae and only variants in detail will be noted in
the description of the individual items.

15. Rock-cut stela, west side of the ancient road between
Aswan and Philae. Bibliography: J. De Morgan, Catalogue des monuments et inscriptions de l'Égypte antique I (Cairo: 1894) 20 nr.
124; KRI I, 303; L. Habachi, "The Graffiti and Work of the Viceroys of Kush in the Region of Aswan", Kush 5 (1957) 27. For
earlier publications, see PM V, 247. (Fig. 15).

In the upper of the two registers, the king, wearing a
simple bag wig and a short kilt of an archaic pattern, grasps a
a kneeling prisoner by the hair. The weapon which he wields is
the maceaxe. The nationality of the prisoner cannot be determined from De Morgan's drawing. No deity is present. Slightly before and over the king's head is a sundisk from which a pair of
uraei emanate, with ꜥnḫs looped around their throats. Over the
head of the slaughtered victim is a pair of vertical cartouches
containing, respectively, the prenomen "Menmareꜥ" and the nomen
"Seti-merneptaḥ". In the lower register, beneath the captive and
and facing toward the king, a man, wearing a long kilt and no
wig, stands with both hands raised in adoration to the king. In
are 3 vertical lines of text, reading:

"Giving praise to your ka, O victorious and triumphant
king, the king of Upper and Lower Egypt, Menmareꜥ,
granted life like Reꜥ. [Made by] the first charioteer

of his majesty, the king's son of Kush, Amenemope".[89]

16. Rock-cut stela, east side of the ancient road between
Aswan and Philae. Bibliography: De Morgan, op. cit. I, 28 nr. 5;
KRI I, 302; Habachi, op. cit. 27. For earlier publications, see
PM V, 245. (Fig. 16).

At the right, facing to the left, the king, wearing a
simple bag wig and an archaic type of kilt, grasps a kneeling
enemy of indeterminate nationality by the hair, to steady him as
he deals the death blow with his ḫpš-sword. No deity is present,

but, at the right, facing the tableau, a man, wearing a long kilt,
kneels in adoration. An ostrich-feather fan, his badge of office,[90] is attached to his belt(?) by two cords. In the field
above and between the prisoner and the adorant, facing to the
left, a pair of vertical cartouches and a short, horizontal line
of text identify the king as;

"the good god, the lord of the Two Lands, Menmareˁ,

the Son of Reˁ, the lord of Diadems, Seti-merneptah,

granted life forever and ever".

Beneath the scene, facing in the same direction as the worshipper,
2 horizontal lines of text identify the latter as:

"the fan-bearer on the right hand of the king, the

overseer of the Southern Land, Amenemope, who will

will be justified".

17. Rock-cut stela, east side of the ancient road between
Aswan and Philae. Bibliography: De Morgan, op. cit. I, 29 nr.
12; KRI I, 302; Habachi, op. cit. 27. For earlier publications,
see PM V, 246.

Although only the feet of the king are preserved, their
striding pose has led both Habachi and Kitchen to assume, un-

doubtedly correctly, that what is preserved is part of the smiting scene. Below the feet are the remains of a single horizontal line of text, reading:

"[-----], the overseer of the Southern Land, the king's

son of Kush, Amenem[ope]".

18. Rock-cut double stela, to the south of the great temple
of Abu Simbel (nr. 24). Bibliography: LD III, pl. 195 b,c; LD V,
pl. 167; KRI III, pp. 104-106. Collated with my own photographs.
For additional bibliography, see PM VIII, 118. (Fig. 17).

a. The north (right-hand) stela:

In 2 registers which are separated by 4 horizontal lines
of text, the body of the stela is deeply recessed within a rectangular frame, the left-hand column of which is also shared by
the adjoing south stela. In the center of the frame's top is the
winged sundisk with "the Behdetite, the great god" on either side.
The right and left jambs of the frame contain identical sets of
the king's titulary, differing only in the qualifying epithet after the nomen. These texts read:

"The Horus, the Mighty Bull, the Beloved of Ma'at, the

king of Upper and Lower Egypt, the lord of the Two Lands,

Wosimare'-setepenre', the lord of Diadems, Ramesses-mi'-

amūn, the Beloved of Amūnre' (var: of Horus, the Lord of

Buhen), granted life".

In the scene itself the king, wearing the Blue Crown from which a
streamer dangles down in back,[91] wields the maceaxe with one
hand, while the other grasps the hair of a pair of prostrate
prisoners, Asiatics, to judge from their features.[92] Behind the
king's upraised left arm a winged sundisk with a single pendant
uraeus hovers protectively. The god Amūn, wearing his double-

plumed crown, faces the king and offers him a ḫpš-sword. In front
of the deity's head a pair of vertical lines of text read:

"Words spoken by Amūnreᶜ, Lord of Karnak: '(I) have given
to you all valour and all victory'."

In the field between Amūn and the prisoners, a single vertical
line of text records that what is happening is "the crushing the
chiefs of wretched Kush".[93] Before the king's head, his prenomen
and nomen are repeated:

"the lord of the Two lands, Wosimareᶜ-setepenreᶜ, the
lord of Diadems, Ramesses-miᶜamūn, granted life like
Reᶜ".

In the field between the back of the king's head and his upraised
arm is "Horus, the Lord of Power". Behind the king's back is his
Horus-name in a serekh, personified by being mounted on a pole
whose butt is the archaic form of the cartouche and from which a
pair of arms emanate, the right hand holding a pole capped by a
bearded head, the left grasping a ḥw-fan.[94] Beneath this scene,
4 horizontal lines of text which separate it from the lower register read:

"Year 38 under the majesty of the Horus, the Mighty Bull,
the Beloved of Maᶜat, the lord of Festivals like his Father, Ptaḥ-tatenen, the Favorite of the Two Ladies, the
one who protects Egypt, who captures the foreign lands,
Reᶜ who engendered the gods, who established the Two
Lands, the Horus of Gold, Rich of Years, Great of Victories, the king of Upper and Lower Egypt, the lord of
the Two Lands, the Master of the Ritual, Wosimareᶜ-
setepenreᶜ, the Son of Reᶜ, of his body, his beloved,
the lord of Diadems, the one who grasps the White Crown,

Ramesses-mi ʿamūn, granted life and eternity upon the
throne of Horus".

In the lower register, at the left, a man wearing an ankle-length
kilt with a long, pleated, triangular apron, and holding an ostrich-feather fan of office with one hand, raises the other in a
gesture of salutation. A text of 7 vertical lines before him
reads:

"The king's son of Kush, Setau,[95] says: 'May your
father, Amūn, protect you with life, good fortune,
and stability! May he grant you Eternity as king
and Forever upon the throne of Horus'! Made by the
king's son of Kush, the overseer of the Southern
Lands, the steward of Amūn, the royal scribe, Setau".

b. The south (left-hand) stela:

The arrangement and composition of the south stela duplicates that of the north stela. In the center of the frame, at
the top, is the winged sundisk, flanked by "the Behdetite, the
great god". The vertical texts on the jambs, starting with that
on the left, read:

"The Horus, the Mighty Bull, the Beloved of Maʿat, the
the lord of Festivals like his father, Ptah-tatenen,
the lord of the Two Lands, Wosimareʿ-setepenreʿ, the
lord of Diadems, Ramesses-miʿamūn'.

In the smiting scene of the upper register, the king wears the
short wig and plumed, horned sundisk.[96] His weapon is the maceaxe. He holds a single, kneeling, cringing prisoner, apparently
a Nubian, to judge from his physiognomy. The god in whose presence the execution is taking place, Horus, human-bodied and fal-
con-headed, wears the Double Crown and offers the king a ḫpš-

sword. A single vertical line before the deity, intersected by his outstretched arm, reads:

"Words spoken by Horus, Lord of Buhen: '(I) have given to you every victory against the South, every triumph against the North'."

Before the king is his titulary:

"the lord of the Two Lands, Wosimare'-setepenre', the lord of Diadems, Ramesses-mi'amūn".

Behind the king is his ka in the form of a personified serekh containing his Horus-name.

The 4 horizontal lines of hieroglyphs which separate the 2 registers are identical to those of the north stela, except that the epithets "Master of the Ritual" in line 3 and "of his body, his beloved" and "the one who grasps the White Crown" in line 4 are omitted. The epithet following the nomen is also different, here being "granted life like Re'".

The only difference in the scene of the lower register is that Setau raises both hands in the gesture of adoration and that his badge of office, the ostrich-feather fan, is missing. However, the 7 vertical lines of text which precede him are quite different in content and tenor from those on the north stela:

"Giving praise to the good god, kissing the earth for the lord of the Two Lands, by the ka of the prince and the god's father, beloved of the god, the privy counsellor of the house of the king, the eyes of the Upper Egyptian king, the ears of the Lower Egyptian king, the intimate of the Horus in his house, the king's son of Kush, Setau".

19. Rock-cut stela to the south of the great temple of Abu

Simbel (nr. 22). Bibliography: Habachi, "King Amenmesse and Viziers Amenmose and Kha⸢emtore: Their Monuments and Place in History", MDAIK 34 (1979) 63 fig. 4; LD III, pl. 204 c. See also PM
VII, 118.

Set within a rectangular frame representing a doorway,
with a cavetto cornice and torus molding executed in high relief,
the two registers of the stela are deeply recessed. In the center of the lintel, beneath the molding, is the hieroglyph ⸢nḫ
which is shared as the initial word by 2 virtually identical
texts which then continue vertically on the jambs. That on the
left reads:

"Long live the good god, the lord of the Two Lands,[97]
Wosikheprure⸢-mi⸢amūn,[98] granted life,[99] the good god,
the lord of the Two Lands, Wosikheprure⸢-mi⸢amūn, the
lord of Diadems, Seti-merneptaḥ, beloved of Amūnre⸢,
the king of the gods".[100]

The sacrificial scene occupies the upper register. The
king wears the White Crown and wields a pear-shaped mace. The
kneeling, supplicant whom he is about to smite seems to be a Nubian. The god before whom the latter is being ceremonially murder-
ed is Amūn. He is offering the king a ḫpš-sword. Over and behind
the king's head a vulture hovers protectively. In the field in
front of and over the deity's head are 2 vertical lines of text,
with a third beneath the god's outstretched arm. These read:

"Words spoken by Amūnre⸢, the king of the gods: 'I give
your ḫpš-sword to you [in order to crush] every land'."
In the field before and over the king's head are his cartouches:

"The good god, Wosikheprure⸢-mi⸢amūn, Seti-merneptaḥ".
Behind his back is:

"Horus, powerful of arm, lord of the ḫpš-sword".

In the lower register, at the left, a man, wearing a long ilt, kneels with both hands raised in the gesture of adoration. efore him are 6 horizontal lines of text, the first 2 of which un the entire width of the stela, the remaining 4 being somewhat horter. These read:

"Long live the Horus, the Mighty Bull, the Beloved of Maꜥat, the one who establishes the Two Lands, the king of Upper and Lower Egypt, Wosikheprureꜥ-miꜥamūn, the Son of Reꜥ, Seti-merneptah, the good god, powerful with his ḫpš-sword, Hero, Valiant like Montu, the lord of strength like the son of Nut, Great of Terror like Amūn, the king of Upper and Lower Egypt,[101] Wosikheprureꜥ-miꜥamūn, the Son of Reꜥ, Seti-merneptah, the ruler of Thebes, [the Beloved of] Amūnreꜥ, the ruler of the gods, granted life like Reꜥ".

t the end of the last pair of these lines, in front of and over he adorant's head a vertical and horizontal line, with another orizontal line behind his back, identify him and record that he stela was "made by the legate, Mery, of Wawat".[102]

D

The scene common to all of these stelae contains the roy-l motif of the triumphant king slaying enemies in the presence f a god, but this is a motif which one really should **not** expect o find on a private monument. And, in fact, although several re certainly commissioned privately by the people who are pict-red and/or named on them,[103] the majority, at first glance, uld seem to be royal, rather than private monuments. Such an ssumption, however, is rather misleading. It should be noted that on the indisputable <u>royal</u> stelae of this genre, rock-cut and free-standing alike, the deity before whom the sacrifice is carried out is usually accompanied in the scene by a speech "Words spoken by (the god) NN: 'I give (or: have given) to you all victory, etc.'".[104] Such speeches are absent on the free-standing private stelae,[105] most of which are relatively small in size, nowhere near the monumental dimensions normally associated with royal stelae.[106] They are, however, present on some of the rock-cut private stelae. None of the private stelae have accompanying texts which could be characterized as royal as, e.g. those found on stelae Cairo JE 13715,[107] which begins with the king's titulary and concludes with an encomium on his power, or Munich Gl. 29,[108] which begins in the same way and then continues with an exchange of speeches between the king and the god. Although it is true that the text of stela nr. 8, Cairo JE 88879, does begin with the king's titulary and continues with a decree awarding a grant of land by the king to the shield-bearer Wosimare'nakht, it can be reasonably argued that it was Wosimare'nakht, not the king, who had been responsible for the erection of the stela.[109] The other seemingly-royal stelae, all of which are more or less complete, have, at best, only the identifying captions of the figures and might be considered royal mainly because they picture the king.[110] While none of this, by itself, is sufficient to warrant postulating a private origin for the stelae in question, when taken together with the facts that the scene appears on obviously non-royal stelae of similar non-monumental dimensions, that the god, when present, particularly on the free-standing stelae, is not accompanied by any utterance, and that no royal inscription is present beneath the scene, then I believe that a strong, albeit circumstantial, argument can be made that this was, indeed, the case and that none of the stelae under study here should be considered as other than private stelae. This, in turn, prompts me to ask some probably-new and hitherto-unasked questions about them, foremost among which are the reasons for the appearance of of a royal scene on a non-royal monument, the meaning or significance of the scene, itself, and, particularly, in connection with the preceding question, the source(s) of inspiration and prototype(s) from which it is derived. While this chapter is concerned only with the motif of the triumphant king slaughtering an enemy or a group of enemies in the presence of a god, it is obvious that the answers to these questions, or at least to the first of them, should be equally applicable to other representations of the king and royal motifs on private stelae.

It has been noted in Section B that the ceremonial scene is, on a number of stelae, viewed within the aperture of a doorway or gateway, with empty fields both above and below it, while on the remainder no such portal is represented. We may then pose the question of whether the inclusion or omission of the portal is of any importance. In other words, is it simply an artistic device which takes this pleasing and symmetrical form to serve as an additional frame, and to emphasize the scene which it encompasses, for certainly the scene pictured within it is the most important element of the visual portion of the stela, or is it an integral part of the tableau itself? If the latter is the case, then its absence on some stelae ought to have an import, but this, in turn, depends on the interpretation of the scene as either a symbolic and propagandistic illustration of the royal myth, or as an actual depiction of a real event. I believe that the

latter was the case and, that on these stelae, we are looking at
a specific ceremonial sacrifice which was performed in a specific
temple at a specific point in time. If I am correct in this,
then those instances of the scene where the portal is omitted are
merely abbreviated and simplified, conceptually and ideologically,
versions of those on which this architectural feature is present,
a case of pars pro toto. It can be further argued that the gateway itself is to be interpreted by this principle, if we consider
the scene of a stela (Fig. 20) found by Mariette at Abydos and
now in the Cairo Museum, temp. nr. 16/3/25/12.[111] In the upper of
the two registers, beneath the curve of its top, is a winged sundisk and immediately below this, filling the entire register, is
the pylon of a temple, comprising the 2 towers, each with a cavetto cornice and torus molding, flanking a smaller gateway which,
likewise, is complete with a cavetto cornice and torus molding.
In front of each tower, on either side of the gateway and close
to it, is a pair of flagpoles and in front of these, facing in-
wards towards the gateway, a colossal statue of a king, wearing
the White Crown, stands on a statue base. Viewed through the
gateway's aperture, with a narrow empty field below it, is a
scene depicting a king, wearing the Blue Crown, standing and offering something to the god, Ptah. The upper register is separated from the lower by a double ground line. In the lower register, at the left and facing right, a man kneels before a pair of
heaped-up offering tables, both hands raised in the gesture of
adoration. In front of the offering tables are 4 vertical lines
of text, continued by an additional, horizontal line in the field
over the altars. These read:

"Giving praise to Ptah, the Lord of Ma'at,[112] and kissing

the earth for his ka: 'I send[113] praises for you to[114]
the height of heaven. (I) exalt your beauty. You are
beautiful when you are at rest. May you favour me
every day'! Made by the goldsmith, Ramose".

The temple pylon pictured here exhibits a remarkable degree of realism and also a, perhaps unwitting, degree of perspective, with each of its elements properly positioned in the sequence in which it would be seen by anyone approaching it. Closest
to the viewer is the pair of colossal statues flanking the dromos.
Between and behind them is the gateway projecting in front of the
towers on each side of it. The flagstaves abut the fronts of the
towers, dirctly behind and in line with the statues. The tableau
in the aperture of the gateway is on a direct central axis with
the sanctuary. Since the other architectural elements of the complex are correctly and realistically depicted, it is then not unreasonable to suppose that the scene, within the canon of Egyptian art, likewise depicted an architectural feature of or within
the temple. Its position on the central axis of the gateway,
when taken together with the fact that one of the figures in it
is that of the god, suggests that what the tableau illustrates is
an action within a sanctuary, probably the main sanctuary of the
temple, and that the empty field at its bottom is actually the
forecourt. The figure of the deity, as I have tried to show elsewhere,[115] is not that of the god incarnate, but is rather that
of his cult statue shown in profile in accordance with the traditional canon.[116] If we understand that the worshipper, the
goldsmith, Ramose, is reciting his prayer and making his offerings to the god within the temple, as the text indicates, how,
then, are we to explain the figure of the king? The simplest

explanation is that he, too, is being shown in the act of performing a ceremony before the cult statue of the god within the sanctuary, while Ramose makes his orisons <u>outside</u>, in the courtyard.
This interpretation is supported by the scene of the upper register, unique, to my knowledge, of a stela (Fig. 21) in Berlin (nr.
23077).[117] There, at the right and facing left, a male worshipper, the outline draftsman of Amūn, Nebreᶜ,[118] wearing an ankle-
length kilt with a wide apron and an elaborately plaited wig,
kneels before an offering table, both of his arms raised in the
gesture of adoration. To the left of the offering table the god
Amūnreᶜ sits upon a throne. <u>The figure of the god is superimposed on the facade of a temple, directly before the central axis of
the gateway, which is hidden by his body.</u> The two towers of the
pylons, however, the platform on which they stand, and the pair
of flagstaves which front each tower are clearly seen. The text
of this stela has been the subject of several studies in depth
and, for the most part, does not concern us here,[119] but the
last few lines of it <u>do</u> have a bearing on the thesis of this
study. After a long hymn to the god, praying for mercy and than-
king him for saving the life of his son, Nebre' concludes the
text with the following statement:

"... 'I will make this stela upon your name and I will
inscribe this hymn on its face for you, in writing, for
you have saved the outline draftsman, Nakhtamūn for me'.
So I spoke to you and you hearkened to me. Now see, I am
doing what I said. You are the lord of the one who calls
to him, the one who is content with Truth, the lord of
Thebes. Made by the outline (draftsman) Nebreᶜ and (his)
son, Khay".

In short, the scene on the upper register in all probability pictures Nebre's original prayer on behalf of his son, Nakhtamūn,
when he visited the temple in order to seek the aid of the god.
The only conceivable reason for the presence of the temple on the
stela, behind the god, would be because the prayer took place inside the temple. Since the god, obviously, is more important
than the building, he has pride of place in the scene. Thus he
is portrayed superimposed on the edifice.

On analogy, the same line of reasoning which I have applied to the Abydene stela Cairo 16/3/25/12 and to stela Berlin
23077, should also be applied to the stelae with the smiting
scene. This is numismatically abbreviated on those where the
pylon gateway is shown (note particularly stela nr. 14) and is
even more simplified on those where it is not. The representation
of the cult statue in profile gives the false impression that it
is standing in the temple's forecourt, which, obviously, it is
not. Nevertheless, that the ceremonial execution was carried out
in the forecourt seems certain for several reasons, not the least
among which is the fact that this was the only part of the temple
which was accessible to the lay public.[120] Indeed, not only on
stela nr.14, but also on stela nr. 11, the dedicator is shown
outside the gateway, adoring the king as he performs the slaughter within. On stelae nrs. 3, 4, 6, and 9, and on rock stelae
nrs. 15, 16, 18, and 19, which also picture the dedicator watch-
ing the sacrificial rite, we may assume that these are simplified
illustrations of the ceremony which, pars pro toto, is indicated
by the king, the victim(s) and the cult statue of the god. In
all of these cases, as in that of Cairo 16/3/25/12 and Berlin
23077, for both technical and traditional reasons, the worship-

pers are shown outside the temple or are separated from it by
being placed in the lower register, but it is most likely that
they actually watched the ceremony from inside the temple's forecourt which, as will be shown below, was the normal venue for
ceremonies of this nature.

On his Amada stela, Amūnhotpe II recorded the execution
of 7 Syrian rulers as follows:[121]

"His majesty returned in joy to his father, Amūn, after
he had slain, with his own mace, the 7 princes who had
been in the region of Takhsi, with them placed upside-
down from the prow of the falcon-ship of his majesty.
... Afterwards, the bodies of 6 of these enemies were
hanged from the wall of Thebes, the hands[122] as well.
Then the other enemy was taken southwards, to Nubia,
and hanged from the wall of Napata".

Although it would appear, in this text, that the captives were
executed in Asia, this does not preclude other captive chiefs
from having been brought back alive to Egypt on other occasions[123]
to grace the pharaoh's triumphal return and to figure in his
thanksgiving to the gods, after which, as in Rome millenia later,
they were ceremonially slain. The Amada text strongly suggests,
in view of the treatment of the corpses of the victims, that the
degradation was witnessed by the Egyptian populace, who undoubtedly savoured the humiliating spectacle of the bodies hanging
from the walls of Thebes and Napata (and, we may assume, from
those of other major Egyptian cities). Is it not unreasonable,
then, to suppose that the execution of the captive enemy rulers
was, likewise, an essentially public affair, if not a public holiday? In this respect, the importance of the ceremonial execution

of the defeated enemy leaders is underscored by its prominent occurence on the walls of the temples. Certainly, in the magnifi-
cent series of battle reliefs of Seti I at Karnak[124] and those of
Ramesses III at Medinet Habu,[125] to cite but 2 examples, the final scene in each series is the formal despatch of the conquered
chiefs before the gods.[126] That these particular scenes were,
indeed, the most important within the series which they culmina-
ted is quite apparent from their placement on the temple walls.
Although chronologically they should have come last, inasmuch as
they depicted the final episode of their respective narratives,
their location, usually on the face of the pylon, insured that
that they would be the first scene to be viewed by anyone who approached the temple's entrance. While they obviously presented
the timeless truth of the triumph of the king at all times over
all of his foes, they must also have illustrated a specific act
in a specific ceremony at a specific point in time.

We may now turn to the question asked earlier about the
inspiration, prototype, motivation, and historical reality behind
the appearance of the royal motif of the ceremonial sacrifice on
the non-royal monuments surveyed above. I have already suggested that what was represented pictured an actual event. However,
it may be argued that this was not the case and that what is en-
ailed here is nothing more than a visual illustration of the royal myth demonstrating the inevitable and invincible triumph of
Egyptian pharaoh[127] which normally entered into the repertoire of
the tableaux of royal stelae and then, for reasons unknown to us,
though perhaps by imitation, also entered into the repertoire of
private stelae scenes. In support of such an arguement, one
might cite the well-known scene of Sahureʿ smiting a Libyan chief

in the presence of his wife, Khutyotes, and his sons, Usa and Uni,
with a detailed list of the herds of animals which had been taken
as plunder appended.[128]   Just as this seeming historical statement loses its historical credibility in the light of those showing Pepi I, Pepi II, and Taharka, likewise slaying a Libyan ruler
in the presence of his identically-named wife and children,[129]
the same could hold true for virtually every representation of
the pharaoh smiting an enemy.[130]   Nevertheless, as John Wilson
noted over 2 decades ago, at some point in time an Egyptian king
undoubtedly did slay a Libyan prince in the presence of his wife,
Khutyotes, and his sons, Usa and Uni, an event which subsequently
entered the royal myth.[131]   In other words, in spite of the fact
that the scene ultimately became incorporated into the royal myth,
it did at some particular time illustrate a real event. While
the obvious propagandistic value of the scene, whether it appears
on a temple pylon or wall, on a free-standing or a rock-cut stela,
particularly on the latter which are found in the border marches
of Egypt and beyond, cannot be either minimized or overlooked,
the fact that in many of these latter instances specific, known
individuals commissioned its portrayal, with themselves appearing
as spectators of it, suggests that in these cases, at least,[132]
more than a glorification of the king via the royal myth was intended, and that an actual event was also being shown and commemorated.

Starting, then, from the premise that the smiting does
depict an actual, physical event, as is, indeed, suggested if not
explicitly stated textually,[133] it is then patently obvious that
this event was the inspiration for and the historical reality
which underlays its appearance in art, particularly in monumental

temple art. While it is logical to assume that the temple scene, in turn, was the prototype of the stela scene, this probably was not the case unless, by this assumption, is understood the technical and mechanical aspects of reproducing a real event in a two dimensional picture. It is manifestly evident that the inspiration for the stela scene also would have been the actual ceremony.

It follows, then, that since a real event seems to have been shown on these private stelae, albeit frequently in an abbreviated manner, it must have taken place at a specific time and in a specific building, obviously a temple[134] which must also be depicted in the scene. Consequently, the next points to be determined, if possible, are at what time or times, on what occasion or occasions, and in what temple, or temples?

Only the double-stela of Setau at Abu Simbel has any specific date,[135] namely regnal year 38 of Ramesses II.[136] The text, itself, gives no indication of why this monument was commissioned or exactly what it commemorates.[137] John Schmidt has suggested, most cautiously, that, since year 38 is the earliest known date for Setau, the commissioning of the stela could have marked his installation as viceroy of Kush.[137] Even so, this does not explain why the king is pictured on it in the act of slaughtering several foes. We would expect that the ritual execution of a conquered ruler to take place only after the war in which he had been defeated was ended, and then during the victory celebrations. How soon these would have taken place after the war was over, however, is another question, although, reasonably, we should not expect the time gap to have been very long.[139] We might expect the nationalities of the prisoners to give an indi-

cation of against whom the war had been fought. In the case of
the Abu Simbel double-stela, however, this actually confuses the
issue for, according to the drawing of Lepsius, some of the victims seem to have been Asiatics,[140] but there is no evidence for
any war of Ramesses II in Asia after year 21, the date of his
treaty with the Hittites.[141] Moreover, the adscription to the
prisoners on the south stela identifies them as "the chiefs of
wretched Kush", and this, undoubtedly, was who they were. We may
well assume that the artist who prepared this stela was influenced by what now must have been a stock scene in his repertoire
and gave no really careful attention to whether or not the nationality of the victims was in harmony with what the accompanying
text recorded.[142] Certainly long after that had been any major
war waged by Ramesses II in Nubia, there must have been the more
or less frequent border incidents and engagements which have always plagued the frontier between a civilized state and its bar-
barian neighbour. In other words, what the double-stela commis-
ioned by the viceroy of Kush, Setau, in regnal year 38 of Ramesses II, may have pictured is the ceremonial sacrifice of several
Kushite chiefs taken after a border skirmish, with the reason for
the commissioning of the stela being to mark Setau's installation
as viceroy. In its execution, however, the scene and the event
which it pictured were transformed into the less factual, but more
dramatic illustration of the royal myth. Such an interpretation
could very well be applied to the other rock-stelae erected by
other viceroys and their immediate subordinates,[143] but we are
still faced with the problem of why this same scene of the triumph of pharaoh should figure on the stelae of private individuals of lesser rank, not on the border marches, but in Thebes,

Memphis, and Qantir, from whence most of the free-standing stelae
which contain it originate. Most of those which have **texts** do
not elucidate this point. The texts only indicate that the stela
in question was "made by" so and so and/or contain a short hymn-
let.[144] One, however, the stela of Wosimareʿnakht from Qantir
(nr. 8), the text of which records the bestowal of a grant of
land to him <u>as</u> <u>a</u> <u>reward</u>, provides the key to our understanding of
the rationale for the commissioning of stelae with this scene by
people of lower rank. At first glance, the combination of the
text and tableau of the Qantir stela seems incongruous, the former appearing to have no relation to or bearing on the nature of
the latter. After all, what does the picture of the slaying of
an enemy ruler have to do with the awarding of a land grant by
the king? Seemingly nothing, until we remember that the scene is
a representation of a <u>public</u> ceremony. The inference from this is
clear: what could be more logical at the conclusion of such a public ceremony in which the evil are justly punished, then to con-
fer rewards on the good, on the various loyal and deserving subjects of the king? Likewise, it would be equally logical for the
recipients of such rewards to commemorate both the award <u>and</u> the
the ceremony at which it was given. When viewed in this light,
Schmidt's speculation about the motivation for the commissioning
of the Abu Simbel double-stela of year 38 becomes quite plausible.
Additional support for the probability of this being the correct
interpretation is to be found in the more varied group of stela
scenes to be discussed more fully below, in Chapter 2, which illustrate an entirely different ceremony and its aftermaths.
Stelae Hildesheim 374[145] and Louvre C 213[146] both picture their
dedicators, "the soldier, Mose, of the great company ʿRamesses-

mi῾amūn, the Beloved of Atum'"[147] and "the overseer of the royal harim, Hormin",[148] standing before the window of appearances and receiving gold collars from the king's own hand, Mose from Ramesses II, Hormin from Seti I, in a public ceremony. Stela Cairo CG 34.177[149] shows "the scribe of the offering table of the lord of the Two Lands, Any" riding ih his chariot after the award, his neck laden with similar gold collars. Stelae Cairo CG 34.178 and CG 34.180, both of which also belong to Any, show him wearing these collars as he sits at a table and is attended by a servitor.[150] Although this group of 5 stelae, all of which depict their owners wearing this gold of honour, show incidents related to a ceremony outside the scope of the present chapter, it may nevertheless be noted here that, on 2 of them, a specific public ceremony is recorded and that, on the remaining 3, the fact that the stela's owner is shown wearing the gold, indicates that the awarding of it to him was, without question, a significant and important event of his life. With this in mind, we may then logically conclude that those dedicators of the stelae with the smiting scene would have regarded their mere attendance at the ceremony and their witnessing of the execution as an important event in their lives, one worthy of commemoration. This, of course, is quite consistent with the psychological rationale which underlays the raison d'être of many, if not all, Egyptian stelae.

E

In the preceding Section I have attempted to establish that the smiting scene depicts the very formal occasion, at which the dedicator was present, when captive enemy chiefs were ritually despatched in the presence of a god, that they did not merely commemorate or reiterate in a symbolic manner the eternal triumph, power, and invincibility of pharaoh. Since the time range of the stelae extends from the middle of the 18th Dynasty until, at the least, the beginning of the 20th (assuming that when the cartouche of a king is present, then the stela is to be dated to his reign),[151] it is obvious that, although the same ceremony is being shown, it is being shown at different times and in different places. It would, therefore, be most satisfactory if we could then assign or relate somehow the individual sacrifices pictured on those stelae whose date seems to be firmly assured by the cartouche of a specific king to the triumphant aftermath and the victory celebrations which followed a specific war known to have been waged in the reign of the king in question. In the lifht of our extant evidence, however, this can hardly be more than speculation and, probably, often fruitless speculation at that. Thutmose IV is shown slaying variously a Libyan, a Nubian, and an Asiatic.[152] While there is no evidence, whatsoever, of any campaigning on his part against the Libyans, the Konosso stela of his year 8 records a punitive action against Nubian raiders, as does that of his year 7, unless these two inscriptions, as has been suggested, refer to the same event.[153] Whatever its exact nature may have been, such military activity which this king carried out in Asia, whether in North Syria or in Palestine,[154] seems to have been ended by his regnal year 6.[155] Consequently, the victory celebrations depicted on the stelae dated to his reign might have taken place around year 8 and the stelae, themselves, may have been carved at about the same time.[156]

The only military activity attested for Horemheb **after** he became king (and its nature is debatable for it seems to have been a propagandistic lie rather than a bona fide campaign) **did take**

place in Nubia.[157] Conversely, the only military activities in
Asia in which he may have taken part were most likely carried out
while various of the Amarna pharaohs sat on the throne, but after
gaining the throne himself, Horemheb claimed that even these were
part of his royal achievements.[158]

The captive being slain by Seti I on the rock-cut stelae
at Aswan (nrs. 15-17) was probably a Nubian.[159] While it is true
that his nationality cannot be ascertained from De Morgan's drawings, Seti I is known to have waged at least one real war in the
south, about regnal year 8, against the Nubian country of Irem,[160]
the viceroy of Kush, Amenemope, who commissioned these stelae,
held office for all of Seti I's reign, possibly even into the
opening years of that of Ramesses II,[161] and these rock-cut stelae
are all located on the frontier of Egypt and Nubia where, if only
for reasons of propaganda and of intimidation, we would expect to
see triumphs over Nubians flaunted. Consequently, it is not for-
cing the evidence to associate these scenes of the execution of
a Nubian prince with the Nubian war of Seti's year 8, with the
ceremonial slaughter taking place sometime after year 8, the 13th
day of the 3rd month of the Proyet season, when the victory was
achieved.[162] If, however, this were the case, then it is clear
that the occasion which prompted Amenemope to commission the car-
vings was not his installation as viceroy (as probably was the
reason for the commissioning of the double-stelae of Setau at Abu
Simbel)[163] inasmuch as Amenemope, by this time, had already been
in office for several years.

Excluding the Abu Simbel double-stela, the other non-royal
monument with a smiting scene which can be securely fixed to the
reign of Ramesses II is that of "the scribe in the Place of Eter-

nity, Ramose", from Deir el-Medineh (nr. 6).[164] Here, although
3 distinct ethnic types are shown being despatched simultaneously
by the king, a Nubian, a Syrian, and a Shasu,[165] it is quite
possible that the representation is not real, but only a reitera-
tion of a stock scene. However, since no Hittite is shown among
the victims, it could also very well be that the ceremony which
was represented reflected, retrospectively, events which took
place before the Kadesh campaign against the Hittites in regnal
year 5. In this event, the Nubian captive may be associated with
the victory against the Nubians pictured at the Beit el-Wali temple which seems to date from the earliest years of Ramesses II's
reign, when he was still coregent with Seti I,[166] and also at
the temple of Derr.[167] The Syrian and the Shasu could easily be
associated with a victory in Palestine or Syria during the campaign of year 4, which saw Ramesses reach as far north as the
Nahr el-Kelb near Beirut.[168]

Since the major military activity carried out during the
reign of Merneptah was the repelling of the invasion by the coal-
of Libyans and Sea Peoples in his regnal year 5, it is not at all
surprising to find a Libyan pictured as the sacrificial victim on
the single stela which is more or less firmly dated to his reign,
(nr. 7),[169] and it is not unreasonable,then, to suppose that the
stela in question had been commissioned and set up in this year,
or shortly thereafter.

Virtually nothing is known of the events, either internal
or external, of the short reigns of Amenmesse and Seti II. However, if my interpretation of the historical reality behind and
the inspiration for the smiting is acceptable, then certainly the
the scene of the rock-cut stela which the legate of Wawat, Mery,

set up at Abu Simbel (nr. 19) in honour of Amenmesse and which
was later usurped by Seti II[170] should be taken as an indication
of some military action by, at least, the former, an action then
either repeated or claimed by the latter. Since the prisoner being executed is a Nubian, this, together with the stela's Nubian
provenance and the fact that it was instigated by a high-ranking
official of the Nubian administration, should all lead us to expect that this putative military activity had taken place in Nubia, although it may possibly have entailed nothing more than a
punitive action on the border marches.

The last ruler to whose reign any of the private stelae
are firmly dated is Ramesses III, the stela in question being
that of the shield-bearer, Wosimare'nakht, from Qantir, which has
been discussed in some detail above.[171] The fact that one of the
prisoners shown on it is an Asiatic and the other a Libyan sug-
sests a time after the Second Libyan War of regnal year 11, for
although real warfare on Ramesses' part in Asia, and specifically in Syria, such as is illustrated in the historical reliefs
both at Medinet Habu and at Karnak, probably did not take place,[172]
the suggestion that some sort of military operation was carried
out in Asia following the defeat of the Peoples of the Sea in
year 8, in an attempt to drive them as far as possible away from
Egypt,[173] is quite plausible and undoubtedly contains an element
of truth. This, of course, would explain the presence of the
Asiatic here.

There were, obviously, very good reasons why captives of
a particular national type appear in some smiting scenes, but not
in others, or what on some occasions a single prisoner was shown
and, in other instances several. We do not have here an example

of artistic license or whim. It should be clear that the motif
of the king smiting a victim (in the presence of a god), while
certainly a conventional item in the repertoire of the Egyptian
artists, is to be taken more seriously that it usually is. It is
not to be dismissed as a mere, stock, scene.[174] When used judic-
iously, it can, as I have tried to show above, be a useful historical document.[175]

F

If the sacrifice depicted on the stelae was a real event
which took place at a specific time, after a successful military
operation, in a real temple, it should be possible, perhaps, to
the location of, at least some, of these temples, if not to identify them. On the great majority of the free-standing stelae,
the god in whose presence the execution of the prisoners is being
carried out is the Memphite god, Ptah.[176] Several of these stem
from Petrie's excavations in the great temple of Ptah at Memphis,[177] others were purchased at Giza and in Cairo, and probably
also originally came from Memphis.[178] 2 were acquired at Luxor
and may have originated in Thebes.[179] The provenance of the
others is unknown,[180] although it is not inconceivable that some
of them came from Memphis. It is likewise probable that the execution pictured on all of them was carried out in the forecourt
of the great temple of Ptah in Memphis. This, surely, was the
case with the pieces actually excavated there and, since at
least 1 of those bought at Luxor agrees so closely in its depiction of the architectural detail of the temple in which the ritual
was accomplished with those of unquestioned Memphite origin,[181]
it can scarcely be doubted that it portrays the same incident in
the same locality.[182] Moreover, being purchased in Luxor does

not assure an original provenance from Luxor,[183] but even if it
did, it is not impossible for the dedicator of the stela, who may
have lived in Thebes, to have been present a ceremony in Memphis,
which he later commemorated on a stela in Thebes.[184]

The single stela which pictures Seth as the deity presid-
ing over the execution was excavated by Habachi at Qantir and we
may assume that it was there, in a temple of Seth, that the ceremony pictured on it was carried out.[185]

While no god is shown on the stela from Deir el-Medineh,[186] it is reasonable to suppose that the prisoners shown on
it were actually slain before Amūnreʿ. Although it is difficult
to decide in which of Amūn's Theban temples this might have taken
place, the Deir el-Medineh provenance suggests that it should
have been on the West Bank of Thebes, and the reign of Ramesses
II suggests that it might have been the Ramesseum. However, considering the importance and the emphasis of the ritual slaughter
of the captive enemy chiefs, it is also not inconceivable, on
analogy with the Memphite examples, that it took place in the
most important temple of Thebes, the temple of Karnak.

With regard to the rock-cut stelae, it is most logical to
suppose that the rite depicted on them took place in the most important temple in their vicinity: the great temple of Abu Simbel,
obviously, in the case of the stelae of Setau and Mery.[187] No
deity is depicted on the rock-stelae of the viceroy of Kush,
Amenemope,[188] but since they are situated on the road between
Aswan and Philae, it is not difficult to assume that here the
sacrifice was offered to the most important deity of the region,
Khnūm, possibly in his temple on Elephantine.

Of the stelae of either firmly-assured or presumed Mem-

phite origin and/or connection, those which show the ceremonial
sacrifice as being viewed through the temple's gateway are remar-
kably consistent in detail, except for the numbers and nationality of the victims. These vary from stela to stela.[189] On two
stelae, the inclusion among other details of at least a pair of
and as many as four human ears, seemingly inexplicable at first
glance,[190] allows us to identify the particular manifestation and
cult statue of Ptah before which and to whom the sacrifice is
being consumated as "Ptah, (the pair of ears) who hears petitions".[191] It is probable that this particular manifestation of
the god was among the most important worshipped in Memphis. A
great many stelae have been found there, or are presumed to have
come from Memphis, which picture Ptah in combination with a pair
or several pairs of ears, together with the epithet "(the pair
of ears) who hears petitions",[192] sometimes with the epithet
alone,[193] sometimes with the ears, but not the epithet.[194] In
addition, a large number of stelae have been found, especially at
Memphis, which have no anthropomorphic representation of any god,
but show only a single ear,[195] a pair of ears,[196] or multiple
pairs of ears.[197] While the epithet and the ears are also found
with deities other than Ptah,[198] the stelae picturing only ears
have always been attributed only to Ptah.[199] While this view can
probably no longer be maintained today,[200] it is, nevertheless,
most likely that this was the case with those found at Memphis.
We are dealing here with the thoroughly Egyptian phenomenon of
depicting the same concept simultaneously in various ways, each
capable of standing alone, but, when used in combination with the
others, supporting, reinforcing, and supplementing them. In view
of this, it is then perhaps not too speculative to see this form

of Ptah in every representation of him from Memphis, even without
any other indication being present. Certainly this is the form
of the god on two of the stelae under study and, if all show the
same ceremony taking place in the same temple, it follows that
they should be taking place before the same cultic image and manifestation of the deity. If, in most cases, he is shown without
the accompanying ears or epithet, this is, then, another example
of the principle pars pro toto.

It should also be noted that the epithet "(the pair of
ears) who hear petitions" is, then, implicit in the representation of ears together with a deity. Along with the other gods at
Deir el-Medineh, it is found with Amūnreꜥ, and, although I know
of no instances in connection with Seth, it is found at Qantir
where Seth was an important god.[201] On analogy with the Memphite
examples, it is not unreasonable to suppose that in both Thebes
and Qantir, the cult statue before which this ritual slaughter
was consumated likewise bore the epithet "(the pair of ears) who
hears petitions". Admittedly, this can only be speculation, but
it is logical to offer thanks, by means of a sacrifice, to the
deity "who hears petitions" in the hope and belief that, by doing
so, the god will continue to hear the prayers of him offering the
sacrifice. In the cases under discussion this would have been
for continued victory.[202] Such a reciprocal exchange is even
suggested by the scene of the Qantir stela of Wosimareꜥnakht[203]
and by those on the Abu Simbel rock-cut stelae of Setau[204] and of
Mery.[205] Here, the god in whose presence the prisoners are being
slain is pictured offering the king a second weapon, a motif
well-attested in Egyptian art.[206] Insofar as one normally would
expect a weapon to be offered before it is to be used, and not

<u>while</u> it, or another weapon, is being employed. This action on
the part of the god seems somewhat out of place. The first idea
that comes to mind is that the artist must have conflated two
separate ceremonies which he depicted simultaneously: the ritual
despatch of the captured enemy leader at the conclusion of a war,
together with the giving of the sword and victory to the king,
which marked the divine sanction for the opening of a campaign.
This latter rite is graphically portrayed in the reliefs of Ramesses III at Medinet Habu where, at the beginning of the series
which illustrate the 1st Libyan War, Ramesses is shown standing
before Amūnreʿ. The king of the gods is seated on a throne,
while Thoth and Khonsu stand nearby, as witnesses. As Amūn presents a sword to the king, he says:

> "My beloved son, take for yourself the sword, that you
> may smite the heads of the rebellious countries! ...
> Forward, (my) son, to cast down him who attacks you, to
> slay (----)".[207]

Like the sacrificial rite, the ritual of conferring the
sword on the king at the beginning of a war figures as the scene,
often in an abbreviated and simplified form, on both royal and
private stelae.[208] However, this ceremony is <u>not</u> what is being
pictured in the tableaux of the Qantir and Abu Simbel stelae, nor
do we have here a conflation of the two rites, conferring the
sword and smiting the foe, in a single scene. What <u>is</u> being
shown is a more elaborate version of the triumphal sacrifice.
As was pointed out in the preceding Section, the first scene to
to greet anyone approaching the temple from the front was that of
the sacrifice, even though, chronologically, it should have and
would have concluded the narrative series of scenes of the king's

victory.[209] In its most expanded form on the temple wall, while
the king slaughters a host of cringing enemies, the god offers
him the sword and, at the same time, leads still more enemies to
the king to be slaughtered,[210] these being symbolically by the
anthropomorphic name-rings, each containing a different toponym.
On royal and private stelae, even on scarabs, it occurs in a much
abbreviated form, with the number of victims drastically reduced
and the additional captives which are presented by the god alto-
gether omitted.[211] The speeches of the god make it clear that he
has already granted victory to the king and that he shall con in-
ue to do so, as the following excerpts indicate:

"I cause the chiefs of the Southern Countries to come to
you, ... that you may give the breath (of life) to whomsoever you wish, but to slay whomsoever you wish, as you
desire. ... I will give to you my sword (here) before
you to overthrow the (Nine) Bows".[212]

"Take for yourself the sword, O victorious king! Your
mace has smitten the Nine Bows. ... I will give you
power. I will place the fear of you in every foreign
land and the dread of you in the hearts of their chiefs.
I will make your boundaries wheresoever you wish!"[213]

While this is, of course, highly symbolic hyperbole, it is, nevertheless, clear that the scene and the ceremony which it depicts
had a very real origin, one whose occurence is so graphically
recalled on some of the private stelae of the New Kingdom.

Footnotes:

7. See now B.G.Trigger, "The Narmer Palette in Cross-Cultural
    Perspective", apud M. Görg and E. Pusch, eds. <u>Festschrift
    Elmar Edel 12 März 1979</u>. (Bamberg: 1979) 409.

8. See J. Śliwa, "Some Remarks Concerning Victorious Ruler Rep-
    resentations in Egyptian Art", <u>Forschungen und Berichte</u> 16
    (1974) 97-117 and, earlier, H.Schäfer, "Das Niederschlagen
    der Feinde. Zur Geschichte eines ägyptischen Sinnbildes",
    <u>WZKM</u> 54 (1957) 168-176. Unfortunately, since I read neith-
    er Russian nor Polish, I have been unable to make use of
    either V.I. Avdiev, "Religionznoje opravdanie vojny v drev-
    neegipetskom iskusstvie, Sceny triumfa", <u>VDI</u> 4 (9) 1939,
    103-117, or Śliwa, "Zagadnienie przedstawieńzwycięskiego
    władcy w sztuce egipskiej", <u>Zeszyty Naukowe Universytetu
    Jagiellonskiego</u> 330 (1973) 7-22. This latter, however, ap-
    pears to be an expanded earlier version of his 1974 study.
    For the royal myth itself, see J.A. Wilson, "The Royal Myth
    in Ancient Egypt", <u>Proceedings of the American Philosophi-
    cal Society</u> 100 nr. 5 (1956) 439-442, and my "Beyond the
    Fringe: Sources for Old Kingdom Foreign Affairs", <u>JSSEA</u> 9
    (1979) 88.

9. See, e.g. <u>LD</u> III, pls. 61, 129, 140, 144; H.Ranke, <u>The Egy-
    ptian Collections of the University Museum</u>. (Philadelphia:
    1950) 15 fig. 2, 103 fig. 62; <u>ANEP</u> 102 fig. 312; The Epigra-
    phic Survey, <u>Medinet Habu II: Later Historical Records of
    Ramesses III</u>. (Chicago: 1932) pls. 101, 102, 114, 120-122.

10. See, e.g. J. Černý, A.H.Gardiner, and T.E.Peet, <u>The Inscr-
    iptions of Sinai</u>. 2nd ed. (London: 1952) pls. 1, 3, 5, 8; <u>LD</u>
    III, pls. 69 c, 81 g-h; <u>LD</u> IV, pl. 197.

11.   See, e.g. A. Rowe, A Catalogue of Egyptian Scarabs ... in
      the Palestine Archaeological Museum (Cairo: 1936) nr. 578;
      H. R. Hall, A Catalogue of Egyptian Scarabs, etc. in the
      British Museum I (London: 1913) nrs. 1108-1110, 2211; E.
      Feucht, Die Königlichen Pektorale (Ph.D. dissertation, Mu-
      nich: 1967) pl. 4, nr. 5; Śliwa, "Some Remarks ...", 101
      fig. 4; Pritchard, ANEP 101 fig. 310; C.R. Williams, The
      New York Historical Society. Catalogue of Egyptian Antiqui-
      ties ... Gold and Silver Jewelry and Related Objects (New
      York: 1924) pl. 8 nr. 26c; Staatliche Museen Preussischer
      Kulturbesitz, Aegyptisches Museum Berlin (Berlin: 1967)
      fig. 590; Rijksmuseum van Oudheden, Kunst voor de eeuwig-
      heid (Leiden: 1966) pl. 24; W.C. Hayes, The Scepter of Eg-
      ypt II (New York: 1959) 369 fig. 233.

12.   For examples of both types of royal stelae see, e.g. stelae
      Munich Gl. 29 and Cairo JE 13715, both published b W.Barta,
      "zwei ramessidische Stelen aus den Wadi Sannûr", MDAIK 20
      (1965) 98-101 and pl. 35; stela Gulbenkian Museum, Durham,
      1964/176, published by H.S. Smith, The Fortress of Buhen:
      The Inscriptions (London: 1976) 143, pls. 37 nr. 1 (drawing)
      and 77 nr. 3 (photograph); LD III, pls. 69, 81, 197.

13.   While, undoubtedly, I have not exhausted the literature on
      stelae, I have looked at the published monuments of the fol-
      lowing collections: The British Museum, Hieroglyphic texts
      from the Egyptian stelae, etc. in the British Museum 10 vols
      (London: 1911-); A. Moret, Catalogue du Musée Guimet. Gal-
      erie égyptienne, stèles, bas-reliefs, monuments divers (Paris:
      1901); E. Leqrain, Les monuments égyptiennes de la Biblio-
      thèque Nationale (Paris: 1879-1891); T.G. Allen, Egyptian

Stelae in the Field Museum of Natural History (Chicago:1936);
H.F. Lutz, Egyptian tomb steles and offering stones of the
Museum of Anthropology and Ethnology of the University of
California (Berkeley: 1927); O. Koefoed-Petersen, Les stèles
égyptiennes (Copenhagen: 1948); P. Lacau, Les stèles du Nou-
velle Empire (Cairo: 1909); W. Spiegelberg, B. Pörtner, and
K. Dryoff, Aegyptische Grabsteine und Denksteine aus süd-
deutsche Sammlungen 3 vols. (Strassburg: 1902-1906); B. Pör-
tner, Aegyptische Grabsteine und Denksteine aus Athen und
Konstantinopel (Strassburg: 1908); P.A. Boeser, Denkmäler
des Neuen Reiches, Dritte Abteilung. Stelen (Leiden: 1913);
J. Cerny, Egyptian Stelae in the Bankes Collection (Oxford:
1958); R. Tosi and A. Roccati, Stele e altere epigraffi di
Deir el Medina (Turin: 1972); H. Stewart, Egyptian Stelae,
Reliefs and Paintings from the Petrie Collection 3 vols.
(Warminster: 1976-1976-1983); E. Bresciani, Le stele egiziane del Museo Civico Archeologico di Bologna (Bologna: 1985);
P. Ramond, Les stèles égyptiennes du Musée G. Labit à Toul-
ouse (Cairo: 1977); J.M. Saleh, Les antiquités égyptiennes
de Zagreb (Paris: 1970); S. Bosticco, Museo Archeologico di
Firenze. Le stele egiziane 3 vols. (Florence: 1965-1972). In
addition, I have gone through my own collection of about 1000
photographs of mostly unpublished stelae and I have perused
the major journals, excavation reports, Festschrifts, and the
published handbooks of the collections and special exhibit-
ions other than those listed above, but these are too numerous to include here, though some are cited in various notes
throughout this study.

14. See above, n. 8. Of the unpublished studies, one is by E.S.

Hall, "The Pharaoh Slays his Foes" which was slated to appear in the alas, now-defunct, Miscellanea Wilbouriana, a second is D.R. Seton, The king of Egypt annihilating his enemies: a study in the symbolism of ancient monarchy (unpublished University of Birmingham M.A. thesis). I am aware also that there is a Munich PhD dissertation, written under the supervision of D. Wildung by S. Schoske, but, unfortunately, no details about it have been available to me.

15. See below, Section B, stela nr. 8, which is almost a meter high.

16. See below, Section B. stelae nrs. 3, 6-9, 12-14.

17. See below, Section B, stelae nrs. 1, 2, 4, 5, 10, 11.

18. See below, Section B, stelae nrs. 1-5, 7, 10-11, 13, and Section C, stelae nrs. 15, 16, 18b, and 19, all of which picture a single captive. The remainder of the stelae show several.

19. Except for nr. 8, where the god is Seth, nrs. 18a and 19, where he is Amūn, and 18b, where he is Horus of Buhen. No deity is shown on nrs. 6, 15-17.

20. With the combination maceaxe, see stelae nrs. 1, 2, 7, 9, 12, 15, 18a-b; With the ḫpš-sword, see nrs. 3-5, 8, 10, 13, 14, and 16. On stelae nrs. 6 and 19, the weapon is the pear-shaped mace. On nr. 11, where that portion of the scene where it appeared is lost, there is no way of knowing what it may have been. For the rather curious weapon which I call the maceaxe, see H. Bonnet, Die Waffen der Völker des Alten Orients (Leipzig: 1926) 41-42.

21. On stelas nr. 8 and 18b, the king wears the Blue Crown. On nr. 19 it is the White Crown. On nrs. 16-16, it is a bag wig. On all of the others it is the short, valenced Nubian

wig, the so-called "military wig" (for which see C. **Aldred**, "Hair Styles and History", <u>BMMA</u> N.S. 15 (1957) 141-147) which, with the exception of stela nr. 13, is surmounted by the horned, plumed **disk**. For this headdress see the next note.

22. See M. Aly, F. Abdel-Hamid, and M. Dewachter, <u>Le Temple d'A-mada</u> IV (Cairo: 1967) 18, where this headdress, listed separately from the crowns worn by the king, is called "the coiffure with ostrich plumes". It is not discussed under the entry <u>Kronen</u> in <u>LdAe</u> III, 811-816, but is briefly alluded to under the entry <u>Federn und Federkrone</u>, ibid. II, 142-144, particularly n. 10.

23. E.g. B. Bruyère, <u>Rapport sur les fouilles de Deir el Médineh (1935-1940)</u> (Cairo: 1952) 62; Bosticco, <u>Museo Archeologico di Firenze</u> 57. What argues against identifying this headdress as the atef-crown is that fact that in every case where it is shown, it lacks the concial crown to which the feathers and horns are affixed.

24. See stelae nrs. 1, 2, 6, 9, and 18a. On nrs. 8, 18b, and 19 the streamers appear to be affixed to the crown which the king wears. On nr. 4, although I can make out no streamer behind his head, I do seem to detect a trace of its end below his upraised arm. More curious is what appears to be a long tasseled object dangling vertically from the crook of his bent right-elbow. This looks like the long tasseled streamer sometimes affixed to the crown worn by Asiatic gods.

25. See stelae nrs. 3, 6-8, 10-12. On nrs. 1 and 5 the collar is summarily indicated by a single curved line at the king's neck.

26. The recessing and the cornice are clear on Petrie's photograph, but not on his drawing, where the former comes out as a three-sided frame and the latter seems to be a horizontally-hatched border.

27. Although exactly like the feather headdress referred t o above in n. 22 (save that no uraei rear up from the horns), Petrie's drawing does not show the sundisks. These, however, are just visible on the photograph.

28. Although visible in his photograph, in Petrie's drawing the projecting tops of the tails of the ms-sign are omitted, and the s is reversed.

29. For the New Kingdom writing of bity here with the Red Crown, see Wb. II, 330, 5, right hand column.

30. K3 nḫt.w rather than k3 nḫt is written, with both the quail-chick and the plural strokes clearly legible.

31. J.H. Walker, the translator of the texts published in Petrie, Memphis I, was unable to read anything here and dismissed the traces with the comment "indistinct titles". However, it is not unlikely, particularly in the light of the poor orthography and misspellings in the text itself, and also in the light of the poor quality of the drawing (see above, n. 25, and below, nn. 32, 33), that he just did not understand what was written. On both Petrie's and my own photographs, the beginning of the line is obscured by the shadow thrown by the projection of the right jamb, but I seem to see the scribe's reed pen and the traces which are visible suggest the rest of the hieroglyph sš.

32. Petrie's drawing shows a large t over the house sign, this followed by an illegible group consisting of a horizontal

stroke on top, with a hornlike sign curving up to meet it from below. On the photograph, however, the t is clearly the horizontal m. The indistinct group which follows is pitted and weathered, but I seem to make out nb "gold".

33. After the s of ms, Petrie's drawing shows an indistinct trace consisting of a tall, vertical stroke, crossed by a wide x, the lower left arm of which is lost. After this the balance of the line is left blank. The photograph, however, reveals the indistinct trace to be the determinative of the seated **man** holding a flail. In the supposedly empty space which follows this, the tip of the di-loaf and the entire and the entire ʿnḫ are quite clear. For the very common name, Ramose, see <u>PN</u> I, 218, 3.

34. Misspelled ḥ-t-p.

35. The loop of the ʿnḫ is missing.

36. Occasionally the open door(s) of the naos can be seen, see stelae Hildesheim 429 (published by L. Habachi, "Khataʿna-Qantir: Importance", <u>ASAE</u> 52 [1952] pl. 36B), Copenhagen AeIN 1346 (see Koefoed-Petersen, <u>Les stèles égyptiennes</u> pl. 30), Philadelphia E 13626 (Memphis find nr. M-4344), 29-65-563 (Memphis find nr. M-2768), Cairo JE 45552 (Memphis find nr. M-2904), and Brooklyn 19.91 (these last four all unpublished). Usually, when the naos is intended to be shown with the doors open, this is done by not completely indicating the its front, as on stela nr. 3, and see also stelae University College, London, 14573 (published by Stewart, <u>Egyptian Stelae</u> I, pl. 28 nr. 2), ex-Metropolitan Museum of Art 08.203.2E (published by Petrie, <u>Memphis</u> I pl. 11 nr. 19), passim. On the other hand, when the doors of the naos are meant to be

closed, this was accomplished by showing the naos' front
from the base to its cornice, see, e.g. stelae British Museum 262 and 263 (published by T.G.H. James, Hieroglyphic
texts IX, pl. 35), University College,London, 14392 (published by Stewart, op. cit. pl. 41 nr. 2), passim.

37. Normally one would expect an apotropaic statement here. If
this is such, then we should restore mry "beloved of" at its
its end. Otherwise, the sentence is another identifying la-
bel of the king. One wonders, however, if a different reading is not possible if what has been taken as the loop of
the t is not a scratch or pit in the stone. If this were the
case, then, on the authority of Wb. II, 227, 3, the falcon
could be read as nb "lord" with the two horizontals beneath
it as t3.wy "(of) the Two Lands". M3 remains unchanged, but
the horizontal line beneath its determinative, which really
does not look like the ʿ-arm, would be read as t3, the entire sentence then reading: "the lord of the Two Lands offers the land" which, after all, is exactly what the king is
doing via the person of the captive enemy chief.

38. For this rather rare title, see Wb. III, 139, 7, where, however, hry is written with the face and not the sky sign.

39. For the name, see PN I, 41,8.

40. The head of the .f-viper is obscured and touches the column
divider to its right.

41. Difficult to see, but certain. For other examples, see PN
I, 389, 22, where he suggests that it may merely be a variant of Ti3, ibid. 337, 18.

42. See PN I, 140, 9, where it is attested only as a masculine
name.

43. Hardly noticeable here, but certain.

44. The present whereabouts of the stela is unknown. It was
    last seen in 1921 when a listing of the Art Institute's Egy-
    ptian collection was made. It was not included among those
    Art Institute pieces which were acquired by the Oriental In-
    stitute of the University of Chicago and, since there is no
    record of its ever having left the Art Institute, it can
    reasonably be assumed that it is still there, misplaced in
    one or another of the Museum's storerooms (Personal Communi-
    cation of 18 February 1981, from Dr. Louise Berge, Assistant
    Curator, Department of Classical Art of the Art Institute).

45. Allen, loc. cit., while noting that it "was received through
    M. Emile Brugsch", suggested that it most probably came from
    Thebes, from somewhere near the mortuary temple of Thutmose
    IV, and $\underline{PM}$ II^2, 446, accepts this provenance. Allen, how-
    ever, gave no reasons for assigning a Theban origin to it
    and Bryan, loc. cit., is undoubtedly correct in suggesting a
    Memphite provenance for it on stylistic and iconographic
    grounds.

46. The long hair of the prisoner insures that he was an Asiatic,
    but the scale of the photograph and the seeming lack of any
    detail of his dress preclude a more specific identification.
    The lack of the beard suggests a Hittite, but other nation-
    alities are equally possible.

47. Sketchily indicated, but certain, the front wall of the naos
    can be traced at the bottom, between the back of the prison-
    er and the w3s-staff of Ptah. Its upper part is clearly
    visible above the captive's head and the god's arms. Its
    topmost part is somewhat covered by the tip of the staff.

For other examples of naoi with the doors closed, see above, n. 36.

48. Compare stela nr. 5 below, where the sky-hieroglyph again appears, but this time covering only the right half of the the tableau, and also stela nr. 2,above, where the scene within the aperture of theportal is inclosed by a thick, raised border. What appears to be the triangular projection of the left end of the sky is caused by a break in the stone immediately below. Nevertheless, both here and in the corresponding place on the right, I seem to detect a slight diagonal thickening of the uprights, as if, indeed, they were melding into the ends of a sky-hieroglyph. For the possible significance of these clear instances of this sign at the top of the scene, see below, n. 120.

49. Probably just a spelling error of no special significance, it occurs not infrequently with the name of Ptah, compare stelae Philadelphia E 12507, University College, London, 14393, and Rochedale Museum, number unknown (all published by Petrie, Memphis I, pls. 12 nr. 24, 10 nr. 9, and 11 nr. 15), ex-Museum Scheuleer S 995 (published by H.P. Blok, "Remarques sur quelques stèles dites 'à oreilles'", Kemi 1 (1928) pl. 9 nr. 2), Berlin West 14666, ex-Metropolitan Museum of Art 90.6.146, and Philadelphia E 13619 (all unpublished), all of which show this retrograde spelling. Note also stela Louvre E 13072 (published by Ledrain, Les monuments égyptiens pl. 19 nr. 2) where the god's name is misspelled t-p-h, and see also n. 34 above.

50. With enough room in the field below for a vertical cartouche to have been inserted. There is no possibility of reading

this group as "Lord of Maᶜat" and taking it as the epithet qualifying the name of Ptah. In that case it should have been written inside the naos together with the name of the god.

51. I possibly see a t3i-bird at the top, followed by a pair of horizontal signs below, but this is very uncertain. Until the stela can be located and can be physically studied, it is best to leave open the question of whether there had been an inscription here.

52. Unusual is this arrangement in which the woman is portrayed before the man, as if it were she who was the principal worshipper, even though it was he who explicitly dedicated the stela.

53. For the name, see PN I, 5, 24. Allen, loc. cit. transcribed it as "Yu", apparently misreading the aleph-vulture as the quail chick.

54. For the name, see PN I, 98, 17, where it is found in a somewhat different spelling. Allen, loc. cit. followed by Bryan, loc. cit. read the name as "Ist(u)", apparently reading the initial hieroglyph as the reed leaf, but the foot is very clear on the photograph. My old friend, Klaus Baer, also had no hesitation in reading this sign b, as is clear from a handcopy of the photograph which he had earlier sent me. Furthermore, there is no reason to inclose the -u of the name in brackets as Allen did. It is quite clear on the photograph.

55. Compare Alexander Badawy, A History of Egyptian Architecture. The Empire (The New Kingdom). From the Eighteenth Dynasty to the End of the Twentieth Dynasty. 1580-1085 B.C.

(Berkeley: 1968) 265 fig. 142 (the temple of Amūnre ʿ-Montu at Karnak North), and 271 fig. 145 (the temple of Hathor at Deir el-Medineh). For a representation of such a stairway with sidewalls (at the entrance to a periptal temple), see ibid. 281 fig. 156 and pl. 36 (from the tomb of Ipuy at Deir el-Medineh). For an ancient three-dimensional model of such a cult temple, complete with stairway (Brooklyn 49.183), see Badawy, "A Monumental Gateway for a Temple of King Sety I, An Ancient Model Restored", Miscellanea Wilbouriana 1 (1972) 1-20.

57. In general for the various types of Asiatic dress and natioalities, see Pritichard, ANEP 14-19 figs. 41-62 and 254-257. For earlier studies, see idem. "Syrians as Pictured in the Paintings of the Theban Tombs", Bulletin of the American Schools of Oriental Research 122 (April 1951) 36-41. For a stimulating and perceptive study on the accuracy and reliability of Egyptian representations of foreigners, see N. de G. Davies, "The Egyptian Expedition 1929-1930, The Work of the Graphic Branch of the Expedition", Bulletin of the Metropolitan Museum of Art (December 1930) 29-42 and idem. "The Egyptian Expedition 1928-1929, The Graphic Work of the Expedition", ibid. (November 1929) 38-41. Because of my inability to read Russian, I was unable to make use of I. V. Bogoslovskaya, "The Dress of the Ethnic Groups Settled in Canaan as Depicted in Egyptian Art of the Sixteenth to Twelfth Centuries", VDI 3 (153) 1980, 117-141.

58. The prenomen appears to be written Ḏsr-ḫpr.w-rʿ followed by an additional vertical stroke alongside those of ḫpr.w, and with a pair of horizontal lines, the lower of which is n, below. Undoubtedly these are to be read stp-n-rʿ, see Urk.

IV, 2113, 2118, 2120, passim. The nomen is garbled. The
falcon Ḥr and beneath it, at the left, the ḥb-sign are all
right, but behind the falcon is an n?, written with the Red
Crown, a second, similarly-written n, but facing in the op-
posite direction, is to the right of the ḥb and at the bottom of the cartouche is a horizontal n. Clearly, in view of
the prenomen, the scribe wanted to write *Ḥr-m-ḥb-mry-imn or
the like, but was probably defeated in this by the minute am-
ount of space available to him.

59. The foe at the left is certainly a Syrian, and the enemy in
the center a Nubian. The other prisoner, at the right and
facing the king, can be identified from his beard and from
his headcloth, the latter held in place by a fillet, more
closely as a Shasu, see E.F.Wente, "Shekelesh or Shasu?",
JNES 22 (1963) 167-172.

60. On this well-known individual, see now Černý, A Community of
Workmen at Thebes in the Ramesside Period (Cairo: 1973) Appendix B: The Scribe Raʿmose, 317-327.

61. So Bosticco, o. cit. citing Rosellini, and Berend, op. cit.
84 n. 1, citing a manuscript of Migliarini.

62. Op. cit. 508: "The prisoners, represented bearded, should
stand for Asiatics, but to what country of Asia they apper-
tain is difficult to say". But see above, nn. 46, 57, 59.

63. He has the short pointed beard and the neck-length curled
hairdo so characteristic of the Libyans, see O.Bates, The
Eastern Libyans (London: 1914) figs. 10,12, 20, 22-24, 49,
and pls. 1-3.

64. See ibid. 132 and the literature cited there.

65. Loc. cit., but dress and facial features alone do not fully

warrant such an identification. In my "The Winged Reshep",
JARCE 16 (1979) section B (71-73), I point out that virtually all of the Asiatic gods worshipped in Egypt, Reshep, Kes-
erty, Mikal, Baʿal, and Baʿal-Ṣaphon, look alike, are dress-
alike, and, if no identifying caption is present, can be
distinguished from one another only through their characteristic poses. But in these instances, it is the cult statue
of the god which is being represented, while here, on stela
nr. 8, if the offering of the sword by the god has any significance, it should be that of the god himself, rather than
his cult statue. Hence the pose is of no help in determing
who he was. Nevertheless, the provenance of Qantir for the
stela virtually assures that he was Seth. See, also, below,
nn. 185 and 201.

66. With the god's name written in honorific transposition.

67. Habachi, op. cit. 509 n. b, takes ⁓ as a writing for 𝖝 ⌐
    via confusion from hieratic, but it is more likely that it
    was confused with ↩ , see Wb. IV, 356, right hand column.

68. Here written without the final .t, but with the determinati-
    ve of the man with his hand to his mouth and plural dots.

69. For the name, see PN I, 85, 16. I do not take ḫꜣswty, as
    did Habachi, loc. cit. as a plural noun, connected with the
    preceding krʿ.w in his title by a direct genitive, but rat-
    her as a nisbe, here singular, "dweller of a foreign land",
    "outlander", on the authority of Wb. III, 236, 1, under-
    standing the following ↵ᵈ as the determinative. In other
    words, Wosimareʿnakht was not an Egyptian from a mountain
    region, but a foreigner in Egyptian service. This is con-
    firmed by the formulation of his name which has as an ele-

ment the prenomen of the king (see W.Helck, _Zur Verwaltung des Mittleren und Neuen Reiches_ [Leiden: 1958] 273). While none of the other men of this name known, are explicitly attested with the title "shield-bearer", it is most probable that both "the brigade commander, overseer of the foreign countries of Tonetjer, and overseer of the palace, Wosimare ͑nakht, of Tjeku" (fragment of a tomb jamb from Tel er-Retabeh published by Petrie, _Hyksos and Israelite Cities_ [London: 1906] pl. 31) and "the royal scribe,Wosimare ͑nakht, of the army" (hieratic ostracon from Qantir mentioned by Habachi, op. cit.511), both of whom had this same foreign origin and both of whom served under Ramesses III, are to be identified with him. For the title kr ͑.w "shield-bearer", see my _Military Rank, Title, and Organization in the Egyptian New Kingdom_ (Berlin: 1964) pars. 171-172 and refs. 477-478.

70. For the identification of this place with the village of Es-Sama ͑na, 2 kilometers to the southeast of Qantir, see Habachi, op. cit. 512-514, where other attestations of it are cited, but with a slightly different spelling.

71. Following Habachi, ibid. 509-510, textual note f.

72. Identified by Habachi, ibid. 486-487, with the well in Qantir.

73. Petrie, _Memphis I_, 8, assigned this stela to Munich, but it, somehow, entered the von Bissing collection and, ultimately, was acquired by the Kestner Museum along with many other sculptures and reliefs from this collection.

74. There is no reason to assume, as Bryan, loc. cit. has, that stelae nrs. 1 and 9 are of the same date and were dedicated by the same man. The Ramose of the Brussels stela and the

the Ramose of the Hannover piece each have quite different
titles which, unlike those of the various Wosimare'nakhts,
cited above in n. 69, have nothing in common. That the Brussels stela dates to the reign of Thutmose IV seems assured
by his cartouches, but see below, Section E, n. 151. However, no such explicit chronological indicators are present
on stela 9. Any attempt to date it can be done only on stylistic grounds, but there is nothing in the orthography or
paleography of the hieroglyphs, in t he composition and arrangement of the registers, or in the dress and details of the
figures to indicate a more specific date than late 18th or
early 19th Dynasty. If the name of the dedicator alone is
the basis for assigning both stelae to the same man, we then
should also assign stela nr. 6 to him, a patent absurdity
since this piece is firmly dated to the reign of Ramesses
II.

75. See above, n. 21.

76. Although neither Petrie's drawing on pl. 8 nor his photo on
pl. 9 show the cross bars of the sistrum's loop, the object
can hardly be anything else. If it had been a menyit-neck-
lace, we should expect the looped part to drape downward
over the woman's hand. And it certainly is not a flaming
brazier.

77. Petrie's photograph is on too small a scale here to be clear,
and his drawing is inaccurate. The sign to the left of the
di-loaf, as my own 1:1 scale photograph shows, is clearly
 . The sign following the n of sn, which looks like a
badly-carved grg or fnd, really does not exist. Actually,
it is a deep, diagonal pit which runs from the infinitival

ending .t of sn to just to the right of the middle of the following t3-hieroglyph.

78. Though not apparent in Petrie's drawing or photograph, the t shows clearly on my own photograph, as does the tail of the bird which is clearly the vulture and not the quail chick. The name is not attested in PN, but it does occur for a woman in the 18th Dynasty on a stela in the British Museum, nr. 322), see J. Leiblein, Dictionnaire des noms hiéroglyphiques I (Christiana: 1871) 225 nr. 675. There is just enough room in the now-missing 7th line to restore m3ʿ-hrw.

79. See above, n. 73.

80. For the significance of ears on stelae, see now my "Reshep Times Two", in W.K.Simpson and W.M.Davis, eds., Studies in Ancient Egypt, The Aegean, and the Sudan: Essays in honour of Dows Dunham on the occasion of his 90th birthday, June 1, 1980 (Boston: 1980) 164-165, nn. 52-54, and, earlier, M. Sandman-Holmberg, The God Ptah (Lund: 1946) 69-73, Blok, op. cit. 123-135. That the ears are all from the same side of the head, rather than being in pairs, is apparently of no particular import, since they are almost as frequently attested on stelae in this manner as in pairs and multiple pairs. See also stela nr. 11 and, also, Section F, nn. 190-200, below.

81. For the epithet, see my "Reshep Times Two", n. 54, and, especially Sandman-Holmberg, op. cit. 74-75. One wonders if, in the multiplicity of the ears, there is not a rebus, with the first pair to be read msdr.wy "the pair of ears" and the second sdm.wy "the ones which hear (scl. prayers)". Such a suggestion is even more tempting in those instances where

more than four ears are pictured, e.g. stelae Hildesheim
375 (published by Habachi, op. cit. pl. 34 B), ex-Metropolitan Museum of Art 08.205.2E (published by Petrie, Memphis I,
pl. 11,nr. 19), Copenhagen AeIN 1016 (ibid., pl. 13, nr. 20),
University College, London, 14398 (ibid., pl. 20, nr. 48),
passim. In such cases, the additional ears might also be
read as a participle, only this time in the passive rather
than the active voice, and as a plural sdm.w "that which is
to be heard". Support for such an interpretation is, perhaps, to be found in the famous passage in the Maxims of
Ptahhotpe, lines 534-563 (published by Z. Žába, Les Maximes
de Ptahhotep [Prague: 1956] 58-61) where the key word sdm is
repeated over and over, each time with a different nuance,
in a literary masterpiece of the type of punning which the
Egyptians so loved.

82. While it is not possible on the evidence of the name alone,
without the title or other corroborating data, it is, nevertheless, tempting to identify him with the well-known royal
butler under Ramesses II, Ramessesashahebsed. On the latter,
see now the stimulating article of **Spalinger**, "A Fragmentary
Biography", The SSEA Journal 10 (1979-1980) 215-228.

83. Starting at the right of the lintel and facing to the right,
one can, perhaps, with a strong imagination, discern the
trace of vertical sign, followed by a cartouche containing
a name ending in -ms-s(w), with a number of faint, indistinct
vertical hieroglyphs following. Although inscriptions on
representations of gates on stelae are not particularly common, they are attested, e.g. stelae nrs. 1 and 4 above each
show a pair of vertical cartouches in the center of the lin-

tel. Admittedly, the possible traces on the lintel of stela
nr. 14 are of a horizontal inscription, but horizontally inscribed lintels are also known to exist, e.g. lintel Philadelphia E 13573, unpublished, from the University Museum's
1915-1923 excavations at Memphis, find nr. M-4363, consists
of two horizontal lines: above is the winged sundisk, flanked by the epithet "Behdety" and below, facing an ʿnḫ in the
in the center are, at the left, the prenomen of Seti I, "the
king of Upper and Lower Egypt, Menmareʿ, the Beloved of
Amūn" and, at the right, his nomen, "the Son of Reʿ, Seti-
merneptah, the Beloved of Mūt".

84. The reed leaf of i̯3w and the body and arm of the seated man
with his hand raised in the salutation are clear at the beginning of the lacuna. The curved underside of the ḵ-basket,
together with its handle, here reversed so that it is on the
left, are still visible. There is just enough room in the
break to restore the plural strokes of i̯3w and the horizontal n.

85. For the name, see PN I, 251, 8.

86. As on stelae nrs. 1, 3, 4, 6, 8, 9, 11, and 14.

87. Omitted are the rock-cut stela of the viceroy of Kush, Amenemope at Kasr Ibrim, the Aswan stela dated to year 2 of Ramesses II, and the lesser Abu Simbel stelae (nrs. 12 and 13).
All are included below in the Appendix to this study, where
the reasons for their exclusion from Section C will be given.
However they shall, on occasion, be referred to in some of
the notes which follow.

88. The men who commissioned these monuments were the heads of
the Nubian provincial administration: the viceroy of Kush,

the legate of Wawat, and possibly a fortress commander.

89. On this personage, see G.A. Reisner, "The Viceroys of Ethiopia", JEA 6 (1920) 38-40, H. Gauthier, "Les 'Fils Royaux de Kouch' et les personnel administratif de l'Éthiopie", Rec. trav. 39 (1921) 201-205, and Habachi, "The Grafitti and Work" 26-27. For his monuments, see KRI I, 302-303.

90. For the fan as a badge of office, see Reisner, op. cit. 80-82 and pls. 9-10.

91. Not apparent in Lepsius' drawing, but clear on my own photograph.

92. So, from Lepsius' drawing. My own photograph, unfortunately, is not clear on this point. See, however, the next note.

93. It is only on this stela that what the king is doing is explicitly stated in the text, unless the suggestion made in n. 37 above, that the text behind the king on stela nr. 3 is to be read: "the lord of the Two Lands offers the land" is correct. If so, then "offering the land" would mean the same as "crushing the chiefs" of the land involved, here the chiefs of Kush or, rather, of certain Kushite tribes.

94. This actually was the ka of the king, as was shown by P. Barguet, "Au sujet d'une représentation du ka royal", ASAE 51 (1951) 205-215. For a clear representation of the royal ka in a fully anthropomorphic guise, see tomb relief University College, London, 14481 + 14581, published by Stewart, op. cit. pl. 45 nr. 1.

95. For the most recent discussion of this well-known viceroy of Kush, see M. Dewachter, "Remarques à propos d'huisseries en pierre retrouvées au temple Nord de Ouadi es-Séboua", CRIPEL 7 (1985) 23-37. For his monuments and the earlier studies

see my "Setau at Memphis", The SSEA Journal 8 (1977-1978) 42-44, and KRI III, 80-111.

96. Not really clear in Lepsius' drawing, but quite visible on my own photograph.

97. The right hand text has nb ḫ‘w "lord of Diadems" here. T3.wy is recorded in Lepsius', but not in Habachi's drawing.

98. Habachi's drawing here and in every other instance where a royal name is given in the text omits the later usurpation of Seti II in order to show the original elements of the name of Amenmesse. I have retained the usurpations in my translation, since they are what are seen today. That the rock-stela was cut during Amenmesse's reign is certain, see Habachi's convincing arguments, op. cit. 62-64.

99. The corresponding right hand text here simply mi R‘ "like Re‘".

100. The corresponding right hand text here has mry Hr nb Mi‘m "the Beloved of Horus, lord of Miam".

101. Bity is written simply with the Red Crown, for which writing see Wb. II, 435, right hand column.

102. Habachi's drawing shows, vertically, h-W3-w3, where h is obviously an error for the tall n, for, inasmuch as the following pair of w3-signs make it certain that the toponym "Wawa-(t) was to be read, the preceding sign should have been a genetival n. For the office and function of the legate of Wawat, see Gauthier, op. cit. 229-230, where the legate Mery is discussed, and Reisner, op. cit. 84-85.

103. See above, n. 86, for examples.

104. As, e.g. on stelae Gulbenkian Museum, Durham, 1964/176, Munich GL 29, and Cairo JE 13715, see above, n. 12, for the

references.

105. And also on those rock-cut stelae which do not picture the sacrifice being offered in the presence of a god, see nrs. 15-17.

106. The preserved portion of the Durham stela measures 70 x 89 cm. The similarly incomplete stela Munich Gl. 29 measures 135 x 87 cm. A stela found at el-Alamein in 1942 and now republished by Habachi, "The Military Posts of Ramesses II on the Coastal Road and the Western Part of the Delta.", BIFAO 80 (1980) 20 and pl. 7, measures 70+x x 90+x cm. The only other free-standing royal stela known to me on which the smiting king motif appears, Cairo JE 13715, is intact and measures 144 x 75 cm.

107. See above, n. 12, for the publication. The text reads:
    "Long live the Horus, the Mighty Bull, the Beloved
    of Maᶜat, the sovereign, great of festivals like
    Tatenen. When he appears, everyone lives, the
    likeness of Reᶜ, the king of Upper and Lower Egypt,
    Wosimareᶜ-setepenreᶜ, the Son of Reᶜ, Ramesses-mi-
    ᶜamūn, who captures all lands in valour and vict-
    ory. None can oppose him. His sword is powerful".

108. See above, n. 12, for the publication. The text reads:
    "Long live the Horus, the Mighty Bull, the Beloved
    of Maᶜat, the lord of festivals like his father,
    Ptah-tatenen, Reᶜ who engendered the gods, the one
    who established the Two Lands, the king of Upper
    and Lower Egypt, the lord of the Two Lands, Wosi-
    mareᶜ-[setepenre'], the Horus of Gold, Rich of
    Years, Great of Victory, the Son of Reᶜ, the lord

of Diadems, [Ramesses-]mi῾amūn. Words said by Seth,
the Great God: 'My beloved son [-----'..Words said
by the king (or the like)]: 'I have come out of
love of you, O Great of Strength. May you be satis-
fied, for there is made for you [----]'".

It should be noted that I differ in some details from Barta
who, loc. cit., translates line 2: "den Re geboren hat, dem
die Götter die beiden Länder gegründet haben". The royal
character of such texts is also demonstrated by the very
fragmentary preserved portion of the el-Alamein stela (see
n. 106 for the reference):

"[-----], the Son of Re῾, Ramesses-mi῾amūn [-------]
enemies, together with [their] families(?). He over-
threw [------] upon his right hand of fighting, the
king of Upper and Lower Egypt, Wosimare῾-setepenre῾,
the Son of Re῾ [------] he captures the land of Libya
in an instant. He is powerful, the one who makes
[------]".

It should be noted that I differ greatly in my translation
from that of Habachi, op. cit., 20.

109. But on his own initiative and not by royal command, as was
the case with the overseer of treasurers, Neshi, who erected
the Kamose stelae, certainly the second and probably the
first, at Karnak, as is related at the end of the second
stela, see now Helck, Historisch-Biographische Texte der 2.
Zwischenzeit und Neue Texte der 18. Dynastie (Wiesbaden:
1975) 97 and, earlier, Habachi, The Second Stela of Kamose
and His Struggle against the Hyksos Ruler and His Capital
(Glückstadt: 1972) 44:

"His majesty commanded the prince and count, the
privy counselor of the palace, the chief of the
entire land, the royal treasurer, the conductor
of the Two Lands, the overseer of the companions,
the one who is powerful of arm, Neshi: 'Cause
that all which my majesty did in valour be made
upon a stela which will rest in its place in
Karnak in the Theban nome forever and ever!'
Thereupon he (**i.e.**, Neshi, who is pictured and
named at the end of the text) said before his
majesty: 'I will act in accordance with all that
has been commanded and that which is praised in
the presence of the king'."

110. But, if we were to carry this argument to its logical end,
we would then have to conclude, absurdly, that any tomb
scenes in which the king is pictured are, because of such
clear indications, royal tombs!

111. Published by A. Mariette, <u>Monuments divers recueillis en Égypte et en Nubie</u> (Paris: 1879) pl. 30a.

112. Written Pth M3ʿt nb, probably for harmonious reasons.

113. While such a meaning is not really attested for ḏb3 "to
dress", "to equip", <u>Wb</u>. V, 556, 1-558, 8, or for ḏb3 "to
"to replace", "to repay", ibid. 555, 1-556, 10, it, nevertheless, seems justified from the context. Ramose is doing
something with praises to the height of heaven, while he ex-
alts the beauty of Ptah. This can only be something like
"sending" or "singing" them to the god.

114. One would expect the preposition r to be employed here for
a place, rather than n, but, according to <u>Wb</u>. loc. cit.

neither verb d̠b3 appears to have been construed with r.

115. See my "Reshep Times Two", Section C, and my "The Winged Reshep", Section B, nn. 32-29.

116. See my "Reshep Times Two", Section C, nn. 52-55.

117. Published by A. Erman, "Denksteine aus der thebanischen
Gräberstadt", Sitzungberichte der Preussischen Akademie der
Wissenschaften zu Berlin, philosophisch-historische Klasse
(Berlin: 1911) 1087-1097 and pl. 16; idem., "Zwei Weihgeschenke aus der thebanischen Nekropole", Amtliche Berichte aus
den Königl. Kunstsammlungen 33 (1911-1912) cols. 15-20 and
fig. 14.

118. For other monuments of this man, see Erman, "Denksteine...",
1096, W. Spiegelberg, Aegyptische und Andere Graffiti (Inschriften und Zeichnungen) aus den thebanischen Nekropolis
(Heidelberg: 1921) 127 nr. 136. For the name, see PN I,
186, 1, and for the title, A.H.Gardiner, Ancient Egyptian
Onomastica I (Oxford: 1947) 71* nr. 180.

119. See Erman, "Denksteine...", 1087-1110.

120. It may be noted that the front faces of some of the Osiride
pillars in the first courtyard of the Medinet Habu temple
symbolically picture the sacrifice of the defeated enemy
ruler (see Medinet Habu II [Chicago: 1932] pls. 118A, C, E,
and 119A). In each of these instances, the depiction of the
execution is accompanied by a brief statement of the identity of the victim, respectively: "the wretched chief of the
land of Nubia", of "Temeh", of "Ta-sety", of "Peleset", of
"Kush", of "Kode", of "Kush" a second time, and of "Hatti".
Moreover, the full sacrificial scene is shown on the inner
faces of the columns on the south side of the same court-

yard, ibid. pls. 120-122. On these Ramesses is shown smiting Syrians, Libyans, Hittites, various Nubian types, and various other Asiatic (Palestinian) types in the presence of Amūn of Karnak or of Re ꜥ-Horakhty. As the king is smiting, the god simultaneously offers him a sword (on this, see below, Section F, nn. 206-213). Since the decoration of a particular part of the temple frequently reflected or indicated the particular services, activities, and ceremonies carried on in it, we may accept these pillar-base and column scenes as strong evidence that the ceremonial sacrifice of the defeated enemy prince was one of the functions which was carried out in the first courtyard, i.e, the forecourt, of the temple. This is confirmed, moreover, by certain iconographic details pictured on those stelae which actually take the shape of, or show, the pylon gateway (above, stelae nrs. 1, 2, 4, 5, 10-12, 14) where the actual scene of the slaying is always set off horizontally by a very broad and usually empty field at the bottom (though on stela nr. 4 kneeling worshippers are shown here), and by a much narrower empty field above. On stelae nrs. 2, 4, and 5, the upper field is either replaced or capped by the sky-hieroglyph. This runs across the full width of the gate's aperture on two of them, while on the third it covers only the right half of the scene. The sky-hieroglyph should have something more than just a decorative meaning here. I submit that it is a clear and obvious indication that the action which is depicted beneath it is taking place outside, in the open air. The curious empty rectangle below the scene can then be understood as picturing the part of the forecourt itself in which, on stela nr. 4, the spectators are actually shown.

121. Urk. IV, 1279, and most recently Černý, Le temple d'Amada.
Cahier V. Les inscriptions historiques (Cairo: 1967) 6-7 and
pls. 2, 7. The same barbarous treatment of the corpse of an
enemy chief is likewise recorded in the tomb biography of
Ahmose, the son of Ebana, at the outset of the 18th Dynasty
(see Urk. IV, 9):

> "Then his majesty (Thutmose I) sailed northwards,
> every land in his grasp, that wretched Nubian hang-
> ing head downwards from the prow of his falcon-ship
> and landed at Karnak".

It was not only dead enemy rulers who were transported to
Egypt to be humiliatingly exhibited there. An Amarna talatat from Karnak pictures a captured Syrian chief shut up in
a cage and hanging from the sailyard of a royal ship, see H.
Chevrier, "Rapport sur les travaux de Karnak, 1952-1953",
ASAE 53 (1955) pl. 7, and M. Abdul-Kader Mohammed, "The Administration of Syro-Palestine during the New Kingdom",
ibid. 56 (1959) pl. 1. Compare, also, S. Schott, "Ein unge-
wöhnliches Symbol des Triumphes über Feinde Aegyptens", JNES
14 (1955) 97-99, for the ideological meaning of such scenes.

122. The taking of hands and phalli as trophies and as evidence
for the bodycount of the dead is well-attested, both textually and pictorially, throughout the New Kingdom. Ahmose,
the son of Ebana, boasts of the separate occasions when he
"carried off as booty" hands (see Urk. IV, 3-5, 7), as does
Ahmose-Pennekhbet (ibid. 35-36). Before Megiddo, Thutmose
III notes of his soldiers (ibid. 659) that "they brought
the booty which they had carried off, consisting of

hands, of living prisoners, of horses, and of chariots".
The loot taken at Megiddo itself (ibid. 663) included "83
hands" and in a list of plunder taken on his final campaign
in Asia (ibid. 730-731) includes "29 hands". Amūnhotpe II
claims on separate occasions (ibid. 1304, 1307, 1308) and,
on the first of these "20 hands were (affixed) to the fore-
heads of his horses" as he travelled in his chariot. In the
Ibhet campaign of Amūnhotpe III (ibid. 1660) "312 hands"
are recorded in the list of booty. In the badly damaged
Karnak inscription of Merneptah (KRI IV, 8) "250 hands"
were taken from the Shekelesh and "790" from the Teresh. At
Medinet Habu, after the conclusion of the 1st Libyan War,
the scribes of Ramesses III are pictured in a pair of scenes
(Medinet Habu I, pls. 22, 23) recording the totals (running
into the thousands) of the hands taken during the fighting.
Likewise they are shown doing this after the 2nd Libyan War
(ibid. pl. 75). In fact, the triumphal recording of the
severed enemy hands and their presentation to the king, even
on the battlefield,is frequently attested in Ramesside art,
see ibid. pl. 42 and W. Wreszinski, Atlas zur altägyptischen
Kulturgeschichte II (Leipzig: 1914-1935) pls. 25, 62a, 64,
70, and 169, all of which show the same incident at the battle of Kadesh as portrayed on different temple walls. An
Amarna block from Karnak (see J. Leclant, "Fouilles et travaux en Égypte, 1952-1955", Orientalia 23 [1954] 65, and
Helck, "Abgeschlagene Hände als Siegeszeichen", GM 18 [1975]
23-24 with fig.) pictures a file of Egyptian soldiers marching, each with human hands spitted on his spearpoint, and in
a Kadesh scene (see Wrezinski, op. cit. II, pl. 70) an Egyp-

tian officer carries a coil of rope to which a number of severed hands are threaded. The great Karnak inscription of
Merneptaḥ (see KRI IV, 7) describes:

> "asses ... laden with the uncircumsized phalli of
> the land of Libya, together with the severed hands
> of [every?] country which was with them",

and a passage in a Ramesside literary text, P. Anastasi II,
5, 3-4, in praise of Merneptaḥ gloats:

> "How pleasant is your going to Thebes, victorious
> (nḫt.ti, which is crossed out in the original text),
>
> bowed down with hads and with chiefs pinioned in
> front of you. You will offer them to your glorious
> father, Amūnkamūtef".

In view of the foregoing, the walls of Thebes and of the
other Egyptian cities must have presented a revolting spectacle, festooned with these gruesome tokens of victory.

123. This certainly would have been the case with the Syrian chief
suspended in a cage from a ship's yardarm (see n. 121,above)
and, in fact, the stela of year 4 of Merneptaḥ from Amada
(published A. Abd-El-Hamid Youssef, "Merneptah's fourth Year
Text at Amada", ASAE 58 [1965] 273-280, and more recently by
Černý, Le temple d'Amada 1-3 and pls. 4, 5, 8), though dam-
and corrupt, and applying to the followers rather than to
their rulers, graphically depicts this:

> "There was no occasion for their survival. All of
> the people of Libya were carried off. ... They were
> given to the [----] in hundreds of thousands and tens
> of thousands, the remainder being impaled to the
> south of Memphis, destroyed. Everything was carried

off to Egypt. ... The Medjai(?) were carried off
to Egypt and fire was hurled against their multi-
tude in the presence of their relatives(?). (As
to) the remainder, their hands were cut off because
of their crime, and others had eyes and ears removed".

Since impalement was also inflicted on the defeated Nubians
of Ikayta after the Nubian war of year 12 of Akhenaton (see
stela Durham 1966/188 + 1966/213 + Philadelphia E 16022 A-B,
published by H.S. Smith, The Fortress of Buhen 124-125 and
pls. 29 and 75 nrs. 3-4, and most recently in my "The Nubian
War of Akhenaton", L'Égyptologie en 1979: Axes prioritaires
de recherches II (Paris: 1982) 300-302), we may well assume
that it was a regular feature of the punishments meted out
to Egypt's defeated enemies. The reference to the Libyans
being "impaled to the south of Memphis" makes it clear that,
like those defeated chiefs whose bodies were hung from the
walls of Thebes and Napata, the humiliation of the conquered
foe, dead or alive, provided a public spectacle for the Egyptians to gloat over.

124. Published by the Epigraphic Survey, The Battle Reliefs of King
Sety I pls. 2-14, 22-36. The most recent publication of the
texts is KRI I, 6-11, 13-15, 17-32. The most recent study of
them is that of W. Murnane, The Road to Kadesh. A Historical
Interpretation of the Battle Reliefs of King Sety I at Karnak.
(Chicago: 1985). See also below, n. 477.

125. Published in Medinet Habu I, pls. 9-11, 13-24, 26, 29-44, and
II, pls. 62-78, 87-99. The most recent edition of the texts
is that of KRI V, 8-20, 27-37, 43-54, 78-87. The best study,
translation of them, and critical commentary is still that of

W.F. Edgerton and J.A. Wilson, Historical Records of Ramses
III (Chicago: 1936).

126. For the arrangement of the Seti I scenes, compare the conve-
nient schematic drawing of their placement on the north and
east walls of the great Hypostyle Hall, between the 2nd and
3rd Pylons at Karnak published by Breasted in ARE II, 39:
the campaigns against the Shasu and Syrians, begins on the
northern end of the east wall and continues along the north
wall, with the sacrificial scene, the largest in the series,
positioned immediately to the left of the doorway in the
center of the north wall. Correspondingly, the series illustrating the wars against the Hittites and the Libyans,
which occupies the western half of the north hall, with the
final scene, the sacrifice, positioned just to the west of
the doorway. Even more telling is the placement of these
scenes at Medinet Habu. The historical series covers the
faces of the north and south outer walls, starting at the
back and ending on the exterior faces of the south and north
towers of the pylon, each of which bear only the single picture of the king smiting his foes. This, on a truely monumental scale, fills the vast expanses of the faces of the
towers. This scene is repeated, moreover, on the exterior
of the 1st Pylon of many other temples, Luxor, Edfu, and
Philae, to cite but a few.

127. See above, n. 8, and the literature cited there and add Bruyère, Rapport sur les fouilles de Deir el-Médineh (1935-1940)
61-64, "Note 8: Le roi vainqueur des peuples étrangers".

128. Published by L. Borchardt, Das Grabdenkmal des Konigs Sahu-
Re' II (Leipzig: 1913) pl. 1.

129. For the Pepi I version, see J. Leclant, "La 'famille libyenne' au temple haut de Pépi Ier", Livre du centenaire 1880-
1980 (Cairo: 1980) pl. 2. For the Pepi II version, see G.
Jequier, Le monument funéraire de Pépi II I (Cairo: 1938) pl.
8. For the Kushite version of Taharka, see M.F.L. Macadam,
The Temples of Kawa. II. History and Archaeology of the Site
(Oxford: 1955) pl. 15. For the implication of the repetition
of this particular scene and its potential value as an historical document, see my "Beyond the Fringe: Sources for Old
Kingdom Foreign Affairs", The SSEA Journal 9 (1978-1979) 87-
88 and, earlier, Wilson's pioneering study, "The Royal Myth
in Ancient Egypt", Proceedings of the American Philosophical
Society 100 (1956) 439-442.

130. See G.A. Gaballa, Narrative in Egyptian Art (Mainz am Rhein:
1976) 94-131 (= chap. 7) which is mainly concerned with Ramesside war scenes, for a particularly illuminating and en-
lightening discussion on this point. His trenchant comments
on the nature of such "historical" scenes and texts, particularly those of Ramesses III (128) are worth quoting:

"... the texts of Ramesses III are rather rhetorical
and very rarely give any specific event, location or
characters. Instead they concentrate almost wholly
upon the divine personality of the king. These
qualities are more or less repeated in the reliefs.
The scenes are repetitive and conventional. Each
scene is mainly centered around the heroic figure of
the king. His commanding, dominating image is every-
where we turn and always attracts our attention more
than the event depicted. ... In such composition

where the king is absolutely victorious and the
enemy is utterly defeated, the divine power of
the king meets no real challenge. ... Even the
presence of Egyptian and foreign troops in the
battles does not reduce the supremacy of the king".

131. Op. cit. 439.

132. These were made by "the ⌐scribe⌐ in the house of ⌐gold⌐, Ramose" (nr. 1), "the ḥry-wr-priest, Iry" (nr. 3), "the wᶜb-
priest of Ptaḥ, Bestu" (nr. 4), "the scribe in the Place of
Eternity, Ramose" (nr. 6), "the shield-bearer, the one from
the foreign land, Wosimareᶜnakht who will be justified" (nr.
8), "the overseer of weavers, Ramose" (nr. 9), "Ashahebsed"
(nr. 11), "Hori" (nr. 14). On the other hand, stelae nrs.
15-17 were dedicated by "the first charioteer of his majesty,
the fan-bearer on the right hand of the king, the overseer of
the Southern Land, the king's son of Kush, Amenemope", nrs.
18a-b were commissioned by "the king's son of Kush, Setau",
and nr. 19 by "the legate of Wawat, Mery".

133. See above, nn. 121-123, and the references cited there.

134. Although in the case of the Amada text of Amūnhotpe II (n.
121, above) the implication seems to be that the prisoners
were clubbed to death before the king returned to Thebes,
the text is not as to whether this took place on the battlefield. Were they first captured during the campaign and
then slain by the king after the final battle, or were they
killed by him during the course of several battles? There is
evidence for both possibilities.

135. See above, stelae nr. 18a-b.

136. Just the year is given. See, however, n. 140, below.

137. The text following the year date on each of the duplicates of the stela contains only the titulary of Ramesses II. Those accompanying the figure of Setau contain a pious wish for the king, on the one hand (nr. 18a), and a statement that Setau praises him (nr. 18b), on the other. Nothing more.

138. See J.D. Schmidt, Ramesses II: A Chronological Structure for His Reign (Baltimore: 1973) 49.

139. While, of course, this is only speculation, it may be noted that the execution of the Libyans taken in the war of Merne-ptah's year 4 took place in that same year, and that the Nubians of Ikayta captured in Akhenaton's Nubian War of year 12 were also dispatched in year 12 (see above, n. 123, for references).

140. See LD III, pl. 195b-c. On both of the stelae the prisoners seem to have long hair and beards. If so, they can hardly be Nubians. However, my own photograph of the captive on the south stela clearly shows a Nubian. Moreover, Lepsius' drawing shows only a single prisoner on the north stela when there are actually two. The Asiatic nationality of the captives on the north stela was possibly deliberate on the part the artist to balance the Nubian triumph on the south stela.

141. For the wars of Ramesses II, see KRI II, 151 (the dated documents) and 152-222 (the undated documents). For the probability that the undated documents of the Asiatic wars refer to events after the battle of Kadesh but before year 18, see my "Aspects of Ramesside Diplomacy: The Treaty of Year 21", The SSEA Journal 8 (1977-1978) 125-126, nn. 32-33. It is not impossible that the events recorded in some of the un-

dated documents referring to Nubian wars may have taken
place around year 38, but if this were so, it cannot be pro-
ven in the light of the present extant evidence.

142. But see the end of n. 140, above.

143. Habachi, "The Graffiti and Work..." 27, saw the rock-cut
stelae of the viceroy, Amenemope, at Aswan (abve, nrs. 15-
17) as evidence for a Nubian victory of Seti I which Faulkner, CAH 3rd ed. II chap. 23, **224** , connects with the pane-
gyric at Kasr Ibrim (below, Appendix, stela nr. 31) and the
Nubian War of Seti's year 8? which is recorded on a stela
from Amarah West and on its duplicate from Sai, see KRI I,
102-104 and, for the reading of the date, K.A. Kitchen, "Historical Observations on Ramesside Nubia", in E. Endesfelder
et ali., eds. Aegypten und Kush (Berlin: 1977) 214-219 and J.
Vercoutter, "Un campagne militaire de Seti I en Haute Nubie",
Rev. d'Eg. 24 (1972) 201-208; see also nn. 162 and 166 below. In this they are followed by Spalinger, "Traces of the
Early Career of Ramesses II", JNES 38 (1979) 276-281. Spalinger also sees the Nubian war pictured at the Beit el-Wali
temple of Ramesses II (see H. Ricke, G.R. Hughes, and E.F.
Wente, The Beit el-Wali Temple of Ramesses II (Chicago: 1967)
pl. 8) and also the Aswan stela dated to "year 3, month 3 of
Shomu, day 26" of Ramesses II (below, Appendix, stela nr. 22)
which was dedicated by an official (possibly a fortress commander, if the restoration of KRI II, 345 n. 10b is correct)
whose name is too illegible, for me at least, to read. In
this they are certainly correct, for, in spite of the arguments of T. Säve-Söderbergh, Aegypten und Nubien (Lund: 1941)
168, that the rock-stelae only contained stereotyped inscrip-

tions of the king, devoid of any real historical context, it
is difficult, if not impossible, to disassociate the Aswan
rock-cut stelae from that at Kasr Ibrim. That the latter
did reflect a real war is effectively argued by R.A. Caminos,
The Shrines and Rock-Inscriptions of Ibrim (London: 1968) 86.
The Aswan inscription of year 2 of Ramesses II, which contains an encomium to the king similar to that of the Kasr
Ibrim text, has been taken as a straightforward historical
document (e.g. ARE III, 204-205, pars. 478-479) although
there is only a bare allusion in it, and then only in the
most conventional terms, to the crushing of both Nubians and
Temehu Libyans. Nevertheless, these inscriptions, even without the positive confirmation of the Amarah West and Sai
stelae, or the implied confirmation possibly supplied by the
Nubian warscenes at Beit el-Wali (see Spalinger, loc. cit.
for these illustrating a war waged under Seti I, even though
Ramesses II appears in them as king), more than circumstan-
tially attest a Nubian war of Seti I. The Sai and Amarah
West stelae allow us to locate it more precisely in his reign.
The figure of the viceroy of Kush, Amenemope, is crucial to
this, since we know that he was followed in office by the
viceroy Iuny, probably in Seti's 9th or 10th regnal year according to Spalinger, loc. cit. 285, although I see no reason
why this could not have taken place as late as year 11, the
year Seti died. Reisner, "The Viceroys of Ethiopia..." 38,
allowed Amenemope a tenure of some 15 years, from ca. 1315-
1290. If Seti's Nubian war took place in year 8 and he came
to the throne around 1318 (following Faulkner's chronology
in CAH), then, even considering that the dates in question

are only approximate, it is still not improbable that Amenemope acceded to the viceroyalty previously held by his father, Paser, just around the time of Seti's war in Nubia.
Since his presentation of the tribute of Nubia to and his
reward in the presence of Ramesses II pictured at Beit el-
Wali (see below, Chapter 2, Section A, n. 215) are not to
be accepted at face value as having taken place under the
latter, but, according to Spalinger, op. cit. 280-281, reflect, rather, his activity under Seti I, he certainly
would have participated in this war. I leave open the question, however, of whether it was he or Ramesses II as crown
prince who commanded the Egyptian forces. With the Aswan
and Kasr Ibrim rock-stelae, then, Amenemope would have commemorated not only the king's victory and his own role in
it, but also his installation in office. This same rationale may be applied to the Aswan inscription of Ramesses II's
year 2 as well, for while it may and should have some sort

of historical basis insofar as it was commissioned by a private individual, it seems reasonable to suppose that there
there was another reason for its commissioning other than
those furnished by its generalized historical allusions.
This could very well have been the appointment of its dedicator, whatever his name might have been, to his post.

144. See above, n. 123.

145. See below, Chapter 2, Section B, stela nr. 21.

146. See below, Chapter 2, Section B, stela nr. 20.

147. For the unit called the "company" (s3) and its importance
within the structure of the Egyptian military establishment,
see my Military Rank 26-30 pars. 46-59. For the rank borne

by Mose, w⁽w, see ibid. 36-37 pars. 77-83. It is most probable that, in the case of Mose, here w⁽w did not indicate
a specific rank, but simply meant "soldier" in the most general sense, see ibid. 37 par. 82. As a distinct rank, w⁽w
"infantry soldier" was that of an ordinary ranker, the low-
est of the low within the military hierarchy. Mose, on the
other hand, was clearly a high-ranking officer of the unit
and probably even commanded it.

148. For the name, see PN I, 248 nr. 19. For his other monuments
see KRI I, 310-319.

149. See below, Chapter 2, Section B, stela nr. 22.

150. See below, Chapter 2, Section B, stela nr. 26.

151. While this is undoubtedly the case with the rock-cut stelae,
it does not always seem to have been so with respect to the
free-standing monuments. Stela Hannover 1935.200.230 (see
above, nr. 3) while clearly bearing the cartouches of Thutmose IV, nevertheless on stylistic grounds, particularly in
the treatment of the figures and the details of their dress,
looks to be of a later, Ramesside, date and is, in fact, so
dated by Munro, Städel-Jahrbuch N.F. 3 (1971) 35, a date
also accepted by the editors of PM (Personal Communication
from Dr. J. Málek dated 20 November 1980) and subequently
confirmed by conversations with various colleagues at the
Brooklyn Museum, notably James Romano, Richard Fazzini, and
Betsy Bryan, in March of 1981. Obviously a Ramesside date
for a stela bearing cartouches of an 18th dynasty ruler
would seem to present difficulties for the thesis which I
have proposed above in Section E above. Dr. Bryan, however,
has made the quite plausible suggestion to me that, since we

know that there was a cult of the deified Thutmose IV in the
Ramesside period, it could very well be that the scene on
Hannover 1935.200.235 pictures a reenactment within the cultic ritual of a major event from the lifetime of the deified
king, in other words, a reenactment of the original actual
ceremony with a priest playing the role the king in much the
same way as the Myth of Horus at Edfu reenacts the triumph
of Horus over Seth (see, most recently, H.W. Fairman, The
Triumph of Horus: An Ancient Egyptian Sacred Drama [London:
1974]). While it is true that most of what we know about
the cults of deified kings is in regard to their functioning
as oracles (see Cerny, "Egyptian Oracles" in R.A.Parker, A
Saite Oracle Papyrus in the Brooklyn Museum [Providence:
1962] 41-44), such a drama and portrayal of the important
events of their lives and reigns could quite plausibly have
been part of these rituals. The cults of the deified Amūnhotpe I and the deified Ahmose-Nefertari have been well-stu-
died, see Černý, "Le culte d'Amenophis Ier chez les ouvriers
de la nécropole thébaine", BIFAO 27 (1927) 159-203. That of
the deified Thutmose IV is less well-known. To the best of
my knowledge, it is mainly attested by representations of
offerings being made to his cult statue, see, e.g., stelae
Philadelphia E 11486, published by W.L.S. Loat, Gurob (London: 1905) pl. 16 nr. 2, Leiden AP 62, published by Boeser,
op. cit. (above, n. 13), and Cairo CG 24.170. For the cults
of deified kings other than those of the New Kingdom rulers,
see D. Wildung, Die Rolle ägyptischer Könige im Bewusstsein
ihrer Nachwelt (Berlin: 1969) and most recently his Egyptian
Saints: Deification in Pharaonic Egypt (New York: 1977) where

he also deals with the non-royal personages, Imhotep and
Amūnhotpe son of Hapi. For the personnel attached to a typical cult statue of a deified king in the Ramesside period,
see my "A Cult of Ramesses III at Memphis", JNES 22 (1963)
177-184 and Helck, "Zum Kult am Königsstatuen", ibid. 25
(1966) 32-41. It should be stressed that this explanation
for the Ramesside date of Hannover 1935.200.230 supports,
rather than challenges, my idea that the scene involved portrays a real event. If, however, this is not acceptable,
then the only logical alternative left to me, if my basic
premise is correct, is to assume that the Ramesside date is
incorrect. I am loath to do this in spite of the fact that
dating on stylistic grounds is not always absolute and that
many of the features used to support a Ramesside date for
the stela do appear already in the 18th Dynasty.

152. See above, stelae nrs. 1 (a Libyan), 2 (an Asiatic or a Libyan), 3 (a Nubian and an Asiatic), 4 (an Asiatic).

153. Urk. IV, 1545-1548. For a fuller bibliography see PM V, 254,
and for the most recent treatment Bryan, op. cit. 417-422.
For opposing views on the date of the Konosso stela, see
Helck, Urkunden der 18. Dynastie. Uebersetzung zu den Heften
17-22 (Berlin: 1961) 148 n. 2 and D.B. Redford, "The Chronology of the Egyptian Eighteenth Dynasty", JNES 25 (1966)
120.

154. For the most recent and best study of Thutmose's military
activity in Asia, see the penetrating analysis of Bryan, op.
cit. 417-422, in which she corrects all the misconceptions
offered by R. Giveon, "Tuthmosis IV and Asia", JNES 28
(1969) 54-59. Bryan has convincingly and persuasively dem-

onstrated that he waged only a single campaign, in Syria, and that any activity carried out in Palestine was nothing more than a "showing of the flag".

115. Assuming that the now mostly-lost text of the Konosso stela of year 7 did refer to some sort of military activity in Nubia, see Urk. IV, 1555-1556, and also assuming with both Redford and Bryan, loc. cit. that the date is not to be emended as Helck, loc. cit. proposes to year 8, then it still does not seem likely, given the probable logistical abilities of a New Kingdom army, even when led by the king in person, to have been able to have successfully campaigned in both Asia and Nubia in the same year. The most aggressive and energetic 18th Dynasty rulers, Thutmose III and Amūnhotpe II, did not attempt to war in both the north and the south in the same regnal year. With this in mind and remembering that the highest date attested for Thutmose IV is regnal year 8 on the Konosso stela (against Baer's supposed year 20 of this king, see Bryan, op. cit. 5-9), then some time during regnal year 6 is clearly the latest possible date for his military activity in Asia to have taken place.

156. Certainly we should not expect to find pictures of Nubians being ceremonially sacrificed before the campaigning against them had been concluded victoriously. It is perhaps significant in this respect that, of the four stelae bearing the cartouche of Thutmose IV, three, nrs. 1, 2, and 4, are iconographically so similar in showing the actual pylon gate as to suggest that they were carved at the same time. Stela nr. 3, which seems to be Ramesside in date and which pictures a ritual reenactment of the ceremony pictured on the other

three (see n. 151) obviously was carved long after the actual event took place.

157. See my "A Private Triumph in Brooklyn, Hildesheim and Berlin", JARCE 7 (1968) 34 and particularly n. 37 with the literature cited there.

158. See my "ʿAnkhesenamūn, Nofretity, and the Amka Affair", JARCE
15 (1978) 46 and nn. 17-22, especially 22.

159. See above, stelae nrs. 15 and 16. However, on the stela
which Amenemope had carved at Kasr Ibrim (Appendix, nr. 31)
the prisoner is clearly a Nubian.

160. See above, n. 143, also for references. While Säve-Söderbergh, loc. cit. argues that since no indications of this
war are included in the historical scenes and lists of Seti
I at Karnak, it could hardly have been more than a simple
"showing of the flag". In this he is followed by A.J. Arkell, A History of the Sudan from the Earliest Times to 1821
2nd ed. (London: 1961) 95. Faulkner, loc. cit. likewise
sees this as nothing more than a punitive enforcing of the
Egyptian peace in the South. However, it might be noted on
the one hand that Sai and Amarah West where the two copies
of the inscription recording this fighting were found are
relatively close to each other, so that a case could be made
for their having been erected there for purely local consum-
ption. On the other hand, the Nubian region against which
Seti campaigned has not been located with certainty as being
in the vicinity of Amarah West or Sai. For Irem as a place
and not a tribal name, as Faulkner assumes it to bee, see K.
Zibelius, Afrikanischer Orts- und Völkernamen im hieroglyph-
ischen und hieratischen Texten (Wiesbaden: 1972) 84-85.
Moreover, if the Nubian victory of the king alluded to at

Kasr Ibrim and suggested by the rock-cut stelae at Aswan also refer to the same war, we may safely assert that Seti's
triumph was proclaimed throughout the length of Nubia, something we would not expect to have been the case for a mere
punitive action. Clearly, then, Seti I's Nubian war, even
though not attested at Karnak, was a major **small war**, a colonial war. For the distinction between small colonial wars
and major wars, see my "The Nubian War of Akhenaton" Sections
A and C.

161. See above, n. 143.

162. The date, badly damaged, is preserved only in the Amarah
West version (see <u>KRI</u> I, 102). It reads:
It is more likely that it is to be restored to anything other
than　or　, with the former more likely. For the restoration of year 9, the upper five integers would have had
to have been squeezed very closely together to fit the available space, but see n. 166 below.

163. See above, n. 138.

164. See above, stela nr. 6.

165. See above, n. 59 with the literature cited there.

166. See W.J. Murnane, <u>Ancient Egyptian Coregencies</u> (Chicago:
1977) 67-70, where the arguments both for and against the
early dates of these scenes and hence the coregency are
clearly given. It occurs to me that, since the coregency
seems to have lasted until year 2 of Ramesses II and to have
overlapped the two years of Seti I (Murnane, ibid., 81-87),
it is not impossible that the Nubian war illustrated at Beit
el-Wali and alluded to in the Aswan stela of year 2 of Ramesses (so Breasted, <u>ARE</u> III, 205 par. 478 and Murnane, op.

cit. 87) was identical to the Nubian war of Seti, in which case the damaged date of the Amarah West stela is to be restored as regnal year 9, in spite of my remarks in n. 162, above.

167. For the Nubian war pictured at Derr, see A.M. Blackman, The Temple of Derr (Cairo: 1913) pls. 13-20. For additional bibliography, see PM VII, 85.

168. See KRI II, 1 (the middle stela of year 4 of Ramesses II at the Nahr el-Kelb) and for additional bibliography, PM VII, 385.

169. See stela nr. 7 and n. 61 above.

170. See n. 98 above. The name of the stela's dedicator, Mery, has not been altered. This suggests to me that he continued in office as the legate of Wawat after Seti II came to power. In fact, he may even have been responsible for the usurpation of Amenmesse's name, perhaps as a protestation or affirmation of loyalty to the new regime.

171. See above, Section D, end.

172. So Gardiner, Egypt of the Pharaohs (Oxford: 1961) 288. Faulkner, op. cit. 243, however, suggests that there may have been a grain of historical reality underlaying these Syrian war scenes. For the historicity of Ramesses III's wars in general, see now L.H. Lesko, "The Wars of Ramses III", Serapis 6 (1980) 83-86.

173. So Faulkner, loc. cit.

174. See above, n. 8 with the literature cited there, but note also the comments of Gardiner and Černý, The Inscriptions of Sinai 27-28.

174. E.g., while nowhere among the other documents preserved from

his reign is there any other evidence of activity of Thutmose IV in Libya or against Libya, that fact that a Libyan is depicted on one (nr. 1) and possibly two (nr. 2) of the stelae unequivocally dated to his reign should have some meaning. While it is, at best, indirect evidence, it nevertheless is evidence for an implied hostile action against Egypt's unruly eastern neighbours in the reign of Thutmose IV. Similarly, stela nr. 19 provides at least one new hiscal datum for the little-known reign of Amenmesse, an action in Nubia which then, implicitly through the replacement of his name by that of Seti II, allowed this same action to be attributed to the latter.

176. See above, stelae nrs. 1-5, 7, 9-14.

177. Stelae nrs. 1, 2, 9, 10, 13.

178. Stelae nrs. 11 and 14.

179. Stelae nrs. 4 and 12.

180. Stelae nrs. 3, 5, 7.

181. Stela nr. 4. See n. 45 for its probable Memphite origin.

182. It is on these grounds that Bryan, op. cit. 241, assigns a Memphite provenance to it.

183. I attribute a Memphite origin to stela nr. 11, which was purchased at Giza, and possibly also to nr. 14, which was purchased from a Cairo dealer, not because they were acquired in the Memphite region, but because of the homogeneous stylistic and iconographic attributes which they share with those excavated at Memphis (above, n. 177). In the case of nr. 4, a Theban provenance has been postulated without any such basis only on the assumption of Allen, see above n. 45, and this, probably wrongly, has become fixed in the literature. For the

ramifications of such arbitrary attributions of the origins of objects, see the brilliant and penetrating study of O.W. Muscarella, "Ziwye and Ziwye: The Forgery of a Provience", Journal of Field Archaeology 4 nr. 2 (1977) 197-218.

184. A reasonable and not unprecedented assumption, see my "A Memphite Stela, The Bark of Ptah...", 87 n. 8, 90.

185. Stela nr. 8.

186. Stela nr. 6.

187. Stelae nrs. 18a-b, 19.

188. Stelae nrs. 15-17. A god is present in the Kasr Ibrim scene (Appendix, stela nr.31), but since his upper body and head are missing, his identity is in question. Probably, however, he was Horus of Miam, in which case the sacrifice could have taken place in his temple, possibly located across the river, in Aniba.

189. See stelae nrs. 1, 2, 4, 5, 10-12. Of these, only nrs. 10 and 12 picture two prisoners. Where the nationalities can be identified, they are a Libyan (nrs. 1, 11, 12), an Asiatic (nrs. 4, 12) and either an Asiatic or a Libyan (nr. 2).

190. Stelae nrs. 10 (four ears) and 11 (at least two ears).

191. See above, n. 81.

192. See stela Rochedale, number not known (published by Petrie, Memphis I pl. 11 nr. 15) and statuette-stela Cairo JE 45555 (published in my "Reshep Times Two" 165 fig. 3). On a number other stelae on which both Ptah and ears are pictured, there is no way of determining if the epithet was also present since these are too fragmentary or otherwise damaged, e.g. stelae Dublin 518-9.08 (published by Petrie, op. cit. pl. 13 nr. 29), ex-Metropolitan Museum of Art 08.2052B (ibid. pl.

10 nr. 13), <u>Memphis I</u> pl. 11 nr. 20 and <u>Riqqeh and Memphis</u>
<u>VI</u> pl. 55 nr. 13, the locations of both which are unknown,
Cambridge EGA 4256.1943 (unpublished), Hannover 1935.200.203
(= ex-Museum Scheurleer S-995, published by Blok, op. cit.
pl. 9 nr. 2) and Hannover 1935.200.205 (= ex-Museum Scheur-
ler S-60, published ibid. pl. 8 nr. 2).

193. The only examples known to me all come from the 1915-1923
excavations of the University Museum of the University of
Pennsylvania at Memphis and all are unpublished: stelae
Philadelphia E 13570 (find nr. M-4374), E 13594 (find nr.
M-2753), E 13604 (find nr. M-2794), E 13613 (find nr. M-
2970), E 13624 (find nr. M-3142), E 13628 (find nr. M-4375),
29-75-564 (find nr. M-2776), and 29-75-565 (find nr. M-2812).

194. E.g., stelae British Museum 1472 (published by Petrie, <u>Mem-</u>
<u>phis I</u> pl. 10 nr. 14), ex-Metropolitan Museum of Art 08.20-
52E (ibid. pl. 11 nr. 19),British Museum 589 (published by
James, op. cit. pl. 31), British Museum 1466 (published by
E.A.W. Budge, <u>A Guide to the Egyptian Galleries (Sculpture)</u>
(London: 1909] 304-305, Hildesheim 375 (published by Habachi,
"Khata‘na-Qantir..." pl. 34B), Hannover 1935.200.687 (= ex-
Museum Scheurleer S-27, published by Blok, op. cit. pl. 8 nr.
1), Berlin 13271, unpublished, but see Königliche Museen zu
Berlin, <u>Ausführliches Verzeichnis der ägyptischen Altertumer</u>
<u>und Gipsabgüsse</u> 2nd ed. (Berlin: 1899) 34.

195. E.g., stelae University College, London, 14393 (published by
Petrie, op. cit. pl. 10 nr. 9) and Louvre E 24852 (unpublished), both of which bear a single ear along with the name
of Ptah. For those stelae picturing a single or multiple
ears and which are usually attributed to Ptah but, in fact,

have no divine name written on them, see nn. 198-199, below.

196. See stelae Manchester 4905.8 (published by Petrie, op. cit.
pl. 10 nr. 10) and Dublin 518-9.08 (ibid. nr. 12). The Manchester stela has the epithet as well as Ptah's name and the
the ears.

197. E.g., stelae Philadelphia E 12507 (published by Petrie, op.
cit. pl. 12 nr. 24), ex-Metropolitan Museum of Art 08.2052D
(ibid. pl. 12 nr. 22), Brussels E 4498 (ibid. nr. 21), Brussels without number (ibid. nr. 25), British Museum 1471
(ibid. pl. 30 nr. 30), Copenhagen AeIn 1017 (ibid. pl. 11 nr.
18), Cairo JE 35175 from Mit Rahineh (unpublished), University College, London, 14398 (published by Petrie, op. cit. pl.
20 nr. 48), Manchester 4909 (published ibid. pl. 13 nr. 49),
Edinburgh 1908.363 (ibid. pl. 11 nr. 17), and Bristol E 2218A
(ibid. pl. 11 nr. 16).

198. See, e.g., stelae Turin 50051 (published by Tosi and Roccati,
op. cit. 282): Soped; Turin 50052 (ibid. 283): Khonsu; Cairo
JE 43691 (published by Bruyère, "Quelques stèles trouvées par
M.É. Baraize à Deir el Médineh", ASAE 25 (1925) pl. 2 nr. 2),
Manchester 4910 (published by Petrie, op. cit. pl. 18 nr.
21); Bankes 16 (published by Černý, Egyptian Stelae pl. 16):
Hathor; Brooklyn 37.1515E (published by S. Sharpe, Egyptian
inscriptions from the British Museum and other sources 2nd
series (London: 1841) pl. 39), Brooklyn 37.1534E (unpublished), Berlin 7354 (published by A. Erman, Die Religion der
Aegypter (Berlin: 1934) 145 fig. 53), and Cairo JE 43566
(published by Bruyère, op. cit. pl. 2 nr. 1): Amūnreʿ; British Museum 358 (published by Budge, Sculpture pl. 21): Min
or Minamūn, the figure is clearly that of the ithyphallic

Min, but the caption names him "Amūnreʿ, the Bull of his mother, the king of the gods"; Turin 50026 (published by Tosi
and Roccati, op. cit. 270): Nebethetep; Turin 50027 (ibid.
275) and Louvre E 662 (mentioned by Bruyere, op. cit. 85):
the deified Ahmose-Nefertari; British Museum 276 (published
by H.R.Hall, Hieroglyphic texts ... V, pl.43 nr.2): Haroeris;
Munich 287 (published by Habachi, "The Qantir Stela of the
Vizier Rahotep and the Statue Ruler-of-Rulers", Festgabe für
Dr. Walter Will Ehrensenator der Universität München (Köln:
1966) 68): the cult statue of Ramesses-miʿamūn-Ruler-of-Rul-
ers"; Brussels E 3047 (published by J. Capart, "Stèles égyptiennes", Bulletin des Musées Royaux du Cinquantenaire 12
(1913) 62 fig. 3): a cult statue of Ramesses II, possibly
"Ramesses-montuemtowe"; University College, London, 14409
(published by Stewart, op. cit. pl. 31 nr. 2): the Osiris
emblem; Metropolitan Museum of Art 08.202.34 (unpublished,
but see W.C. Hayes, The Scepter of Egypt II (New York: 1959)
384), Cairo JE 72294 (published by S.Hassan, The Great Sphinx
and Its Secrets (Cairo: 1953) 43 fig. 31 nr. 9), two small
stelae, whereabouts now unknown, but which were described
by A. Kamal, "Rapport sur les fouilles du Comte du Galarza",
ASAE 10 (1910) 117-118 , and Cairo JE 72267 (unpublished but
described by C. M. Zivie, Giza au deuxième millénaire (Cairo:
1976) 246-247): the Sphinx; Cairo JE 72297 (published by Hassan, loc. cit. nr. 8) and JE 72298 (ibid. nr. 1): Haramachis;
Cairo JE 72293 (ibid. 42 fig. 30 nr. 4): Hormerty; Cairo JE
25417 (published by N.Aimé-Giron,"Adversaria Semitica (III).
VII—Baʿal Ṣaphon et les dieux de Tahpanhès dans un nouveau
papyrus phénicien", ASAE 40 (1941) pl. 42): Baʿal Saphon;

Hildesheim 402 (published by Habachi, "Khataʿna-Qantir..."
530) and Hildesheim 1092 (ibid. 533) picture the statue of
Ramesses-montuemtowe and the epithet, but no ears are shown.
This is also true for Hildesheim 1100 (ibid. 541) and Berlin
14662 + Turin 50067 (published by B. Grdseloff, Les debuts
du culte de Rechef en Égypte [Cairo: 1942] pl. 2), both of
which picture Reshep and the epithet, but do not show any
ears.

199. So Sandman-Holmberg, The God Ptah 70.

200. The following examples were excavated by Petrie at Memphis:
stelae Manchester 4905-4908 (Memphis I pls. 10 nr. 6 and 13
nrs. 27-28), Philadelphia E 12506 (ibid. pl. 10 nr. 11),
University College,London, 14394 (ibid. pl. 13 nr. 26), British Museum, number unknown (ibid. pl. 10 nr. 7), and stela
Riqqeh and Memphis VI pl. 55 nr. 14, present location unknown.
All of these could very well have been dedicated to Ptah.
However, stela Cairo JE 72296 (published by Hassan, op. cit.
43 fig. 31 nr. 11) and an unnumbered stela now in a Giza
magazine (ibid. nr. 12) were excavated by Hassan near the
Sphinx and, although anepigraphic, were probably dedicated
like the other ear stelae from Giza (see preceding note) to
one or another of the manifestations of Horus worshipped
there. Stelae Berlin 19789 and 20437, both unpublished, are
said to have come from Abusir. Stela Brooklyn 16.95 was purchased at Abu Tig, and stelae Oriental Institute, Chicago,
11105 (unpublished) and Stockholm MM 10002 (published by B.
J. Petersen, "Aegyptische Stelen und Stelenfragmente aus
Stockholmer Sammlungen", Opuscula Atheniensia 9 [1963] 100
fig. 5) are both of unknown provenance. Although stelae

University College, London, 14432 and 14433 (published, but not illustrated by Stewart, op. cit. 38) are said to have possibly come from Memphis and stela Oxford 1892.1093, unpublished, is thought to come from Sakkara. These attributions, however, were probably made on analogy with the excavated Memphite examples, but the truth is that, like the Chicago and Stockholmn stelae, their provenance is really not known. They could easily have come from a site other than Memphis. As the case of the two Giza examples suggest, when Ptah is not attested either pictorially or textually on an ear stela, it is quite misleading to assume that it was dedicated to him and to assign such an anepigraphic ear stela a Memphite origin. Other provenances and other deities are equally possible.

201. For Amūnreʿ at Deir el-Medineh, see stela Cairo JE 43566 and for the epithet at Qantir, stelae Hildesheim 1100 and Berlin 14662 + Turin 50067 (Reshep), or Hildesheim 402 and 1092 (Ramesses-montuemtowe). For the exact references, see n. 198 above.

202. This do ut des "I give that you may give" concept of reciprocity is well-attested in the htp-di-nswt formula, see W. Federn, "Htp (r)dj(w) (n) ʿInpw: zum Verständnis der vorosirianischen Opferformel", MDAIK 16 (1958) 120-130. That the king's grattitude and offering to the god went far beyond the mere sacrifice is amply demonstrated textually, see Gardiner, "Tuthmosis III Returns Thanks to Amun", JEA 38 (1952) 6-23.

203. Above, stela nr. 8.

204. Above, stelae nrs. 18a-b.

205. Above, stela nr. 19.

206. E.g. LD III pl. 29 (north outer wall of the great temple of Amūn at Karnak); ibid. pls. 139a, 140a (temple of Redesyeh, first room); ibid. pls. 144 (north outer wall of the great temple of Amūn at Karnak), 145a (south outer wall at Karnak), 185b (temple of Derr, forehall, left rear), 184a (ibid. right rear), 186 (Abu Simbel, great temple, left side of east wall of room F), pl. 187b (Nahr el-Kelb, middle stela), 207d (temple of Ramesses III at Karnak), 209c-d (Medinet Habu, first pylon), 211 (ibid. second pylon), stela Philadelphia 29-107-958 (published by A. Rowe, The Topography and History of Beth Shan [Philadelphia: 1930] pl. 46), passim.

207. See Medinet Habu I pl. 13.

208. E.g. stelae Philadelphia 29-107-958 (above, n. 206), Cairo CG 34.025 verso, Oriental Institute, Chicago, 14310 (published by U. Hölscher, The Mortuary Temple of Ramesses III II [Chicago: 1951] pl. 14 C), British Museum 66668 (published by Smith, The Fortress of Buhen pl. 79.

209. See above, n. 126, and compare Hölscher, op. cit. 5-6.

210. See, e.g. LD III, pls. 129, 144, 145, 207d, 209c, d, 210a, passim.

211. For scarabs, see, e.g., Jerusalem J907 (published by Rowe, Catalogue of Egyptian Scarabs pl. 15 nr. 579), British Museum 39215 (published by Hall, Catalogue of Egyptian Scarabs ... British Museum 109 nr. 1109), 47053 (ibid. nr. 1108), 47099 (ibid. nr. 1110), 17124 (ibid. 221 nr. 2211), passim.

212. From the outer face of the north tower of the first pylon. For the full text, see Medinet Habu II pl. 102.

213. From the south face of the vestibule of the second pylon at

Karnak. For the full text, see K.A. Kitchen and G.A. Gaballa, "Ramesside Varia II", <u>ZAeS</u> 96 (1969) pl. 8 and fig. 8,
and for an excellent discussion of such "Ramesside Triumphal
Texts", ibid. 23-28.

Chapter 2. The Giving of Gold Collars as a Reward

A

Unlike the scene of the king smiting an enemy in the presence of a god, which does not at all figure in the tomb art of the New Kingdom, that in which a faithful official is personally rewarded by the king (and, in one instance, his wife by the queen) with gold, usually in the form of gold collars, is one of the most popular and important autobiographical motifs found in the private tombs of the New Kingdom from shortly after the middle of the 18th Dynasty through the Ramesside period, with the most numerous examples attested in the rock-cut tombs of Tel el-Amarna,[214] It is also found, in at least two instances, carved on a temple wall, once at Beit el-Wali[215] and once at Karnak.[216] In this scene, the personage who is being honoured, accompanied by several friends and attendants, is shown in the presence of the king (and, often, also the queen) who either sits in a small kiosk[217] or stands at the window of appearances in the palace.[218] In some cases the king and/or the queen are depicted in the very act of handing down the gold collars[219] and in virtually every instance the recipient is shown with his hands raised in an attitude of jubiliation, his neck bedecked with the collars, while a pair of attendants annoint him and adjust them to sit properly around his throat and over his shoulders.[220] In the texts which accompany this scene, the speech of the king usually gives his reasons for the bestowal of the reward and that of the rewardee contains his gratitude in reply to his royal master.[221] In most instances the king wears the Blue Crown, but once his headdress is the simple nemes-headcloth[222] and, in another, the nemes surmounted by the atef-crown.[223] Mostly the king is clad in his normal daily dress, but in the last-cited example he appears in the mummiform gestalt of Osiris.[224] The garb and headgear of the queen varies from representation to representation, regardless of whether she is alone or is accompanying the king.[225] The gold collars which are the principal item being bestowed are of the type which the Egyptians called šby.w. They comprised up to four strands of tightly-strung, heavy, biconical gold beads.[226] When they are shown being worn in both relief and painting (i.e. two-dimensionally)[227] or in sculpture in the round (i.e. three-dimensionally),[228] they are immediately recognizable in two ways. Unlike the broad floral collar which presents an unbroken silhouette at the neck and shoulders of the person wearing it, the curved profile of the last visible bead in each strand of the šby.w characteristically bulges above the line of the shoulder and, since more than one one of these collars is worn at the same time, their overlapping curves present a scalloped effect across the chest and shoulders of their wearer. Although other items of reward and honour are not shown actually being conferred in these tomb scenes there are indications in the accompanying texts and ancillary sub-scenes that they included of other pieces of gold jewelry, in one case a pair of linen gloves, gifts of cattle, promotion to higher offic, and, as we have seen in the previous chapter, grants of land.[229]

Receiving a reward in the presence of or from the very hand of pharaoh, himself, clearly was a high and memorable point in the life and career of the recipient. Obviously this was the reason it occupied pride of place among the autobiographical scenes of his tomb. Frequently it is not only the actual moment of the brstowal which was depicted. A series of additional tableaux and subscenes continued the narrative, with the recipient, wearing his gold of honour, returning home in his chariot,[230] receiving the acclamation of his colleagues, friends, family, and retainers upon his arrival,[231] and, still proudly wearing the gold collars, feasting at a table.[232] In a few Amarna tombs he is even portrayed wearing the collars while he performs an act of worship having nothing to do with the ceremony of reward on the reveals of the tomb's doorway.[233]

Like the ceremonial sacrifice of a captive enemy prince or its ritual reenactment[234] which the dedicator of a stela witnessed in person and at which he may have been, himself, rewarded,[235] so the ceremony of his reward and/or promotion at the king's own hand was also commemorated by the recipients on stelae. Though not as numerous as those with the smiting scene, all of the examples known to me have been collected and studied in Section B of this chapter. These, however, do not at all present the homogeneous tableau found on the sacrificial scene stelae, but rather include the actual awarding of the gold and some of the narrative stages of its aftermath. Moreover, unlike the stelae with the smiting scene, where the majority of those whose provenance is assured by controlled excavation and which come from a temple,[236] most of those which picture the various stages of the rewarding with gold which also have a firm provenance through controlled excavation come from the tomb.[237] But although they do have a certain mortuary significance, these are not the conventional funerary stelae which contain the stereotyped htp-di-nswt formula to insure offerings for the well-being of their deceased owner in the Afterworld. However, some of them do contain invocations of a kind to the ka-soul of the person to whom they were dedicated[238] and one, stela nr. 30, clearly pictures a funerary repast in the Afterworld.

B

20. Stela Louvre C 213, provenance not known. Limestone, with no traces of colour. 100 x 92 cm. text and scene in sunken relief. Bibliography: Ch. Boreux, <u>Musée National du Louvre: Dép-artment des antiquités égyptiennes: guide-catalogue sommaire</u> I (Paris: 1932) 80 and pl. 8, and, earlier: E. Ledrain, <u>La stèle du Collier d'or</u> (Paris: 1876); P. Pierret, <u>Recueil d'inscriptions inédités du Musée du Louvre</u> II (Paris: 1878) 10; S. Gabra, <u>Les conseils de fonctionnaires dans l'Égypte pharaonique. Scenes de recompenses royales aux fonctionaires</u> (Cairo: 1929) 42-43, pl. 2; <u>KRI</u> I, 309; Gaballa, <u>Narrative in Egyptian Art</u> 130 n. 238. (Fig.22).

Although this rectangular stela is complete, it somewhat disconcertingly appears unfinished. A wide, empty, horizontal field runs across the width of its top, almost as if the artisan who had carved the monument had left this portion deliberately unworked, so that it could either be fashioned or fitted into a cornice. Below this blank space, occupying a little more than three-fifths of the remaining area is the scene with its attend-ant texts. At the left, facing right, "the king of Upper and Lower Egypt, Memareʿ, the Son of Reʿ, Seti-merneptah" stands at a window of appearances. Since the lower part of his body is con-cealed by the balcony, it is clear that he is standing behind the window and looking out. He wears a simple nemes-headcloth,with a uraeus affixed to his brow, a broad collar, and a sleeved garment over his upper body. Leaning forth out of the window, his left hand resting on the edge of a wide cushion which covers the win-dowsill, he gestures downward with his right hand at a pair of

3by.w-collars and at a long rectangular object (an ingot of prec-
ious metal?) which sit on the plate of a high table with openwork
sides. A falcon, its wings outspread and its claws clutching a
fan, hovers protectively over and the king, and a pair of vertical cartouches behind his back contain his nomen and prenomen.
The window is unadorned, save that its upper sill is capped by a
cavetto cornice and what appears to be a torus molding. At the
right, before the table with the collars, a man stands and looks
up at the king, his arms raised high in the gesture of jubiliation, his feet set firmly on a ground line. He wears a long, el-
aborately-pleated wig and a long sleeved-garment with a wide, triangular apron. He is attended by a pair of shaven-headed retainers, each wearing a calf-length pleated kit with a long pleated
apron. One adjusts a gold collar around the jubiliant's neck,
while the other whose hands are above and below his waist looks
as if he is about to pick up something, possibly another collar,
from the table. This, in reality, would have been right next to
the trio, but due to the conventions of Egyptian art, it seems to
be at a distance from them. However, on the basis of parallels
to the scene, the second attendant may simply be anointing his
master with oil.[239] In the field above the men, ten vertical
lines of text contain the speeches of both the king and the jubiliant. The of the king, the three lines to the left, reads:

"Words spoken by his majesty to the nobles who are at his

side: 'Give much gold to the one who is praised, the over-

seer of the royal harim, Hormin,[240] him whose lifetime is

long, whose old age is happy, him without blemish and

without fault in the palace, whose utterance is sound,[241]

whose comings and goings are at their place,[242] who shall

endure[243] with a goodly burial'".[244]

The response of Hormin, contained in the remaining seven lines, is as follows:

"That which the overseer of seal-bearers,[245] the over-seer of the royal harem, Hormin who will be justified, said: 'Your appearance is beautiful,[246] O goodly ruler! Amūn loves you,[247] for you are here[248] forever, like your father, Re', making his lifetime, O ruler who has made me [great] among men, the one[249] who has created me by his ka. There is joy and happiness[250] for the ones near you,[251] those who hear[252] your teaching. I am a humble man, one whom you have caused to be a great man by what you have done. I have achieved a happy old age without (any)one having found fault (in me)'."

Below the entire scene are four horizontal lines of hieroglyphs running the entire width of the stela and reading:

"May the king give an offering to Ptah, the Lord of Ma'at, Divine Ba who lives on Ma'at, who made the gods and men,[253] All-lord who illuminates the lands, that he may give a happy life and endurance upon earth, the passing of a goodly lifetime in peace, and a happy burial which comes from the king, that he may allow the Osiris, the overseer of the harem of the king, Hormin, who will be justified, to appear among the imperishable stars and to shine among the indefatigable stars. A great hecatomb will be made for you in his (i.e., Ptah's) place, the one in which you will be.[254] Your corpse will be glorious like the corpse of the Eternal One.[255] You shall be a ba and it shall enjoy provisions in the place of Wennofer.[256] Anubis

will do the embalming for you and Isis will pour out her
milk for you. The (ceremony of) Opening-of-the-Mouth
will bring joy to your ka in every good place. The ritual
priest will perform the Opening-of-the-Mouth and the Great-
est-of-Artificers[257] will cause your ka to be raised up.
The haunch of beef will be cut for your ba and it (i.e.
the ba) shall be divine in the necropolis. Wennofer
shall love you and shall exalt you in the presence of the
Ennead".

21. Stela Hildesheim 374, probably from Qantir. Limestone,
with no traces of colour. 67 x 47 cm. text and scenes in sunken
relief. Bibliography: H. Kayser, Die ägyptischen Altertümer im
Roemer-Pelizaeus-Museum in Hildesheim (Hildesheim: 1973) 59-60
and pl. 51. Earlier, A. Ippel and G. Roeder, Die Denkmäler des
Pelizaeus-Museums zu Hildesheim (Hildesheim: 1921) 96 fig. 33,
Roeder, "Ramses II als Gott", ZAeS 61 (1926) 65-66 and fig. 2;
idem., "Der Schmuckwert der ägyptischen Hieroglyphen", Buch und
Schrift 3 (1928) 2 fig. 4; Habachi, "Khata'na-Qantir..." 535;
idem., Features of the Deification of Ramesses II (Glückstadt:
1969) 30 fig. 17; Kayser, "Söhne des Sonnengottes", Zeitschrift
des Museums zu Hildesheim N.F. 23 (1971) 43-44; Gaballa, loc. cit.
n. 239; KRI III, 263-264. (Fig. 23).

Both registers of this round-topped stela are somewhat
marred by horizontal breaks which run obliquely upward from the
left edge to the right edge, with a large chip of the surface
gouged out at the right end of each. This has caused some loss
to the scenes above and below. The upper of the two registers
contains a double scene. In the center, facing to the left, "the
lord of the Two Lands, Wosimareʿ-setepenreʿ, the lord of Diadems,

Ramesses-miꜥamūn stands and offers a small figure of Maꜥat to
"Ptah, the Lord of Maꜥat, the king of the Two Lands, he who hears
petitions".[258] The king wears the Blue Crown with uraeus and
pendant streamer, a broad collar, and a sleeved, calf-length, diaphonous overgarment beneath which his knee-length kilt is clearly visible. The mummiform god stands on a pedestal inside of an
open naos, the front and doors of which are not indicated.[259] The
other scene of the register is to the right of this. In the center, facing to the right "Wosimareꜥ-setepenreꜥ Ramesses-miꜥamūn"
stands at a window of appearances and throws down a pair of gold
šby.w-collars to a man who stands below, adoring him. Since Ramesses' entire body, clad as before, is shown, it is clear that he
is being viewed from inside the window, looking out. The window's
enclosed balcony, which occupies about two-fifths of its height
and which is capped by a cavetto cornice and torus molding, is
covered with a thick cushion upon which the king rests his left
arm, while he raises his right hand to throw out a collar. The
upper part of the window is framed by a pair of jambs which support a corniced lintel capped by a frieze of sundisk-crowned uraei. Just to the right of the right jamb, i.e., just outside it,
are four vertical lines of incised hieroglyphs, the first of
which faces towards the other three is interrupted by the second
of the gold collars which the king presents. These read:

"The king, himself, is giving silver and every good thing
of the palace to the ⌜overseer of the scribe(s)⌝ [who ---]
for the army,[260] the one who gives satisfaction on account
of that which comes forth from his mouth, Mose [----]".[261]

Mose stands at the far right of the register. His figure has
been badly damaged by the large gouge in the right edge of the

stela, which was caused by the vertical fracture at the bottom of
the register. Only his arms, upraised in the gesture of adoration, his lower legs, and the hem of his kilt are still preserved.
Between him and the window are various offerings or, more likely
in view of the text, gifts. These seem to include three ingots
of metal[262] contained in two nb-baskets, and a haunch of meat.
They are placed upon and below a table.[263]

The lower of the two registers has but a single scene. At
the left and filling its entire height is "Ramesses-mi'amūn-the-
Sun-of-Rulers", a colossal statue of the king.[264]   It depicts
the king seated upon a square, high-backed throne and wearing the
Double Crown on top of a nemes-headcloth.[265] In the field in
front of it, his feet on a level with its waist, the king stands,
clad as in the upper register. He holds a hk3-scepter in his
left hand and, with his extended right hand, offers a gold šby.w-
collar. At the right, on a level with the base of the statue and
facing it and the king is a large group of men, some bending down,
the others looking upward and stretching their hands towards the
king in an attempt to catch the various gold collars and other
objects[266] which he has showered down upon them. In front of
this company and slightly apart from them is their leader, surely
the Mose of the upper register. He thrusts himself forward, the
hands of his outspread arms cupped to receive the rewards cascad-
ing down about him. Since all of the men, including Mose, wear
the so-called "military kilt" with the large, inverted triangular
apron,[267] and with several also wearing the so-called "military
wig",[268] it is obvious that they are soldiers. This is confirmed by the text which is in the field over their heads. It consists of twelve vertical columns of incised hieroglyphs which con-

tain two separate speeches. The four lines at the left which
face in the same direction as does the king record his speech to
the assembled soldiers. The remaining eight lines contain their
reply. The speech of the king is as follows:

"Words spoken by his majesty to the army: 'Now see the
things which the soldier[269] Mose, whom his majesty loves,
has done in the presence of Pharaoh! How good are the
things[270] which he has done so very greatly'."

To this, the assembled soldiers reply:

"Words spoken by the entire army at the honouring of
their leader:[271] 'You are Reʿ! You are like Him when
you appear.[272] We live because you look at that which
was done by(??)[273] the soldier Mose of the great company of Ramesses-miʿamūn "[Beloved of] Atum",[274] [in
the presence of][275] ⌐his statue⌐ Ra[messes-miʿamun]-
the-Sun-[of-Rulers" belonging to][276] Ra[messes-]miʿ-
amūn'".

22. Stela Cairo CG 34.177, from the tomb of Any (nr.23) at
Amarna. Limestone, with colours well-preserved. 27 x 23 cm.
scene in sunken relief, text incised. Bibliography: N. De Garis
Davies, The Rock Tombs of El Amarna V (London: 1908) 10 and pl.
22. Earlier, G. Daressy, "Tombeaux et stèles-limites de Hagi-
Qandil", Rec. trav. 15 (1895) 45; G. Steindorff, "Vier Grabstel-
en aus der Zeit Amenophis' IV", ZÄeS 34 (1896) 65-67 and fig. 3;
U. Bouriant, G. Legrain, and G. Jequier, Monuments pour servir à
l'étude du culte d'Atonou en Égypte (Cairo: 1903) pl. 25. See also M. Sandman, Texts from the Time of Akhenaton (Brussels: 1938)
68 where, however, it should be noted that her identification of
this and the other stelae from the tomb of Any as British Museum

objects is incorrect. The numbers are Cairo Museum Journal d'en-
trée numbers. Those cited by Steindorff, op. cit. are the old
Giza Museum numbers. (Fig. 24).

The scene, set within a blue border which parallels the
outline of this small round-topped stela pictures its owner and a
charioteer standing a moving chariot.[277] The passenger, wearing
a robe with short, pleated sleeves, and a wavey shoulder-length
wig, steadies himself by leaning both hands on the upper edge of
the vehicle's box.[278] A cone of perfumed incense sits on top of
his head and, in addition to an earring and a bracelet on his
right wrist, he wears four gold šby.w-collars around his neck.
The shaven-headed driver is bare to the waist and holds the reins
with both of his outthrust hands. He seems to be leaning himself
forward in an attempt to urge the team of horses from a walk to a
faster gait. The chariot, the typical light car of the 18th Dynasty, with six-spoked wheels, has a closed, painted-leather bowcase affixed to its sidepanel.[279] Outside of the usual head and
shoulder harness, the chariot-horses show no other equipment. The
background of the stela is painted yellow, the heads and arms of
the two men and the body of the charioteer are red, as is the
leather of the sidepanel and the leather insets of the bowcase.
The two horses are likewise painted red. The passenger's hair
and eye are black. In the field above there are six vertical
lines of blue-painted hieroglyphs and beneath the fourth of these
are three additional short, horizontal lines. These last serve
as the caption for the charioteer. The main text reads:

"The real scribe of the king, his beloved, the scribe of
the offering table of the lord of the Two Lands,[280] the
steward, Any, who will be justified. (He says): 'I return

in peace with the rewards of the king.[281] He has commanded a goodly burial for me and he has granted that I
shall reach the state of reverence in peace'".
The short text over the head of the driver identifies him as "the
charioteer of the royal scribe Any, Tjay".[282]

23. Stela in Giza, number not known. From the Sphinx amphitheater at Giza. Limestone, with no traces of colour. Dimensions
not known, scene and text in sunken relief. Bibliography: S.
Hassan, The Great Sphinx and Its Secrets (Cairo: 1953) 61 and fig.
52; Ch. M. Zivie, Giza au deuxieme millenaire 254 nr. 6; Schulman,
"A Memphite Stela, The Bark of Ptah..." 101 nr. 48. (Fig. 25).

Only a fragment of the scene of this small votive stela[283]
is preserved. In the center, resting on a ground line and facing
to the left are the hind legs and tails of a standing team of
horses. These are yoked to a chariot seen immediately to their
right. Of the chariot itself, all that is preserved are its pole,
visible between the rumps and tails of the horses, a four-spoked
wheel whose spokes cross in such a way as to suggest that the intent of the artist had been to carve six but, for some reason,
did not, the frontpanel of the car and the lower part of a bowcase affixed to the sidepanel. A man stands in the chariot. Only
the lower part of his pleated kilt is preserved. At the left a
pair of attendants face the vehicle. The nearer of these, standing behind the horse-team, wears a calf-length pleated kilt and
bows down. His arms, superficially looking like the anthropomorphic rays of the Aton, are pressed against the apron of his kilt.
The second attendant, standing just to the left of the horses'
forelegs and dressed like his fellow, is more erect. Probably his
hands were raised in adoration.[284] At the right of the scene,

time on a larger scale than the other two, a third man stands facing the rear of the chariot. His body is preserved from the buttocks down. He wears a calf-length kilt and sandals.[285] His sash has been gathered up at his no-longer visible belt, its bunched-up, peplumlike effect making it look as if it were a second apron worn higher over the regular apron of his kilt.[286] The butt and lower part of the shaft of a fan which he holds is inclined in such a direction so as to insure that he is holding it to shade the occupant of the chariot. The remains of a vertical column of hieroglyphs, facing left, stand between the fan-bearer and the man in the chariot, but there is no way of determining to which of them it belongs. What can be read of the mutiliated text is: "the overseer of [----] of the lord of the Two Lands, [----], Pashed".[287]

24. Stela Cairo CG 34.176, from the tomb of Any (nr. 23) at Amarna. Limestone, some colour preserved. 42 x 28 cm. scene and text in sunken relief. Bibliography: Davies, op. cit. 10 pl. 21; Daressy, op. cit. 44; Steindorff, op. cit. 65 and fig. 2; Bouriant-Legrain-Jequier, op. cit. 50 and pl. 25; Sandman, op. cit. 67. (Fig. 26).

Both registers are inclosed by a border which parallels the outline of the stela's round-top. Above, at the right and facing left, "the real scribe of the king, his beloved, the scribe of the offering table of the lord of the Two Lands, Any, who will be justified" stands erect in a very formal, almost statuelike attitude, his right arm bent at the elbow, the hand holding a staff, the left arm hanging straight down at his side, its hand clutching a handkerchief.[288] Any wears a quarter-sleeved upper garment over his long, calf-length kilt. Its lower part has been

gathered through his belt so that it gives a peplumlike appearance at his knees.[289] His wig curves naturally over his shoulders and on his feet are sandals. "The scribe, Nebwawi",[290] shaven-headed, bare-chested, barefoot and wearing a short knee-length
kilt, stands facing Any. His right hand is extended in a gesture
of address. His left hand grasps a roll of papyrus. "He says:
'Look at the ox, the one of which it was said to bring it'". In
the lower register, which is separated from the upper by a double
ground line, Nebwawi, dressed as before, leads a short-horned ox
by a halter, presumably into the presence of Any in the upper register. The bovine's throat is festively bedecked with a broad
collar. This, in turn, is adorned with a lotus flower and two
buds.[291] In the field over this scene are eight vertical lines
of text which read:

> "The scribe Nebwawi, he says: 'We have seen the beauti-
> ful things which the goodly ruler has done for his scribe
> of the offering table. He has ordained a happy burial
> for him in Akhetaton'".

Traces of dark red colour are still visible on the flesh of the
men and the hide of the ox. The horns of the animal originally
had been gilded.

   25. Stela Cairo CG 32.178, from the tomb of Any (nr. 23) at
Amarna. Limestone, some colour preserved. 27 x 23 cm. scene in
sunken relief, text incised. Bibliography: Davies, op. cit. 10
and pl. 22; Daressy, op. cit. 44; Steindorff, op. cit. 67 and fig.
4; Sandman, op. cit. 67-68; De Meulenaere, Le règne du soleil:
Akhenaton et Néfertiti (Brussels: 1975) 83 nr. 22. (Fig. 27).

   The scene of this small stela is set within a frame which

parallels the outline of its round-topped shape except on its
left side. Here it is replaced by the right side of a doorway,
i.e. the right jamb, the right corner of the lintel with its cornice. Davies, possibly rightly, identified this as "the latticed
door of the shrine in his (i.e. Any's) tomb".[292] To the right of
this doorway and facing left, Any sits on a folding stool, the
legs of which terminate in ducks' heads and the seat of which is
covered with an animal skin.[293] He wears a diaphonous ankle-
length pleated robe with pleated half-sleeves, bracelets on his
wrists, armlets on his biceps, and four gold šby.w-collars around
his neck. His sandal-clad feet rest upon a platform which also
supports the base of the doorjamb behind him, the legs of the
stool, and the visible leg of a rectangular, openwork-sided table
laden with various kinds of food and floral bouquets. The left
side and leg of the table are concealed by his feet and the lower
part of his robe. His left hand is raised in a gesture of what
looks to be salutation. On the other side of the table and facing
him is a retainer who offers a large jar with a prominent collar.
The flesh of the two men is painted red,as is the jar and the
legs of the stool. Any's adornments were overlaid with gold
leaf. In the field above the scene are eight vertical lines of
text which comprise two adscriptions to it. The five lines at
the left belong to Any and, when taken in conjuction with the
action performed by the attendant (which we may read as a rebus
for the Egyptian words meaning "to make a libation", to pour
out")[294] then read:

"Making a libation for the ka of the real scribe of the
the king, his beloved,[295] the scribe of the offering
table of the lord of the Two Lands, the steward, Any,

who will be justified".

The two lines of text at the extreme right identify the man who
is making the liquid offering and record that the stela was "made
by the servant of the scribe of the king, Any, Anymen".[296] The
line preceding this contains his speech to Any: "Let wine be
poured out for you".

26. Stela Cairo CG 34.180, from the tomb of Any (nr. 23) at
Amarna. Limestone, some colour preserved. 41 x 27 cm. scene in
sunken relief, text incised. Bibliography: Davies, op. cit. 9-10
and pl. 22; Daressy, op. cit. 45; Steindorff, op. cit. 63-65 and
fig. 1; Bouriant-Legrain-Jequier, op. cit. pl. 26; Sandman, op.
cit. 67. (Fig. 28).

Unlike the others from the tomb of Any previously discussed, the scene of this round-topped stela is not set off by a
border. At the left and facing right, Any sits on a high-backed,
lion-footed chair with openwork sides. He wears the usual diaphonous robe, the pleats and apron of which the artist has attempted, albeit unsuccessfully, to portray in a realistic manner
with the apron laying flat on his lap and the pleats gathered and
bunched up. A cone of perfumed incense surmounts his wig. Several thick gold šby.w-collars encircle his neck, bracelets are on
his wrists, and sandals on his feet. His right hand is held formally to his side, its fist clutching a napkin or handkerchief.
His left hand is extended, palm down, perhaps to touch or take
one of the offerings which are heaped in front of him in a large
nb-basket. This sits on a low square, openwork-sided stand, the
left leg of which is concealed by Any's feet. Its right leg,
Any's feet, and the feet of his chair all rest on a narrow pedestal or mat. The contents of the basket are various types of food

together with a floral bouquet of which only the stems are visible. To the right of these a man stands facing Any and offers a bouquet of flowers to him. He wears a shoulder-length wig and a calf-length pleated and sleeved garment with a pendant apron. The thighs of the robe have been gathered over his sash and hang, peplumlike, over the apron. Traces of red paint are still visible on the feet, arms, and faces of the two men. In the field over their heads eight vertical lines of hieroglyphs comprise two separate texts. The four lines at the left belong to Any and read:

> "the real scribe of the king, his beloved, the scribe of the offering table of the lord of the Two Lands, the steward, Any, who will be justified[297] with a goodly burial".

The remaining four lines are the speech of the offerant and read:

> "Your nourishment[298] is a bouquet of the Aton! May he give breath to me(sic!). May he unite your body. May you see Re⸍ whenever he appears, and adore. He shall listen to what you say".

Beneath the scene a horizontal line of hieroglyphs records the fact that the stela was "made by the overseer of works, Pakha,[299] who will be justified".

Stela Copenhagen AeIN 897, provenance unknown.[300] Brown sandstone, no traces of colour. 45 x 37 cm. scene in sunken relief, text incised. Bibliography: Koefoed-Petersen, Les stèles égyptiennes 31-32 and pl. 37. Earlier, M. Mogensen, "A Stele of the XVIIIth or XIXth Dynasty with a Hymn to Ptah and Sekhmet", PSBA 35 (1913) 37-40 and pl. 2; A.F.R. Platt, "Notes on the Stela of Sekhmetmer", ibid. 129-130 and pl. 31; Koefoed-Petersen, Re-

ceuil des inscriptions hiéroglyphiques de la Glyptotheque Ny Carlsberg (Brussels: 1936) 57. (Fig. 29).

Since the upper part of the stela is lost, there is no
way of knowing what its original shape was. It seems to have had
two registers. In the upper of these, in the center and facing
right, the god Ptaḥ sits on a high-backed throne which stands on
a pedestal. **The goddess Sakhmet stands behind the throne.** In
front of Ptaḥ, on a base line incised above his foot, the remains
of a rectangular openwork-sided stand are still visible. Of the
god, only the curve of his buttocks, his mummy-wrapped legs, and
his feet, can still be seen. All that is left of the goddess is
her body from the abdomen down, her left forearm and hand holding
a staff, and the 'nḫ which her right hand grasped. The side of
the throne is framed by a reed-mat border, as is the smaller
square inset at its lower left, the face of the latter being decorated with the unification symbol. The sidepanel of the pedestal is covered with a frieze of alternating 𓏞and 𓏞 hieroglyphs.
The goddess wears a tight calf-length sheath. A bracelet encircles her left wrist and a similar piece of jewellery is on each
leg, just above the ankle.

The lower register is separated from the upper by a
doubled register line. At the right, facing left, a man kneels
with both hands raised in the gesture of adoration to the deities
above. A cone of perfumed incense sits atop his long elaborately-
plaited wig, the latter also encircled by a filet. A number of
Over the sleeved diaphonous upper-garment he wears a number of
gold šby.w-collars adorn his neck. His robe is drawn through his
belt at the waist, so that its lower part hangs out in front as
if it were a triangular apron, but the actual apron can been seen

very clearly underneath it.[301] He wears an armlet on each forearm,
just below the crook of the elbow. In front of him, filling the
major part of the register and continuing behind his back, is a
hieroglyphic text of fourteen vertical lines which read:

"The servant here praises your beauty, O great Ptah, he
who is south of his wall, Tatenen who resides in the
walls, august god of the Primeval Time, he who fashioned
man and gave birth to the gods,[302] primeval one, making
the life of mankind[303] so that one says in his heart:
'See, they have come into existence!',[304] he who fore-
tells that which not yet is and who has renewed that
which is,—— nothing at all exists without his not knowing it;[305] he creates the needs of every day in accordance to what he determines[306]——, you[307] have placed the
earth at its statutes like you made it, and Egypt remains
under your command as (it did) at the first time!

And hail to Beautiful-of-Face, the favorite of the
house of Ptah, Great Sakhmet, the lady of heaven, she who
is on the brow of Reᶜ, who makes the northward journey of
his Eye in the great house of Hierankonpolis (pr-wr)[308]
and (that of) his double uraei in the house of flame at
Buto (pr-nsr),[309] who is upon his brow in the evening
bark, who is with him in the dawn bark when she blocks
the approaching attack of the Apophis serpent.[310] Rag-
ing[311] against the ones who are with him (i.e. Apophis),
she has grasped the spear,[312] O Sakhmet, Great One, the
beloved of Ptah, the lady of heaven and mistress of the
Two Lands!

May the two of you grant a happy lifetime without sick-

ness to my limbs.[313] May my face be free from injur-
ies.[314] May my ears be opened. Life will not be
forced open(??)[315] and its totality[316] shall not exist.
I shall be transfigured among the glorious spirits, one
who is praised in ma'at, the [----], the stonemason of
of the king,[317] Merysakhmet".[318]

28. Stela Louvre E 14275 (ex-Museum Guimet 22), provenance
unknown. Limestone, with no traces of colour. 43 x 27 cm. scenes
and text incised. Bibliography: A. Moret, Catalogue du Musée
Guimet. Galerie égyptienne, stèles, bas-reliefs, monuments divers
I (Paris: 1909) 47-49 and pl. 20. Earlier, A. Wiedemann, "On Some
Egyptian Inscriptions in the Musée Guimet at Paris", PSBA 14
(1892) 332-335; also mentioned by Gauthier, "Les 'Fils Royaux de
Kouch'..." 200. (Fig. 30).

In the upper of this round-topped stela's two registers,
at the left and facing right, a man sits on a high-backed, lion-
footed chair with openwork sides. He wears a diaphonous sleeved
upper garment over his ankle-length kilt, the triangular apron of
which sits squarely on his lap.[319] On top of his elaborately-
plaited shoulder-length wig is a large cone of perfumed incense.
The valanced wig is bound with a fillet around the brow. The
man's neck and chest are festooned with massive gold sby.w-col-
lars. His right hand rests on his lap. The left is raised to
his chest, the fist clutching the stem of a lotus, the flower of
which is pressed to his nose. His bare feet rest upon a reed mat,
as does the base of a tall narrow table which, however, is partly
concealed by the feet. This is heaped up with a variety of food
offerings. Facing the table at the right is a second man who
pours a libation from a hs-jar to the seated figure. Bare-chest-

ed, he wears a less elaborate wig, a broad collar around his neck,
and a pleated calf-length kilt with the narrow inverted apron
usually associated with the so-called "military kilt".[320] Behind
the chair at the left is a tall floral bouquet, from the top of
which a lotus flower and two buds emanate. The feet of the libationer, the reed mat, the feet of the chair, and the base of the
bouquet all rest upon a second mat which also serves to separate
the two registers. In the field over the offering table, a little off-center, is the archaic form of the cartouche flanked by a
pair of wedjat-eyes, with two zigzags of water and a basin beneath
the cartouche. Above this group, centered at the arc of the
stela's top, a single horizontal line of crudely-incised hieroglyphs identifies the seated figure as "(the tutor of) the king's
daughter,[321] Paserpanetjer".[322] Below, to the right of the group
and over the libationer's head two short vertical lines record
that the stela was "made by the soldier, Parennefer".[323] This text
is continued by a third vertical line which, curiously, is to the
right, between the offerings and their recipient. This reads:
"for his lord, Paserpanetjer".[324] Behind the chair a single vertical line of text, which is continued behind the bouquet, again
identifies the seat man, but this time with a slightly different
title, as "the overseer of the tutor(s),[325] Paserpanetjer".

In the center of the lower register is a tall narrow cylindrical offering table, to the right and left of which sits a
couple, each on a high-backed and lion-footed couch. The two men
and the woman at the right all wear similar short valanced wigs.
The woman at the left wears the more usual longer woman's wig
which is held in place by a fillet. The two men, each bare-
chested, wear long diaphonous pleated kilts, as does seemingly

the woman of the right hand couple. The other female is clad in
a tight-fitting sheath. The attitude of the two men is identical
with that of Paserpanetjer, but that of their companions differs.
The lady on the left holds the right biceps of the man seated
next to her with her right arm, while her left embraces his back.
This is also the position of the right arm of the other woman,
whose hand can be seen grasping her partner's right shoulder. Her
left arm is pressed to her side, the hand on her lap.[326] On the
table is a large squat jar, flanked by two hs-jars, and some kind
of vegetable. In the field above this, between the two couples
and behind the lady on the left, are six vertical lines of rudely
incised hieroglyphs which identify the two pairs. The couple on
the right are, respectively, "Tuty"[327] and "Meyta".[328] The pair
on the left are "Parennefer" and "his lady, the mistress of the
house, Yeyu,[329] whom the soldier, Parennefer, of [the ship or
unit named][330] [----] sired".

29. Stela Yale University Art Gallery 28.53, from Serabit
el-Khadim. Limestone, with no traces of colour. 70 x 51 cm.
scene and text incised. Bibliography: A.H.Gardiner, T.E. Peet,
and J. Černý, The Inscriptions of Sinai 2nd ed. (London: 1955)
194 nr. 302 and pl. 75; J. Pijoan, Summa Artis. Historia General
del Arte. 3. El arte egipcio hasta la conquista romana. 2nd ed.
(Madrid: 1945) fig. 286. (Fig. 31).

A man stands at the left side of this round-topped stela,
both of his hands raised in a gesture of salutation. Shaven of
pate, he wears an elaborate sleeved upper garment over his long
kilt. This has an equally long triangular apron which is looped
through his belt, the ends of which dangle down asymmetrically
on each side of the apron. On his feet he wears a pair of sand-

als and around his neck are two thick gold šby.w-collars. In
front of him, facing in the same direction as he does, and continuing in the field over and behind his head, are six vertical
lines of well-cut hieroglyphs, the first three of which run the
full height of the stela. The text reads as follows:

"Year 3, third month of Shomu: His majesty commanded his
praised one, his beloved, the intimate[331] of his lord,
the overseer of the treasury of gold and silver,[332] the
privy counselor of the august palace,[333] Sebekhotpe,[334]
who will be justified, to bring for him all which his
heart desired, (namely) turquoise, from his fourth expedition. He said before his lord: 'The Spirits of Pe
and Nekhen rejoice for you and that which the sundisk
encircles worships you,[335] who created (even) the
tribesmen,[336] [-----],[337] who guides the name[338] (of?)
the royal butler,[339] Sebekhotpe, who will be justified".

30. Stela Vatican City 253, provenance unknown. Limestone,
with no traces of colour. 62 x 64 cm. text and scene in sunken
relief. Bibliography: G. Botti and P. Romanelli, Le Sculture del
Museo Gregoriano Egizio (Vatican City: 1951) 77-78 and pl. 49 nr.
125. (Fig. 32).

Only a small, almost rectangular fragment from the left
side of the stela is preserved. It is impossible to determine
what the monument's original shape may have been, how many registers it might have had, or the exact placement of the fragment on
the left side. At the extreme left the scene is bordered by a
nicely modelled vertical reed mat. To the right of this, facing
right, a male sits on a high-backed chair in front of a now-lost
table which had been heaped up with a large variety of meats,

breads, fruits, and floral bouquets. Part of the seat, the back, and the curved cushion of the chair are preserved, the curlique top of the latter breaking the outline of the reed mat border behind it. The man seated on the chair wears a quarter-sleeved pleated and diaphonous upper garment over his long kilt, the pleats of which fall naturally on his lap and thighs. Although his finely modelled facial features are those of a youthful person, horizontal lines indicating the obesity of age[340] are visible beneath his breasts. His elaborately-plaited wig is surmounted by an extra-large cone of perfumed incense. Each of his wrists is encircled by a bracelet and around his neck he wears two kinds of collar. Underneath is a multiple-stranded broad collar of ovid and tubular beads. Over this he wears a four-stranded gold $šby.w$-collar, the ties of which are visible just above his right shoulder. **His right arm is held formally to his right side.** In its clenched fist he holds a handkerchief whose end loops out over the fist, almost parallel to his lap, while its body flows loosely and freely down from the bottom of the fist. His left hand is extended forward in a gesture of salutation, although through an optical illusion it almost looks to be plucking a piece of fruit from the offerings on the **table** before him. In the field in front of his head, above his left arm and the offerings are the remains of a text of seven vertical lines of moderately-incised hieroglyphs. Beneath these is an eighth horizontal line. While none of the vertical lines are complete, it is clear that they contained a text of a religious content. What I can read is as follows:

"[-----] witness(?) the heart. Its (evil) occasion does not exist. [-----] with all the ones who live in it. The

god [-----] on truth. His abomination is falsehood.
[-----] without allowing to sleep another [-----] my
'voice'[341] when it cries out [-----] greatly, greatly.
My voice is not raised approaching and I am not brought
back".

The horizontal line beneath these vertical columns reads:

"[-----],thousands of beer, thousands of beef, thousands of fowl, thousands of milk, thousands of wine,
thousands of ungent, thousands of alabaster and linen,
thousands of every thing".

C

Unlike the scene of the king ceremonially slaughtering
a captured enemy which, other than on the private and public
stelae discussed in the preceding chapter,[342] is found in monumental art only in the temple, that depicting the reward of a favour-
ed and the various stages of its aftermath, although it is on occasion found on temple walls,[343] is, nevertheless, primarily a
genre belonging to the repertoire of tomb art.[344] The reasons
for this seem fairly straightforward when we take into consideration the nature and context of each of the ceremonies being illustrated. In the case of the former, a public event is being recorded, one in which the pharaoh himself is the principal actor,
performing a rite of triumphal thanksgiving to the god(s) on his
own behalf and on that of Egypt for, one may assume, continued
triumph, well-being, and victory. In the case of the ceremony
picturing the rewarding of an official with gold, in spite of the
fact that the king is shown playing a leading role in it at one
particular instant in time, what is being commemorated is, essentially, a private matter. The emphasis is not so much on the

king as it is on the exceptional honour which is being conferred
on the recipient, being rewarded by the king's own hand. The
tangible evidence of this royal largess is immediately apparent
in the form of the gold šby.w-collars worn by the various officials being honoured. The king is present only in those scenes
which picture him in the very act of conferring the collars.[345]

An unique temple scene picturing a ceremony akin to the
one in which rewards are given, but one possibly of a more public
nature, has been reconstructed from a number of Amarna talatat
which had been used as fill in various of the pylons of the great
temple of Amūn at Karnak.[346] There, the king is pictured at the
window of appearances while below, in the courtyard outside, a
number of courtiers and officials enjoy a banquet at the king's
expense. Redford has convincingly shown that this was "probably
one of the many ceremonies of the sd-festival, when the king dis-
tributed his bounty to his officers in a concrete fashion".[347] He
cites a number of texts, the earliest going back at least to the
reign of Amūnhotpe III, which describe such a ceremony,[348] the
most detailed and graphic description being that preserved in the
Decree of Horemheb:[349]

> "I made the regulations for the provisioning[350] of my
> [majesty] with respect to every holiday(?):[351] They
> came around to[352] my majesty three times a month. It
> came to be for them like a festival, every man sit-
> ting down at [his] portion of every good thing, con-
> sisting of good bread, meat, cakes from the royal
> possessions,[353] [their heads] annoin[ted with] oil.
> Their acclamation reached heaven, extolling the good-
> ness of the lord [of the Two Lands].[354] The leaders

of the infantry, every great one of the army, every man
among [-----] without number during the casting down to
them from the window and the hailing of every man by his
name by the king himself. They went away from the Presence rejoicing and provisioned with the goods of the
palace".

In his discussion of the Karnak talatat with this banquet scene
beneath the window of appearances, Redford correctly points out
that the king is not pictured casting down collars and other such
items to the assembled throng below because, while the feast was
indeed a public ceremony, the awarding of gold collars was essentially a private matter.[355]

The respective public and private natures of the sacrificial and reward ceremonies are likewise manifested on the private stelae on which they are found. In this respect it is interesting to note that all of those which illustrate the ritual sacrifice and whose provenance is firmly assured by controlled excavation[356] come from the temple. Conversely, virtually all of
those relating to the ceremony of reward and whose provenance is
equally fixed by excavation come from the tomb.[357] On the stelae
with the sacrificial scene, the dedicator plays no role whatsoever save that of a passive observer and witness. This is true
even for the single exemplar which has a real narrative text, the
Qantir stela of Wosimare'nakht (nr. 8) which records what was
awarded to him, not what he did. The principal focus in the
scenes of such stelae is the ceremony itself and the chief actors,
the only participants in fact, are the king, the victim(s), and
the god. Indeed, the presence of the dedicator is not even always
indicated either pictorially or textually.[358] To the contrary,

on the stelae with the scene of the rewarding and the various
stages of its aftermath, the principal personage, the official
who is being or has been rewarded, and who is not always their dedicator,[359] is almost always shown wearing the gold šby.w-col-
lars.[360] Nor is this obvious pride in being the recipient of such
a reward from the king's own hand confined only to representations
of it on the walls of his tomb and/or on his commemorative stelae.
There are several instances where the men who were so honoured
have left statues of themselves on which they display the collars
around their necks.[361]

D

With the exception of stela nr. 29, of the Ramesside royal
butler, Sebekhotpe, which was erected near the Hathor temple at
Serabit el-Khadim in Sinai, only the stelae which were dedicated
to or by the scribe of the offering table of the lord of the Two
Lands, Any (stelae nrs. 22, 24-26) were actually found in situ, in
his tomb at Amarna along with two others, Cairo CG 34.179 and CG
34.181, which were dedicated to him "by his brother, [Ptah]may"[362]
and "by the servitor, Yay"[363] respectively, though on these last
two, as on nr. 24, Any is not depicted wearing the šby.w-collars.
Four of these six stelae were found set up in niches, three on one
side, one on the other, in the walls of the vestibule of Any's
tomb.[364] However, none of the published accounts specify which
four of the six stelae these were, although one gets the impression from Bouriant's description of the tomb that the four stelae
were nrs. 22 and 24-26.[365] Beyond the vestibule a short passage
leads into the main chamber of the tomb, the walls of which do not
appear to have been decorated save for a cornice running along the
sides beneath the ceiling.[366] At the far end of the corridor is

is the shrine, the major part of which is occupied by the seated
tomb-statue of Any, and the right and left walls of which each
are decorated with a scene showing Any seated behind an offering
table[367] and being offered a libation (in the scene on the right
wall)[368] and a floral bouquet (in the scene on the left wall)[369]
by a servant. Both scenes, together with the texts which accompany them, were found in a badly-damaged state of preservation,
but enough remains of each to allow most of its original appearance to be restored. In the right hand scene, Any, wearing the
cone of perfumed incense on top of his wig, a sleeved upper garment, and sandals on his feet, sits in a formal attitude, one
hand which holds a ḫrp-scepter pressed against his chest, the
other resting on his lap. A woman, probably his wife,[370] stands
behind him while before him, a man purs out the libation from a
high-necked amphora. The text above identifies him as "the servitor and agent[371] of the royal scribe, the justified Any, Meryreꜥ".
Any also appears in this pose on stela Cairo CG 34.179, but there
the dedicator, "his brother, (Ptah)may" is depicted hailing him
with one hand and saying:

> "There is made for you a ḥtp-dí-nswt invocation of bread
> and beer, meat and fowl, and libations of wine.' So says
> (ín) his brother, (Ptah)may".[372]

On stela nr. 25, dedicated by "the servitor of the royal scribe,
Any, Anymen", the latter is also depicted pouring out a libation
from a similar amphora to the seated Any, while saying: "Let wine
be poured out for you". More than half of the twelve lines of the
text representing the speech of the servitor Meryreꜥ as he pours
out the libation are lost. What is preserved reads:

> "[-----] all [-----] you go forth. [-----]. You shall be

as one among [-----]. The king has ordained[373] for you a
happy burial (in) the cliffside[374] of Akhetaton, [in the
Place][375] of Eternity. Its interior shall be for you
the place of your ka.[376] (remainder of the text is corrupt)".[377]

Finally, in connection with this scene it may be noted that on
stelae Cairo CG 34.179 and 34.108 (nr. 26) Any is called "one who
shall be justified[378] with a goodly burial" and, on stela Cairo
CG 34.177 (nr. 22) Any himself says: "I return in peace with the
rewards of the king. He has commanded for me a goodly burial" and
on stela Cairo CG 34.176 (nr. 24) the scribe Nebwawi describes
"the beautiful things which the goodly ruler has done for his
scribe of the offering table: he has ordained for him a happy
burial in Akhetaton".

In the scene on the left wall of the shrine Any is dressed as before, but with the addition of four gold šby.w-collars
around his neck.[379] He sits behind an offering table, one hand
resting on his lap, its fist clutching a napkin or handkerchief,
the other hand, palm down, extended as if partaking of the offerings. Facing him is the same Meryreʿ who this time raises .
one hand in salutation,[380] while he pours out a libation from a
ḥs-jar with the other.[381] The accompanying text, which contains
his speech to Any, though damaged, is better preserved than that
in the scene on the right wall. On the basis of several parallel
texts from the tomb of Ḥuya (nr. 1) at Amarna, much of the missing or corrupt part of it can be restored. It reads as follows:
    "Accept the offerings [of the king's own giving to][383]
    the steward of [ʿAakheprureʿ].[385] [-----][386] every[387]
    shrine of yours. Your name will flourish [-----][388]

which you desire.[389] Every generation which shall come(?)
shall call out to [you].[390] Your name shall not be sought
[in your mansion].[391] You shall be a son for whom is
made[392] the ḥtp-dỉ-nswt invocation consisting of your
bread and your beer of your house, the wine of the house[393]
which has come forth from the Presence, and [-----]".[394]

Any appears in the same attitude and attire on two of the stelae
from his tomb, Cairo CG 34.181 and CG 34.180 (nr. 26). On the
second of these he also wears the gold šby.w-collars. While the
texts of neither of these two stelae can be directly related in
content to the text of the scene on the left wall of the shrine,
one might compare that of stela Cairo CG 34.179 where Any's brother, [Ptah]may says: "There shall be made for you a ḥtp-dỉ-nswt
invocation of bread and beer, meat and fowl, and libations of
wine". Moreover, as we have just seen, the texts of stelae nrs.
22 and 24 make it clear that these benefices which Any shall enjoy come to him by the king's command and, we may even assume,
from the king's own hand.

Although we do not know exactly which of the six stelae
dedicated to Any were set up in the wall niches of the vestibule
of his tomb, it is certain that at least two of them had to have
been from among the group of stelae nrs. 22 and 24-26. If the
impression given by Bouriant that it was all four stelae from
this group is correct,[395] then it is striking that in that portion of the tomb which normally contains scenes depicting those
aspects of the lifetime of the deceased which he deemed important
enough to be repeated for eternity in the Afterworld,[396] four
stelae, each illustrating a single different stage following the
actual ceremony of being rewarded with gold by the king were found

in precisely this part of the tomb. Moreover, there is no reason
to assume that the other two stelae likewise were not intended to
be erected in similar niches, but since the tomb was apparently
never finished, these were never carved.[397] Even were this not
the case, the placement of the four remaining stelae in the niches
of the vestibule with scenes of the various stages of the aftermath of what must have been the most important single event in
Any's career, his being personally rewarded by the king, is para-
lled in a number of other tombs at Amarna where these same scenes
decorate the corresponding walls in them.[398] This almost suggests
that, in the case of Any whose tomb was a relatively modest one,
the stelae in question served here as a simplified and certainly
less expensive substitute form of tomb decoration. Furthermore,
if this suggestion is acceptable, we may then very easily hypotho-
size that those other stelae relating to the rewarding ceremony
also originally may have stood in niches in the corresponding
parts of their tombs, but it must be emphatically stressed that
this can only be speculation.[399] It might also be argued that,
were this the case, we should have expected to find in the tomb
of Any a stela whose scene showed the actual award being made, as
it is depicted on the stelae of Hormin (nr. 20) and Mose (nr. 21),
but we do not. However, such an argument loses most of its force
when we remember that the most important element of the ceremony
was the reward itself, even more than the king's giving of it.

Footnotes:

214. For the most recent study of this scene and its significance
in tomb art, see G.A. Gaballa, Narrative in Egyptian Art 62-
64 (the earlier 18th Dynasty), 72-78 (the Amarna period),
129-130 (the Ramesside period) and compare J. Vandier, Manuel d'archéologie égyptienne. IV. Bas-relief et peintures.
Scenes de la vie quotidienne (Paris: 1964) 638-668, ánd A.
Hermann, "Jubel dei der Audienz. Zur Gebärdensprache in der
Kunst des Neuen Reichs", ZAeS 90 (1963) 49-66. For an earlier
treatment, see S. Gabra, Les conseils de fonctionnaires dans
l'Égypte pharaonique. Scenes de recompenses royales aux fonctionnaires (Cairo: 1929).

215. See H. Ricke, G.R. Hughes, and E.F. Wente, The Beit el-Wali
Temple pl. 9 and, earlier, Hermann, op. cit. 61 and pl. 9c,
Roeder, Der Felsentempel von Bet el-Wali (Cairo: 1938) 35 and
pl. 30f. Interestingly enough, with the exception of Hermann,
none of the other scholars who have investigate the rewarding
scenes have included this one, yet it is identical with them:
the viceroy of Kush, Amenemope, having been led into the presence of Ramesses II sitting inside a kiosk is decorated with
gold šby.w-collars after he has presented the king the booty
taken from the Nubians. For the probability that this scene
is also to be connected with the Nubian war alluded to in the
Aswan inscription of year 2 of Ramesses II (which in turn may
actually have been the Nubian war which took place between
years 7 and 9 of Seti I) and which this same Amenemope commemorated with three rock-stelae near Aswan and a fourth at
Kasr Ibrim, see above, Chapter 1 nr. 143.

216. See Hermann, op. cit. pl. 10 and, earlier, G. Lefebvre, In-

scriptions concernant les grands prêtres d'Amon Romê-Roy et
Amenhotep (Paris: 1929) pl. 2. For the most recent treatment of the texts, see W.Helck, "Die Inschrift über die Belohnung des Hohempriesters 'Imn-htp", MIO 4 (1956) 161-178.
For the possibility that the high priest Amūnhotpe is not being rewarded in the presence and by the hand of the king,
himself, but rather in the presence of a **statue** of the king,
since the royal figure stands on a pedestal, see W. Federn,
"Roi ou statue royale?", CdÉ 34 (1959) 214.

217. See, e.g. Wreszinski, Atlas I, pls. 203-205 (from the tomb
of Khaemhet, nr. 57, at Thebes), Vandier, op. cit. 557, fig.
300 (from the tomb of Paser, nr. 106, at Thebes), Davies, The
Tomb of the Vizier Ramose (London: 1941) pls. 34-37 (from the
tomb of Ramose, nr. 55, at Thebes), idem. "Akhenaton at
Thebes", JEA 9 (1923) 138-139 and pls. 23, 24, 27 (from the
tomb of Parennefer, nr. 188, at Thebes), A. Fakhry, "A Note
on the Tomb of Kheruef at Thebes", ASAE 42 (1943) 488-492
(from the tomb of Kheruef, nr. 192, at Thebes), LD III, pl.
230 (from the tomb of Penno, at Aniba).

218. See, e.g. Davies, The Rock Tombs of El-Amarna II (London:
1905) pls. 10 (from the tomb of Panehsy, nr. 6) and 33 (from
the tomb of Meryre' II, nr. 2); idem. ibid. III, pls. 16-17
(from the tomb of Huya, nr. 1); ibid. IV (1906) pl. 29 (from
the tomb of Mahu, nr. 9); ibid. VI (1908) pls. 4 (from the
tomb of Parennefer, nr. 7), 17 (from the tomb of Tutu, nr.
8) and 29 (from the tomb of Ay, nr. 25); H.Schäfer, "Ein
Relief aus der Zeit Tutanchamuns", Berliner Museen: Berichte
aus den preussischen Kunstsammlungen 49 nr. 2 (1928) 39 fig.
3 (from the Memphite tomb of Horemheb); Davies, The Tomb of

of Nefer-Hotep at Thebes (New York: 1933) pls. 9-13, 16 (nr.
49, of the chief scribe of Amūn), idem. Two Ramesside Tombs
at Thebes (New York: 1927) pls. 27-29 (from the tomb of Ipuy,
nr. 217, at Thebes), Vandier, op. cit. 668 fig. 369 (from the
tomb of the god's father of Amūnreʿ, Neferhotep, nr. 50, at
Thebes), Petrie, Gizeh and Rifeh (London: 1907) pls. 29-30
(from a Ramesside tomb, owner unknown, at Rifeh), PM I part
I 2nd ed.239 (Oriental Institute, Chicago, photographs 3911-
14, 3916 and 10333 of the otherwise unpublished tomb of
Amenemope, nr. 148, at Thebes). In at least three instances
at Amarna the award seems to be taking place with the royal
couple standing in a courtyard, see Davies, The Rock Tombs of
el-Amarna I, pl. 30 (from the tomb of Meryreʿ I, nr. 4),
ibid. II, pl. 41 (from the tomb of Meryreʿ II, nr. 2), and
ibid. IV, pl. 7 (from the tomb of Pentu, nr. 5). For the
window of appearances, see B.J. Kemp, "The Window of Appearance at El-Amarna and the Basic Structure of this City", JEA
62 (1976) 81-99, R. Stadelmann, "Tempelpalast und Erscheinungsfenster in der Thebanischen Totentempeln", MDAIK 29
(1973) 221-242. An earlier, but still excellent study is
that of H. Schäfer, "Der König im Fenster. Ein Beitrag zum
Nachleben der Kunst von Tell El-Amarna", Amtliche Berichte
aus den Preusz. Staatsammlungen 40 nr. 3 (1918) 41-61. See
LdAe II (1977) 14 (article "Erscheinungsfenster").

219. E.g. in the scenes from the Amarna tombs of Meryreʿ, Meryreʿ
II, Parennefer, Ay, and Tutu, and in the tombs of Neferhotep
(nr. 50) and Ipuy. For the exact references, see above, n.
218.

220. Or else he is reaching up to the window, either to salute

the king or else to taking the collars which are being hand-
down, see previous note, as well the scene from the Memphite
tomb of Horemheb, cited in n. 218.

221. Not all of these scenes have texts preserved, and when they
are, the king's speech is frequently couched in such artifi-
cial hyperbole so that the specific reason f or the bestowal
is not easily apparent. But Meryre⸂ I was rewarded "because
of his obeying the teaching of Pharaoh, l.p.h., doing all
that was said", Tutu "because of his love for Pharaoh, l.p.
h." The legate of Miam, Penno was rewarded because he had
erected a statue of Ramesses VI in the temple of Derr and
also for what he had "done in the Neh(s)y lands, the land of
Ikayta, when you had them brought as captives in the presence
of Pharaoh, your good lord", and the god's father of Amūn,
Neferhotep was rewarded "at the command of my lord, Amūn".
(One wonders, in this last case, if this is not an oblique
indication of Horemheb paying off a political debt for the
support of the clergy of Amūn for his usurpation of the Egyptian throne?). There are two scenes in the Amarna tomb of
Huya which show him receiving gold collars. The motivation
for the first of these was his appointment as "the overseer
of the royal harem, overseer of the treasury, and steward in
in the house of the mother of the king". Clearly the bestowal of the collars was a concomitant feature of the promotion.
The replies of those being rewarded, when preserved, adds
little to our knowledge of why they are being so honoured.
In general they consist of encomia and paeans of praise of
the king.

222. In the scene from the tomb of the anonymous Ramesside offic-

ial from Rifeh, see above, n. 218.

223. In the scene from the tomb of Paser, nr. 106, at Thebes, see above, n. 217.

224. This particular scene, in comparison to the others of this genre, is rather unique. It depicts, I believe, the vizier Paser being rewarded in the Afterworld by the deceased and deified Seti I. My reasoning for this brash supposition is based mainly on the fact that the king, in Osiride guise, is depicted accompanied by the goddess Ma'at and the Souls of Pe and Nekhen. Unless the awarding of gold collars here was taking place during a particular religious ceremony, one which called for the king to appear as Osiris and with various priests and priestesses impersonating the deities, one can hardly come to any other conclusion. While there is no speech of the king, that of the goddess Ma'at is rather telling:

"Words spoken by Ma'at, the daughter of Re':
'My hands are behind you in life and good fortune. I give [----] you joy upon the throne'".

The term "throne" s.t-wr.t is written with the determinative of a shrine ⌂ , so that the expression here clearly refers to a sanctuary within the temple and, as the speech seems to be addressed to the king rather than Paser, the inference is that we are dealing with a cult statue of the former resting within a sanctuary within the temple. Since Seti is shown in the Osiride form, this can hardly be a cult statue of the living king. Moreover, the attendants of Paser are all styled imy-ḫnt which **Wb**. I, 75, 1, vaguely renders "priesterlicher Amtstitel" and the speech of Paser, though replete with lacu-

nae and containing the usual praise of the king, is filled
with references to "the Holy Place" (Ḏsr.w) and to the nec-
cropolis. For the latest edition of these texts, see KRI I,
291-293.

225. Once, in the tomb of Neferhotep (nr. 49) at Thebes, she is
shown by herself as she confers gold šby.w-collars on the
wife of Neferhotep, see Davies, op. cit. pl. 14.

226. On these collars, see most recently C. Aldred, Jewels of the
Pharaohs abridged ed. (New York: 1978) 12-13 and, earlier,
A. Wilkinson, Ancient Egyptian Jewellery (London: 1971) 108
pl. 31B. There is an abstract of an interesting unpublished
study by E. Ertman, "The 'Gold of Honor' in Royal Representation", Newsletter ARCE 83 (Oct. 1972) 26-27, which, among
other things, speculates on the possible connection of this
necklace with the cult of Amūn. For the word itself, see Wb.
IV, 439, and for its equation with the so-called "Gold of
Honour", see H. von Deines, "Das Gold der Tapferkeit, eine
militärische Auszeichnung oder eine Belohnung?", ZAeS 79
(1954) 83-86.

227. To the references cited in nn. 217-218 above, add also stelae nrs. 20-22, 25-30 in Section B, below.

228. See, e.g. statues Cairo CG 42126, 42168, and 816, published
most recently by Vandier, op. cit. III: Les grands epoques:
La statuaire (Paris: 1958) pls. 147 nr. 1, 162 nr. 6, and
169 nr. 4.

229. E.g. the king orders the god's father of Amūn, Neferhotep
(tomb nr. 50 at Thebes) "to receive rewards in the presence
of the king, consisting of millions of everything, of silver,
gold, clothing, ungents, loaves of bread, beer, meat, and

cakes (<u>Urk</u>. IV, 2177). Penno, the legate of Miam, was specifically granted two silver bowls and ointment of gum or re-
sin (see Hermann, "Jubel bei der Audienz..." 62-63 and fig.
16). The high priest Amūnhotpe received, among other things,
"one broad collar equipped with two strands of gold beads and
a pectoral, a fillet for the head of an official, and two
tied-together [----], a total of four items of fine gold in
skw-work, weighing ten deben", "twelve silver vessels weighing twenty deben, good bread, meat, [-----], four great amphorae of sweet beer, two hin of sweet ointment" and "twenty
arourae of land with grain" (see Helck,"Die Belohnung..."
167). The last item in Amūnhotpe's reward calls to mind the
grant of land given to the shield-bearer Wosimare'nakht which
was discussed in Chapter 2, Section E, end. The god's father
Ay and his wife (see Davies, <u>The Rock Tombs of el Amarna</u> VI,
pl. 29) are pictured standing and catching the collars which
both Akhenaton and Nofretete are showering down at them,
while other items, previously thrown down, are heaped up at
their feet. These consist of "eighteen double necklaces of
gold beads, at least two of them fitted with pectorals, two
plain necklaces, five collars, no doubt of threaded faience
trinkets, six fillets, probably of the same sort, four gold-
en(?) cups, two with a foot, two without, two metal(?) vases,
five signet rings, one pair of gloves, twelve pairs of plain
armlets" (ibid. 22). Ay was apparently particularly pleased
by the gloves since he is shown in an adjoining subscene
proudly wearing them and showing them off to his admiring
retainers. Gloves may also have figured as one of the items
conferred on the Amarna noble Ḥuya if the horizontal stripes

from the wrist to the elbow on each arm raised to the king
in adoration at the awarding ceremony do not indicate a series of banglelike armlets (see Davies, ibid. III, pl. 17 and
compare the scene from the tomb of Ay just cited). Perhaps
the most telling representation is from the tomb of Meryre⟨
II where, immediately after the rewarding, Meryre⟨ returns
home wearing the šby.w-collars. He is followed by two long
lines of servants carrying tables laden with all sorts of
collars, vessels, foods, jars, flasks, jugs, amphorae, meat,
fish, and cloth (ibid. II, pl. 37). See also stela nr. 25,
below, whose owner proudly records that the king has granted
him "a goodly burial in Akhetaton".

230. E.g. ibid. II, pl. 36 (from the tomb of Meryre⟨ II, nr. 2,
at Amarna), ibid. III, pls. 5 (from the tomb of Parennefer,
nr. 7) and 20 (from the tomb of Tutu, nr. 8); idem. The Tomb
of Neferhotep pl. 16 (from the tomb of Neferhotep, nr. 49,
at Thebes). Also see below, Section B, stela nr. 22. In a
number of ancilliary scenes the chariot is shown parked with
the charioteer waiting outside the locale in which his master is being rewarded, see Davies, The Rock Tombs of El Amarna II, pl. 11 (from the tomb of Panehsy, nr. 6), ibid. III,
pl. 17 (from the tomb of Huya, nr. 1), ibid. VI, pls. 17
(from the tomb of Tutu) and 30 (from the tomb of Ay, nr. 26),
and compare stela nr. 25, below, Section B.

231. See the preceding note for references.

232. E.g. Davies, op. cit. V, pl. 9 (from the tomb of Any, nr. 23).

233. E.g. ibid. I, p s. 35, 37 (from the tomb of Meryre⟨, nr. 4),
ibid. II, pls. 22 (from the tomb of Panehsy) and 31 (from
the tomb of Meryre⟨ II), ibid. III, pl. 29 (from the tomb of

Ahmose, nr. 3), Wreszinski, <u>Atlas</u> I, pl. 189 (from the tomb
of Khaemhet, nr. 57, at Thebes).

234. See above, n. 151.

235. See above, Chapter 1, the latter part of Section E.

236. See above, n. 181.

237. See below, Section B, stelae nrs. 22, 24-26, all of which
come from the tomb of Any at Amarna. Stela 29 which was
found in situ at Serabit el-Khadim is certainly not a tomb
stela.

238. See below, Section B, stelae nrs. 20, 25, 26, and 30.

239. See above, nn. 217-218 for the parallels.

240. See above, n. 148, for the name and for his other monuments.

241. r.f wḏ3. Gabra's rendering, Les conseils 42 "dont la bouche
est saine" is perhaps a little too literal.

242. Gabra, loc. cit. renders this a little more freely: "dont la
marche est à sa place (en bonne direction)". The sense seems
clear enough.

243. <u>KRI</u> I, 309 line 5, reads: ⸗ as against Gabra, loc. cit.

244. Taking n̲ as the instrumental "with" rather than as the loca-
tive "in", see Gardiner, <u>Egyptian Grammar</u> 3rd ed. (Oxford:
1957) par. 162, 7.

245. Gabra's rendering, loc. cit. "le chef du sceau" perhaps attributes more to this title than is permissible. It is probably more preferable to retain the older <u>Wb</u>. V, 637, 11-16
rendering "Vorsteher des Schatzes" or the like.

246. Or, taking ḥꜥ.k as a verb: "You appear beautifully".

247. Reading mr-tw Ỉmn.

248. Taking mỉ with the following ỉw.k dỉ, see Erman, <u>Neuägypt</u>-

ische Grammatik 2nd ed. (Leipzig: 1933) par. 621.

249. Since p3 is written, it is best to reflect this in the translation. It may even have the force of a vocative here: "O
(You)!"

250. Gabra's rendering, loc. cit. 43: "belle est la joie de tes
voisins" presupposes that nfr is a verb here, but from its
physical position in the sentence this is unlikely. It is
better to understand it as a noun cordinate with rsw(t).

251. Literally: "belong to your neighbours".

252. Understanding sḏm as a plural participle with the ending not
written.

253. For the writing of nṯr.w with three stars, see Wb. II, 354,
right hand column and also É. Drioton, "Recueil de cryptographie monumentale", ASAE 40 (1940) 409 nr. 4.

254. Taking irr.tw in the following line, nty twk im-s here, and
all of the following verb forms as various expressions of
the future resulting as a conswquency implied by the htp-di-
nswt-formula "may he grant that....".

255. Gabra, loc. cit. 44, takes nhh as an adjective and shows the
determinative of the entire expression to be the man with
his hand to his mouth. Kitchen, loc. cit. reads the determinative as the seated man with two minsculte strokes below. I
understand the word as a noun since Wb. II does not recog-
nize it as an adjective. However, it is not attested as a
noun there with either of these two determinatives, although
a nhh determined with the seated god is known, loc. cit. 302,
10-11, as the name or nickname of varicus gods.

256. Unlike Gabra, loc. cit. I do not take b3.k as the emphasized
subject of the following hmn.f, with the suffix .f serving

as a resumptive pronoun. There is no reason not to understand b3.k as a verbal form, see <u>Wb</u>. I, 411, 1-3.

257. I.e. the high priest of Ptah in Memphis will, himself, pre-
side at Hormin's funeral. For wr ḥrp ḥmw(.t) (and incident-
ly sm, an office held simultaneously by the former), see
Gardiner, <u>Ancient Egyptian Onomastica</u> I (London: 1947) 38*-
39*.

258. And not as Kayser, <u>Die ägyptischen Altertümer</u> 59, translates:
"Ptah, der Gott der Wahrheit, der die Gebete des Königs der
beiden Länder hört". "King of the Two Lands here refers to
Ptah, not Ramesses II, see Sandman-Holmberg,<u>The God Ptah</u>
chap. 6, 80-86 ("Ptah as King"). For the epithet "he who
hears petitions", see above, nn. 189-202.

259. See above, n. 36.

260. Although not clear in the published photographs, the auto-
graphed copy of the text in <u>KRI</u> III, 263, 14, shows
where the restoration sš admirably suits the traces beneath
imy-r in the first square. There are four military titles
which begin with sš and end with m p3 mšꜥ: ss shw n p3 mšꜥ
"the scribe of the assemblage of the army", see my <u>Military</u>
Rank 66 par. 166 and refs. 238, 240, 468, sš aḥn n p3 mšꜥ
"the scribe who writes commands for the army", ibid. 66 par.
168 and refs. 469-470, ss ḫnrt n p3 mšꜥ "the scribe of the
prison of the army", ibid. 65-66 par. 165 and ref. 467, and
sš dni n p3 mšꜥ "the scribe of the distribution of the army",
ibid. 66 par. 167 and refs. 238, 240). In view of the horizontal trace at the bottom of the second square of the lacuna, just above the clearly visible n, there is room, though
cramped, to restore either shw or shn, both of which are

written with a narrow horizontal determinative. While such a
title "overseer of the scribes who write commands for the
army" or "overseer of the scribes of the assemblage of the
army" is otherwise not known to me, it is clear that it referred to an officer of very high rank. Thus Mose should
have been either a "scribe of the infantry" (sš mnfyt) or a
"scribe of elite troops" (sš nfrw), ibid. loc. cit. See also
nn. 147 above and 271 below.

261. Two more lines follow here, the first a lacuna of two squares
with n-t legible at the bottom of the first. The traces in
the second seem to read Imn ḥr iꜥi "Amūn, washing(??)", with
possibly two more groups lost. I have no real suggestions
for what may have originally stood there or how to translate
what is visible.

262. Probably, from their shape, copper oxhide-ingots, see G.
Bass, Cape Gelidonya: A Bronze Age Shipwreck (Philadelphia:
1967) 52-78.

263. The table is almost completely destroyed by the oblique fracture running across the face of the upper register. Only
its plate is preserved, with the nb-baskets resting on it.
The haunch of meat which sits on the register line conceals
its foot.

264. Habachi, "Khataꜥna-Qantir..." 549-555, distinguishes four
distinct cult statues of Ramesses II: 1) Wosimareꜥ-setepen-
reꜥ-Montu-in-the-Two-Lands, 2) Ramesses-miꜥamūn-the-God, 3)
Wosimareꜥ-setepenreꜥ-the-God, 4) Ramesses-miꜥamūn-the-Sun-
of-Rulers, and mentions a fifth statue, pictured on a stela
in Munich (Gl. 287) perhaps also from Qantir, and named
Ramesses-miꜥamūn-the-Ruler-of-Rulers. This may be related to

the statue Ramesses-miʿamūn-the-Sun-of-Rulers, see the next
note.

265. The statue Ramesses-miʿamūn-the-Sun-of-Rulers is illustrated
on one other statue, Hildesheim 1085, described but not shown
by Habachi, loc. cit. 540. Here the figure of the king is
dressed and crowned as on the stela of Mose, but unlike the
latter, is shown in full profile. From these two instances
may we conclude that this particular colossal statue was a
seated one? It is tempting to suppose that the statue of Munich Gl. 287 (see Habachi, "The Qantir Stela of the Vizier Rahotep..." 67-77 is another example of the statue Ramesses-
miʿamūn-the-Sun-of-Rulers with a variant of the name. How-
such an identification must be ruled out. Not only is there
the difference in the name, the statue of the Munich stela
is that of a standing figure and the known representations of
"Sun-of-Rulers show it to have been a seated statue. It is
this last point which is significant. Habachi, "Khataʿna-
Qantir..." 549-550, has shown that each of the individual
statues is depicted on the Qantir stelae in the same attitude. There is a seated statue named Ruler-of-Rulers, but
this is the southern of the Memnon Colossi Nebmareʿ-Ruler-
of-Rulers which is also illustrated in the rock inscription
of the architect Men, at Aswan, see Habachi, "The Qantir
Stela..." 75-76 and figs. 4-5.

266. It is difficult to determine exactly what these other items
were, but what looks like a bowl can be seen just over the
forehead of Mose, with perhaps three more bowls in the field
between the bottom of the text and the upraised arms of the
assembled men. Over Mose's head one can make out two slender

cylindrical objects, that on the right perhaps a libation vase.

267. See my The Military Establishment of the Egyptian Empire (unpublished M.A. thesis, University of Chicago: 1958) 94-95.

268. See above, Chapter 1, Section A, n. 21.

269. See above, n. 147.

270. For n before the relative form, see Erman, op. cit. par. 835.

271. Literally: "their lord". While nb conceivably may refer to the king, the context here makes it more like that Mose is meant.

272. Taking wbn.k as a virtual relative clause with the preceding twk mi kd.f, rather than the following ꜥnḫ.n.

273. Kayser, loc. cit. translates: "so leben wir von Deinem Blick ..." and notes that "Der Rest der Inschrift ist durch Zerstörung leider nicht mehr verständlich", but the authographed copy of the text in KRI III, 264, shows no hatching over over the last group of line 4 or the first group of line 5 of the reply of the assembled soldiers to Ramesses: hr nty iry which is then followed by the recognizable traces of the title wꜥw and the name Msw. As it stands, I agree that the text is incomprehensible here. If, however, we allow a corrupt text, or rather a corrupt orthography, and assume that is a poor writing of 𓇋𓂝, some sense may be made out of it: n m33.k hr nty i-ir wꜥw Msw, literally: "on account of your looking at that which the soldier, Mose, did".

274. For the "company", see above, n. 147 and the literature cited there. For the meaning of the name of a military unit of this size, see my Military Rank 74-75 par. 187. Other than

the present instance, a company of this name is not known
to me.

275. Accepting the restoration offered in <u>KRI</u> III, 264 n. 6a.

276. Although Kitchen, ibid. n. 6b, points out that lines 7-8 of
the text were completely erased anciently, his autograph at
this point does not reflect this erasure. In line 8 the
sundisk at the beginning and half of the cartouche at the
end are written without hatching, indicating that these
groups, at least, are undamaged and visible. In any event,
the restoration can hardly be anything else.

277. As far as I can determine, it is not until the Amarna period
that <u>Egyptian</u> chariots are shown with two occupants, the
driver and the passenger. In the earlier 18th Dynasty representations, when they are depicted <u>in</u> <u>motion</u>, only a single
chariot rider is shown, see e.g. Wreszinski, <u>Atlas</u> I, pl. 26a
(from the tomb of Userhet, nr. 56, at Thebes), pl. 347 (from
an anonymous tomb, nr. 143, at Thebes), Davies, <u>The Tombs of</u>
<u>Two Officials</u> pls. 6 (from the tomb of Amūnhotpesise, nr.
75, at Thebes) and 24 (from the tomb of Nebamūn, nr. 90), relief Luxor Museum J. 129 (published by Y. Yadin, <u>The Art of</u>
<u>Warfare in Biblical Lands in the Light of Archaeological</u>
<u>Study</u> [New York: 1963] 200), sculptor's model(?) Hannover
2959 (published by I. Woldering, <u>Ausgewählte Werke der ägypt-</u>
<u>ischen Sammlung</u> 2nd ed. [Hannover: 1958] pl. 38); faience
tile Metropolitan Museum of Art 17.194.2797 (published by
Yadin, op. cit. 188). Chariots with only a driver are also
shown on a number of pictorial ostraca, e.g. Cambridge EGA
4287.1943 (published by E. Brunner-Traut, <u>Egyptian Artists'</u>
<u>Sketches</u> [Leiden: 1979] pl. 23 nr. 27), Stockholm MM 14111

(published by Petersen, <u>Zeichnungen aus einer Totenstadt</u> (Stockholm: 1973) pls. 45 nrs. 81, 82, and 46 nr. 83); Brussels E 6438 and E 6440 (published by J. Capart, "Ostraca illustrant des texts littéraires", <u>CdE</u> 16 (1941) 191-193 figs. 2-3), Berlin 21771 and 23678 (published by Brunner-Traut, <u>Die altägyptischen Scherbenbilder (Bildostraka) der Deutschen Museen und Sammlungen</u> (Wiesbaden: 1956) pl. 36 nrs. 102-103), Munich 1551 vso (ibid. nr. 104), Deir el-Medineh 2158 (published by J. Vandier D'Abbadie, <u>Catalogue des ostraca figurés de Deir el Médineh (nos. 2256 a 2722)</u> (Cairo: 1937) pl. 19), ibid. nrs. 2783, 2784, and 2787 (idem. <u>Catalogue des ostraca figurés de Deir el Médineh nos. 2734 a 3053</u> (Cairo: 1959) pls. 105-106). There is, however, no really good way of determining if any of these ostraca can unequivocally be assigned to the 18th Dynasty before the Amarna period. The dating criterion based on the number of spokes in chariot's wheel has been seriously questioned (see Brunner-Traut, <u>Die altägyptischen Scherbenbilder</u> 102 n. 7), but if the proposal of H.A. Liebowitz, "Horses in New Kingdom Art and the Date of an Ivory from Megiddo", <u>JARCE</u> 6 (1967) 18, that in the pre-Amarna 18th Dynasty, all four legs of the horses touch the ground, with fore and hindlegs spread apart to form a narrow-based isosceles triangle is correct, then possibly Munich 1551 vso, Deir el Medineh 2158 and Deir el Medineh 2783 may also date to this period. A number of representations from the earlier 18th Dynasty picture the chariot parked, an attendant next to it, while its owner inspects his harvests, but whether this attendant was a charioteer or a sais is impossible to tell. For these, see e.g. J.J. Tylor

and F.L. Griffith, <u>The Tomb of Paheri at El Kab</u> (London:
1894) pl. 111, Wreszinski, op. cit. I, pls. 191 (from the
tomb of Khaemhet, nr. 57, at Thebes), 231 (from the tomb of
Menna, nr. 69, at Thebes), 260 (from the tomb of Djehuty-
nefer, nr. 80, at Thebes), and 424 (painting British Museum
37982, from an anonymous Theban tomb). That non-Egyptian
chariots at this time carried both a driver and a passenger
is clear from the representations of such on the sidepanels
of the chariot of Thutmose IV, see Yadin, op. cit. 192-193
and compare Bruyère, <u>Deir el Médineh Année 1926. Sondage au</u>
<u>temple de Thotmès II</u> (Cairo: 1952) pls. 3-4.

278. The realistic manner in which the passenger steadies himself
by resting both hands on the edge of the sidepanel is not
without interest. When the vehicle is being used in combat,
the passenger usually holds a shield in one hand and opera-
tes or helps to guide the reins with his other (e.g. Wreszinski, op. cit. II, pls. 62a, 137, 151, 183), maintaining his
balance, one supposes, by spreading his legs squarely apart
and bracing his body against the side of the car. In many
instances, however, (e.g. ibid. pls. 17, 64, 66, 83, 92a,
169) only the arm and hand holding the shield are visible
and it may be assumed that the other either holds on to the
sidepanel on the far side of the chariot (ibid. pl. 128)
or to the body of the charioteer (ibid. pl. 67). When the
vehicle is being driven in a non-military situation and the
passenger has both hands free, he usually steadies himself
as on stela nr. 22, e.g. Davies, <u>The Rock Tombs of el Amarna</u>
II, pls. 26 and 13, ibid. VI, pl. 20, Yadin, op. cit. 213-
214 (the painted box of Tutankhamūn), J.D. Cooney, <u>Amarna</u>

Reliefs from Hermopolis in American Collections (Brooklyn:
1965) 52 fig. 50a (a Ramesside relief from North Sakkara),
Wreszinski, op. cit. pl. 166, Davies, The Tomb of Nefer-Hotep pl. 16. Ofen, moreover, the chariot box is equipped
with handgrips. These are affixed to either its front or
sides and the passenger grasps them instead of holding directly onto the edge of the car, see e.g. Davies, The Rock
Tombs of el Amarna I pl. 19, ibid. II pls. 13, 36, ibid. IV,
pl. 22, ibid. VI, pl. 20.

279. Interestingly enough, while the bowcase, obviously an essen-
tial fixture of the chariot in military situations, is also
usually shown attached to the sidepanel even when the vehicle is used for peaceful pursuits (including, of course,
hunting desert game), the chariot is, nevertheless, shown
without it on occasion. In tomb art I know of only one instance, on the chariot in the tomb of Khaemhet (Wreszinski,
op. cit. I, pl. 191), but on the pictorial ostraca the chariot without the bowcase attached is more common, see ostraca
Stockholm MM 14049 (published by Petersen, op. cit. pl. 65
nr. 126), MM 14112, 14113, Berlin 21771, 23678, Brussels
E 6438, 6440, and Deir el Medineh 2158, 2162, 2169, 2176
(the last three published by Vandier D'Abbadie, Catalogue...
nos. 2256 a 2722 pls. 20, 22, 23) and Deir el Medineh 2783
and 2794 (the latter published idem. Catalogue...nos. 2256
a 2734 a 3053 pl. 106). Where no citation has been given immediately following any of the other ostraca just listed,
the full reference will be found in n. 277 above.

280. For the reading of the title as sš wdhw, see Gardiner, Egyptian Grammar 488, Signlist R3 n. 4. For other examples,

e.g. statues Cairo CG 42235, 42244-42248. For the name Any, see PN I, 2, 11. For his tomb and other monuments, see Davies, The Rock Tombs of el Amarna V, 6-9 and pls. 9-11, 19-23.

281. For ii with the sense of "return", "come back", rather than just "come", particularly in the idiom ii m htp "to return in peace", "to turn home happily", see Wb. I, 37, 33-34. For m hsw.t "with rewards", ibid. III, 158, 2. Davies, loc. cit. translates the following wd.f as "who orders for me" as if wd were a participial form. There is no reason not to take as a sdm.f with with past reference and the beginning of a new sentence.

282. For the name, see PN I, 388, 11. Although we normally tend to assume that "charioteer" is a military designation (see my Military Rank 67-68 pars. 171-173) it is clear from this instance that it occurs in non-military contexts. One wonders if the man driving the chariot of "the royal scribe of memoranda, Tjay" on the fragment of a Ramesside tomb relief from North Sakkara (see above, n. 278) is the personal charioteer of this Tjay, or, since the fragment may picture a military context,—there is a bowman and a second chariot in this register and the feet of marching men in the register above it—, or the royal scribe is actually a passenger in a military vehicle driven by a regular chariotry soldier of the rank.

283. So described by Hassan, loc. cit. On the other hand, Zivie, loc. cit. simply calls it a relief.

284. One can hardly suppose any other attitude. If he had been holding a fan like the third man at the right, we would expect some trace of its shaft and butt to be visible.

285. Which would make him a person of some importance, as is also suggested by his larger size. For the sandal, which is of the newer type with the projection curving upward at the toe, see M. Abdul-Qader Muhammed, <u>The Development of the Funerary Beliefs and Practices Displayed in the Private Tombs of the New Kingdom at Thebes</u> (Cairo: 1966) 156-157.

286. For this rather common mode of dress, see Davies, <u>The Rock Tombs of el Amarna</u> I, 10-11, and compare Abdul-Qader Muhammed, op. cit. 152.

287. For this very common name, see <u>PN</u> I, 119, 13. Unfortunately there is no way of identifying him with any of the many men known to have had this name. Nor do I have any suggestion for what was lost in his title.

288. For the pose, which goes back to the Old Kingdom, see Vandier, <u>Manuel d'archéologie égyptienne</u> IV 67 fig. 20 nrs. 69-73. It is well attested for statues in the round in the Old and Middle Kingdoms, see ibid. III. <u>La statuaire</u> pls. 16 nrs. 1, 3 (statues Cairo CG 14 and 32), 35 nr. 1 (statue Brooklyn 50.77), 43 nr. 1 (statue Cairo CG 80), 45 nrs. 1, 2 (statues Cairo CG 46992 and Copenhagen 1560). However, inasmuch as this pose is <u>not</u> attested by Vandier for any of the New Kingdom private statues, we may then assume that it is Any himself who is being pictured, not a statue of him.

289. See above, n. 286, and the references cited there.

290. For the name, see <u>PN</u> I, 184, 6.

291. For the significance of the bovine, obviously intended as a sacrificial offering, hence the festive decorations, see H. Kees, "Bemerkungen zum Tieropfer der Aegypter und seiner Symbolik", <u>Nachrichten der Akademie der Wissenschaften zu</u>

Göttingen, Phil.-Hist. Kl. (1942) nr. 2, 71-88 and more recently J. Leclant, "La 'Mascarade' des boeufs gras et le triomphe de l'Égypte", MDAIK 14 (1956) 129-145. Although the
decoration of the horns of the various beasts illustrated by
Leclant, figs. 1-21 and pls. 7-8, is missing from that of the
ox on stela 24, the collar and flower adornment of the latter
is shown on a number of his examples, e.g. figs. 1-3, 8, 14-
16, and 18-19.

292. Loc. cit. I have qualified this identification because I
think that Davies was wrong. The entrance of and the shrine
itself with the seated statue of Any are quite well preserved, ibid. pl. 20. For Davies to have been correct, two assumptions have to be made: a) that the representation of the
structure on the stela should be in accord with the actual
physical shrine and 2) that the figure of Any on the stela
is actually that of the statue in the shrine and should look
like it. While the first of these assumptions can, more or
less, be defended by supposing that the cornice of the structure on the stela actually represents the roof of the tomb
and that the curved element beneath this cornice is the roof
of the shrine, curved to conform to the concave contour of
the ceiling of the passage leading to the shrine's entrance,
the horizontal elements then being interpreted as the cavetto
cornice and torus molding so evident on the real doorway, we
have difficulty with the second assumption. The figure of
Any on the stela in no way conforms with his statue in the
shrine. The latter sits on a high-backed chair, set on a
pedestal which rests on a raised dais and is reached by a
short flight of steps. The pose of the statue is quite un-

like the figure on the stela. As far as I can make out, the
statue wears no šby.w-collars and sits rather stiffly, the
arms bent at the elbow and resting on his lap. Compare this
with the animated attitude of Any on the stela which is certainly that of a living person engaged in a vigorous action,
not that of a statue. Even more telling is the fact that
the statue in the niche sits on a high-backed chair while the
figure on the stela sits on a folding stool. Since, to my
knowledge, statues are never depicted seated on the latter
item of furniture, it is then conclusive that the representation of Any on the stela pictures the man himself and not
his statue.

293. In general, representations of people seated on stools are
rare on stelae, and outside of the present instance I have
been unable to find any where the legs of the stool terminate
in ducks' heads. For examples in tomb paintings, however,
see Davies, The Tomb of Ken-Amun at Thebes (New York: 1930)
pl. 17, idem. The Tomb of Two Sculptors at Thebes (New York:
1925) pl. 7 (from the tomb of the chief sculptor, Nebamūn,
nr. 181), Wreszinski, Atlas I, pl. 369 (from the tomb of Yepuy, nr. 217, at Thebes). Apparently it was commonplace
enough to figure on the occasional ostracon, see, e.g. ostracon Munich 1549 (published by Brunner-Traut, Die altägyptischen Scherbenbilder pl. 2 nr. 95). A number of such stools,
some of them in an excellent state of preservation, are extant, e.g. H.Carter, The Tomb of Tut.ankh.Amen. Discovered by
the Late Earl of Carnarvon and Howard Carter III (London:
1933) pl. 33, Berlin 12552 (published in Aegyptische Museum
Berlin (Berlin: 1967) nr. 643), Metropolitan Museum of Art

Hayes, Scepter II, 202 and fig. 116, British Museum 2477, described but not illustrated in British Museum, A Guide to the Fourth, Fifth, and Sixth Egyptian Rooms, and the Coptic Room (London: 1922) 87 and perhaps identical with the British Museum stool illustrated in J.G. Wilkinson, The Manners and Customs of the Ancient Egyptians new ed. I (New York: 1878) 411 fig. 180 nr. 1. For a general discussion and additional bibliography, see Vandier, Manuel d'archéologie égyptienne III, 60 nn. 4 and 7 and earlier Schäfer, loc. cit. n. 3, and Wrezinski, op. cit. I, pl. 39b. Although Hayes, loc. cit. notes that this type of stool was most popular during the 18th Dynasty, its attestation in the Deir el-Medineh tomb of Yepuy clearly shows that it was still in use during the Ramesside period. Finally, for a discussion of the symbolism of the duck's head, see A. Hermann, "Das Motiv der Ente mit zurückgewendetem Kopfe im ägyptischen Kunstgewerbe", ZÄeS 68 (1932) 86-105.

294. See my "The Royal Butler Ramessesemperreʿ", JARCE 13 (1976) 120 (stela Cairo TR 3/7/24/17) and 121 (lintel(?) Brooklyn 35.1315). There, as here, the inscriptions associated with the figures performing the action seem to begin in the middle of a sentence. Hence it is not improbable that the picture of the worshipper's action is to be read as a rebus in combination with the rest of the text. After all, any hieroglyph is a picture en petite. For the pictorial nature of these and conversely the hieroglyphic nature of pictorial representations, see now the brilliant study of H.G. Fischer, "Redundant Determinatives in the Old Kingdom", The Metropolitan Museum Journal 8 (1973) 7-24.

295. A pit has obliterated the left third of the mr-canal which, incidentally, looks more like the š-pool.

296. For the name, which is attested only here, see PN I, 2, 12.

297. I take m3ꜥ-ḫrw here, as I have done virtually throughout the entire study, in an anticipatory sense, i.e. not that he is already dead and thus "justified", but that he will be "justified" in the future, and clearly, "with (m) a goodly burial". See my "The Royal Butler Ramessesemperreꜥ" 119 n. 16 and 122 n. 46.

298. Davies, loc. cit. 1Q, translated: "Unto your ka! A bouquet of the Aten". Steindorff, loc. cit. 65, misread the opening words here and was unable to translate. Davies' translation is poetic but makes little sense. If, however, we understand k3 as "nourishment", "offering" (see Wb. V, 91, 3-13 and ibid. the right hand column for the spelling with the k3-arms and the stroke, but no determinative), then we have a good non-verbal sentence expressing a timeless state of being, and so I have taken it.

299. Steindorff, loc. cit. apparently followed by Ranke, since there is no independent listing for P3-ḫ3 in PN, read the name as P3-ḫ3rw "Pakharu" (see PN I, 116, 17), probably on the basis of the throwstick determinative. But the throwstick only indicates that the man or the name was of foreign origin. I see no reason to emend it and consequently have followed Davies, loc. cit. in reading it as written.

300. It was acquired at a sale of art in Egypt in 1894, but beyond this, nothing is known of its origin. If, however, its owner can be equated with one of the Merysakhmets from Deir el-Medineh (see below, n. 318), perhaps it can be assigned

to the Theban area.

301. See above, n. 286, and the literature cited there.

302. With nṯr.w written in honorific transposition.

303. Koefoed-Petersen, Les stèles égyptiennes 32, translated ir.t
ʿnḫ tm.w as a participal phrase qualifying the preceding
p3w.ty: "Dieu des premiers ages qui crea l'espece humaine".
While the general sense of this is correct, grammatically it
should be noted that ir.t is an infinitive and any translation should reflect this.

304. Koefoed-Petersen did not attempt to translate ḏd.tw m ib.f
m3ʿ ḫpr.sn which seems logically to be the result of Ptah's
creation. The sense seems clear: Ptah is the Primeval One
who fashioned the life of mankind, a fact so acknowledged by
whomsoever stops to ponder on it. Of course, to our modern
ears this is an obvious and cumbersome repetition.

305. Compare Koefoed-Petersen, loc. cit: "pour lui, il n'est rien
qu'il ignore". The text: nn ḫpr.wt nb(.wt) m ḫm.f ḫpr.w,
literally: "there does not exist everything which has come
into existence as that which he does not know their coming
into existence".

306. Ḫpr.f ḫr.t hrw rʿ nb ḫnty s3.n.f. For this transitive use of
ḫpr whereby it has the force of sḫpr, see Wb. III, 264, 16-
17.

307. All of the preceding sentences have, thus far, been descriptive and qualifying epithets of Ptah in line 1. With the
change to the pronoun of the second person singular, the
speaker has arrived at the main thought and clause. This
same structure is repeated in the next section of the text
where Sakhmet is invoked towards the end of line 5, except

that the verb of the main clause of this second section, towards the end of line 8, is now in the dual, its antecedents being both Ptah and Sakhmet.

308. There is a deep gouge in the surface of the text at this this point which has all but obliterated the tall vertical sign(s) which stood there. Koefoed-Petersen, loc. cit. read in the lacuna ⧗▯ , but a careful scrutiny of my own photograph shows that, while such a reading is possible, it is more likely that what stood there according to the preserved traces was ⧨⫤ which is nothing more than the determinative of pr-wr. This is even more probable in light of the mention almost immediately afterwards of the pr-nsr (for which see the following note). For the pr-wr, see <u>Wb</u>. I, 517, 2-4.

309. For the pr-nsr, see <u>Wb</u>. I, 518, 1.

310. The imagery invoked here is striking. Mdr, <u>Wb</u>. II, 187, 7, is used "vom Berg der dem Wind abhalt". Hsfy, transcribed by Koefoed-Petersen, loc. cit. as ⸬⸭⸮ and Mogensen, "A Stele ..." 39 as ⸬⸭⸮, was already correctly recognized by Platt, "Notes..." 132. While it is not attested in the <u>Wb</u>. in this exact spelling and nuance, the sense is clear enough, compare <u>Wb</u>. III, 337,5-338, 1.

311. For the idiom hsi̯ hr "to rage against", see <u>Wb</u>. III, 159, 9. I take the verb here as the 3rd feminine singular of the Old Perfective.

312. For mꜥbꜣ "spear", see <u>Wb</u>. II, 47, 1-3.

313. It is with this sentence that the long invocation to Ptah and Sakhmet ends and the main reason for the prayer of Merysakhmet to them is stated. Only Platt, op. cit. 131, connected ḥꜥw.i̯ "my limbs" with the preceding nn n.f ḫꜣi̯.t

(for the construction, see Erman, <u>Neuägyptische Grammatik</u>
par. 478, end). Mogensen, "A Stele..." 40 and Koefoed-Petersen, <u>Les stèles égyptiennes</u> 32, both assumed that it was
the subject of the following sw m sḏb.w, but this is incorrect grammatically. Merysakhmet is asking the two deities
to grant several things, the first of which, a "happy lifetime" etc. is a noun clause serving as the direct object of
dỉ.tn. After this, however, the remaining desiderata are
expressed by verbal clauses, i.e. **sḏm**.f forms with noun subjects, see Gardiner, <u>Egyptian Grammar</u> par. 70.

314. See the preceding note. The subject of sw is, of course, ḥr.ỉ.

315. Neither Mogensen nor Koefoed-Petersen, loc. cit. attempted
to translate this sentence. Koefoed-Petersen, <u>Receuil.</u> loc.
cit. transcribed the first two hieroglyphs of line 10 as
⌡⌐, but as Platt, op. cit. 132 and pl. 31, correctly noted,
what is actually written is ⌡⌐ . I have rendered this and
the following as independent sentences, but it is quite possible that they are also dependent on dỉ.tn as additional desiderata to be granted by the divine couple. Admittedly, my
translation of wb3 here is a guess and I really do not know
what both this and the following sentence mean.

316. While shwỉ "totality", <u>Wb</u>. IV, 212, **6-15**, is not attested in
this spelling, the word can hardly be anything else. Koefoed-
Petersen's transcription of the text, loc. cit. omits the
plural dots beneath the bookroll determinative, they they are
quite apparent on the photograph.

317. There is a lacuna of at least two squares before the legible
and preserved traces which begin with nswt. Platt's facsim-
ile, loc. cit. pl. 31, confirmed by a careful examination of

the photograph, shows immediately to the right of nswt in
the lacuna the tip and blade of the mdh-axe and beneath this
there is a clear t, thus: . The title, then, is not lost,
but is to be read: mdh nswt m kd which, though not to my
knowledge attested elsewhere, is undoubtedly a variant of
the well-known mdh-kd nswt "stone mason of the king", Wb.
II, 190, 15.

318. For the name, see PN I, 157, 25. While no other "stone mason of the king" of this name is known to me, it is interesting to note that out of thirty-four randomly collected examples of this name, twenty-nine come from Deir el-Medineh
and five of these, Theban graffiti nrs. 356, 466, 1841,
2080, and 2301) belonged to a Merysakhmet who was an "outline
draftsman" (sš kd).

319. Usually the apron is not indicated on the two-dimensional
representations of seated figures. A least a random perusal
of the New Kingdom stelae published in the Cairo Catalogue
Génerale, Tosi and Roccati, Stele ... di Deir el Medina,
Koefoed-Petersen, Les stèles égyptiennes, and Stewart, Egyptian Stelae... have produced no examples. Out of the thus-
far published volumes of British Museum stelae which contain
mostly or completely New Kingdom stelae (vols. 5-10) only
three examples, British Museum 797 (vol. 7, pl. 36), 156
(vol. 9, pl. 28), and 146 (ibid. pl. 47) show the apron
depicted in the same manner as on stela 28.

320. See above, n. 267, and the literature cited there.

321. Weidemann, op. cit. 332-333, believing that the man in question was the viceroy of Kush, Paser I, under Ay and Horemheb (see the next note) assumed that the writing s3t nswt

was an error for s3 nswt and accordingly noted this with sic!
While it is true that nothing precedes s3t nswt, there is, as
will be shown below in nn. 322 and 325, good reason for believing that the sic! was not justified, and that s3t nswt
was indeed intended, although the scribe **did** omit something
in front of it.

322. Wiedemann, loc. cit. read the name as "Paser", understanding
the hieroglyphs p3 ntr as an epithet "the god" which indicated that Paser had been deified. Moret, op. cit. 145, disre-
garded the words p3 ntr, but read the hieroglyph of the seated man on the throne which occurs in one of the three writings of the name as part of it: "Pawerpasep". Gauthier,
op. cit. 200, agreed with Wiedemann that he was the viceroy
Paser I, but suggested that the ntr-sign was actually to be
read as the throwstick and stood for some word for foreigner,
again taking this as an epithet alluding to perhaps a Nubian
origin for the viceroy. While none of the three proposed
readings of the name are attested in PN, that of Moret can
be immediately discarded. The hieroglyph of the man seated
on a throne is simply a variant determinative replacing the
bearded seated man which occurs in one of the other writings.
Since in all three instances, the penultimate sign before the
man determinative **is** the ntr-sign, we must assume that it was
the ntr-sign which the scribe intended. Consequently, we may
also discard Gauthier's proposed reading. If we rule out
the proposed identification with the viceroy Paser I which
is based on both reading the three hieroglyphs following sr
as an epithet, together with the assumption that s3t nswt
which precedes the name once is an error for s3 nswt (see the

preceding note), then I see no obstacle for reading the name as it is written in all three instances: Paserpanetjer.

323. The eyeball of ir is missing. For the name, see PN I, 114, 24, and for the title, above, n. 147.

324. Alternately, it is possible that the two lines "made by the soldier, Parennefer" simply identify the dedicator of the stela and that we should assume that what Parennefer is doing is to be read as a hieroglyph kb, kbh, or the like, meaning "make a libation". Such an ideographic writing is attested for kbh from the Late Period on, see Wb. V, 27, the right hand column. There is no reason why it could not have been so used earlier. If so, then this would be combined with the following line to read: "Making a libation for his lord, etc." However, it should be noted that whichever alternative this line is to read with, it is out of place in respect to whatever precedes it. For reading the combination of the picture + the text, see also above, n. 294.

325. Wiedemann, loc. cit. transcribed the beginning of the line as m rmn followed by the determinatives(?) of the ꜥ-arm beneath which was a disk. I would divide it differently. Starting at the very end, the sign which he read as a disk looks more like the breast ▽ . This, in turn, suggests that the three preceding signs, mn + its phonetic complement n + the ꜥ-arm are to be read as a single word mnꜥ(.t) "tutor", for the writing of which without the final .t see Wb. II, 94, 5, the right hand column. If I am correct, then it is obvious that this title which is frequently associated with the children of the royal family should be connected with the problematic s3t nswt at the beginning of the horizontal line

at the top of the stela. S3t nswt, then, is surely to be as
written, with **the** understanding that the artisan **who** carved
the stela omitted mnʿ(.t) for one reason or another.

326. Wiedemann's statement, loc. cit. that the stela was "of ex-
ceedingly bad workmanship" is nowhere better demonstrated
than here, unless the lady suffered a withered left arm which
is accurately shown in the same manner as is the polio-crip-
pled right leg of the "doorkeeper, Rama" of stela Copenhagen
134,(see Koefoed-Petersen, op.cit. pl. 44). Such sloppiness
of execution, however, is more likely when one looks at the
general layout of the stela, with the off-center cartouche
flanked by the wedjat-eyes, the poorly cut hieroglyphs, and
the strange arrangement of the three lines of text discussed
above in n. 324. Also worthy of note is the fact that this
woman seemingly wears a man's calf-length pleated kilt and a
wig similar to those worn by the seated men. Yet that she is
a woman is clear from the determinative of her name and from
her well-defined breast. For the valanced wig worn by women,
see Aldred, "Hair Styles..." 145.

327. 𓀀𓏤 . The name is not attested in PN, but compare tt,
ibid. I, 383, 21-23.

328. ⳽. The name is not attested in PN.

329. For the name, see PN I, 55, 15.

330. Several illegible traces are evident beneath the name. Unless these were a plene writing of m3ʿ-ḫrw, it is most likely
that they specified the military unit to which Parennefer belonged. This could have been any of the following, the "company" (s3, see my Military Rank 136 ref. 320a-c), a "ship's
contingent (ḥnyt, ibid. 136 ref. 321a-c), the "Residence"

(p3 Ḥnw, ibid. 137 ref. 324), or a "garrison troop" (iw'yt, ibid. 138, refs. 333-334).

331. Following the suggestion of Gardiner, Peet, and Černý, loc. cit. note c, that the horizontal n written here be emended to mḥ.

332. For the imy-r pr-ḥḏ n nbw ḥḏ, compare Gardiner, Ancient Egyptian Onomastica I 26* nr. A90, which deals with the similar title imy-r pr-ḥḏ n ḥḏ nbw, obviously a variant of it (see also Wb. I, 518, 5-8). While a Sebekhotpe (called Panehsy) is known to have held this office in the years 30-36 of Amūnhotpe III (see Helck, Zur Verwaltung des Mittleren und Neuen Reiches [Leiden: 1958] 512 nr. 9), stela nr. 29 is clearly Ramesside in date and cannot have been the same man. However, neither Helck, loc. cit. nor Černý in his supplement to and review of Helck's book, Bibliotheca Orientalis 19 (1962) 140-144, included the latter among the incumbents of this high administrative office. From this we might well assume that the Sebekhotpe of stela nr. 29, though he was an "overseer of the treasury of gold and silver", was not the "overseer of the treasury". Yet he was a royal butler and in the Ramesside period the royal butler ranked among the highest magnates of the land, often performing functions normalexercised by such officials as the vizier or the viceroy of Kush, see my "The Royal Butler Ramessesemperre'" 123-124, and also n. 334, below.

333. On the title ḥry sšt3w in general, see my "Two Unrecognized Monuments of Shedsunefertem", JNES 39 (1980) 305, commentary note g and the literature cited there. Although no other instances of a ḥry sšt3w n 'ḥ šps are known to me, compare Wb.

IV, 299, 7, ḥry sšt3w n nswt, and statue Cairo CG 42164, ḥry sšt3w n pr nswt.

334. For the name, see PN I, 305, 6. The only other instance known to me of a royal butler with this name is found in a papyrus in Turin, see now S. Allam, Hieratische Ostraka und Papyri (Tübingen: 1973) pl. 133, which is dated to a "year 1, month 2 of Shomu, day 7" of an unspecified 20th Dynasty king (but see below) and which reads:

> "the coming of the nobles, the vizier Neferronpe, the first prophet of Amūn, Ramessesnakht, the royal butler Setherwenemef, the royal butler Preꜥnakht, the (over-seer) of the treasury Montuemtowe, the royal butler Atumnakht, the royal butler Sebekhotpe, and the brig-ade commander Payiri"

to bring some mortuary equipment for the royal tomb. If the two Sebekhotpes are one and the same man, as is likely, the naming of him here after the overseer of the treasury Montu-emtowe suggests that, along with the royal butler Atumnakht, he was immediately subordinate to Montuemtowe. If, then, his designation as "overseer of the treasury of gold and sil-ver" discussed above, in n. 332, did not refer to the office held by the head of this administration,——and it probably did not, since on Stela Sinai 302 Sebekhotpe still refers to himself, first of all, as a royal butler——, the title nev-ertheless still indicates his position within the treasury administration. The dates for the two documents can probably be narrowed down with a little more precision. Of the three great officials mentioned in the Turin papyrus, the vizier Neferronpe is attested from year 1 of Ramesses IV to year 13

of Ramesses IX (so Helck, op. cit. 464), and the first prophet of Amūn Ramessesnakht from year 1 of Ramesses IV to at
least the reign of Ramesses VII (so Černý, CAH 3rd ed. II,
chap. 35: "Egypt from the Death of Ramesses III to the End
of the Twenty-First Dynasty" 637 n. 2). The overseer of the
treasury Montuemtowe, however, is attested only from the end
of the reign of Ramesses III or year 1 of Ramesses IV until
year 4 of Ramesses V (so Helck, op.cit. 519). Consequently,
the Turin text and two years later, stela nr. 29, are to be
dated to years 1 and 3, respectively, of the reigns of either
Ramesses IV or Ramesses V.

335. Gardiner, Peet, and Černý, op. cit. 194, translated: "all
that the sun disk embraces praises thee" which, though essentially what the sentence means, is nonetheless somewhat
free. "All" is not present in the Egyptian unless it is inherent in šn, written here with two archaic cartouches, the
first to be read phonetically, the second as the determinative.

336. Gardiner, Peet, and Černý, loc. cit. did not really attempt
to translate this sentence which reads p3 ẖnmw mhw(t), but
did suggest, loc. cit. note d, that it might be rendered
"he who joined the family". What this might mean completely
escapes me. While, admittedly, my own translation is little
more than a guess, in view of the fact that the provenance
of the stela is the mining country in Sinai, it seems plausible to suppose that mhw(t) is better understood in its
meaning of "tribe", "clan of Bedouin", etc. (see Wb. II,
114, 8) rather than in that of "family" (ibid. 114, 7). If
so, the the participle ẖnmw should refer to an action per-

formed by the king in connection with these desert dwellers.
While none of the meanings assigned to ḥnm in **Wb**. III, 377,
3-379, 20, basically all nuances and extended uses of "join",
"unite oneself with", and the like, really suit the king
with regard to the desert tribesmen who, after all, are normally considered hostile to Egypt, there is another, less
common ḥnm "build", "fashion", "create", ibid. 382, 1-3,
which might be suitable here in the sense that it is the king
who creates all, even the Bedouin. Compare the Great Hymn to
the Aton from the tomb of Ay (published by Sandman, <u>Texts
from the Time of Akhenaton</u> 94), although there it is also
true that it is the Aton, not the king, who is pictured as
the universalistic creator:

> "You fashioned the earth as you wished, you alone.
> All mankind, herds and flocks, everything on earth
> that walks on legs, and that which is the heaven
> which flys upon their wings, the lands of Syria and
> Kush, and the land of Egypt. You set every man to
> his place and you make their requirements".

Of course it is also possible that we have here still another verb ḥnm, the meaning of which is unknown.

337. Not translated by Gardiner, Peet, and Černý, loc. cit. What
is written here seems to be a badly-formed ḏ-serpent with a
t underneath it. To be read ḏ.t "forever" and connected
with the preceding phrase?

338. Rn "name" is clear. What precedes it looks like a misformed
ssm. While possibly a title of Sebekhotpe, on analogy with
titles like sšm.w-ḥb "festival leader (<u>Wb</u>. IV, 288, 22-23)
or sšm.w-k3.w "director of offerings" (ibid. 289, 1), it is

more likely, since no such title is attested in the <u>Wb</u>. that this participial phrase also refers to the king, specifying still another benefice of his.

339. To date there have been no exhaustive studies in depth of this title and the office which it encompassed, although I already have touched upon some aspects of it in my "The Royal Butler Ramessesemperreʿ" 123-126, and again in my "The Royal Butler Ramessessamiʿon", <u>CdÉ</u> (forthcoming) Section C.

340. For representations of aged and aging people, see E. Riefstahl, "An Egyptian Portrait of an Old Man", <u>JNES</u> 10 (1951) 65-73.

341. The ḥrw-oar is quite clear. It is followed by a bird-hieroglyph which, however, really does not look like the quail chick (w), but the following double reed leaves and the determinative of the man with his hand to his mouth seem to insure the reading.

342. See above, Chapter 1, stelae nrs. 1-19.

343. See above, nn. 215-216 for references.

344. See above, n. 214, for references.

345. See above, nn. 217 and 218 for references in tomb art, and for stelae, nrs. 20 and 21.

346. See R.W. Smith and D.B. Redford, <u>The Akhenaten Temple Project I. Initial Discoveries</u> (Warminster: 1976) 132-134, pls. 63-65.

347. Ibid. 134.

348. Ibid. nn. 86-88. The texts in question are <u>Urk</u>. IV, 811, 1459-1460, 1867, and Papyrus Boulaq 18, 37, 1-2, and 45, 1.

349. <u>Urk</u>. IV, 2158, Helck, "Das Dekret des Königs Haremheb", <u>ZÄS</u> 80 (1955) 125-126. For translations, see Smith and Redford,

op. cit. 134, Helck, op. cit. 126, and, earlier, K. Pflüger,
"The Edict of King Haremheb", <u>JNES</u> 5 (1946) 266.

350. Helck, loc. cit. translated mkt as "protection", a meaning
well-attested for it, see <u>Wb</u>. II, 160, 22-161, 4, but in the
light of what follows, "protection" is hardly appropriate.
Pflüger's rendering, loc. cit. "(wants) to protect" is also
unsatisfactory since mkt <u>is</u> clearly a noun. Redford, loc.
cit. is probably correct in assigning a meaning of "provisions", "provisioning", or the like for it, based on mk "provisions", "nourishment", <u>Wb</u>. II, 162, 5.

351. Helck's "für jeden (Ersten]", loc. cit. makes no sense here.
If his restoration of the text at this point (hrw t)p or (r⸢
t]p, depending on how the sundisk is to be read (see <u>Urk</u>.
IV, 2158), is correct, the allusion is certainly to a specific point in time, literally "every first day". However,
since Horemheb's officials came "three times a month", as the
following sentence relates, then "every hrw/r⸢ tp" obviously
cannot have been "every first day" of the month. It is not
improbable that the phrase did mean something like "holiday"
as both Redford and I have taken it.

352. While the antecedent of the suffix .sn in ph̲r.sn was probably
expressed in the lacuna at the beginning of the line, it is
clear that .sn refers to the officials who were present at
the banquet outside the window.

353. Redford's "at royal expense", loc. cit. is perhaps a bit too
free.

354. Loc. cit.

355. By his use of "........" Helck, loc. cit. suggests that the
lacuna between nb and hry.w tp nw mnfyt was a very large one.

Actually it is only one square wide, just enough room for the restoration t3.wy proposed by both Pflüger and Redford, loc. cit.

356. See above, stelae nrs. 1, 6, 8-10, 13, and possibly 2, as well as the rock-cut stelae nrs. 14-19. Of all of these stelae with firm provenances, only nr. 6 was found in a tomb.

357. See above, stelae nrs. 22, 24-26. Those which do not come from a tomb are nrs. 23, from the Sphinx amphitheater at Giza, and nr. 29, from outside the Hathor sanctuary at Serabit el-Khadim.

358. See above, stelae nrs. 2, 5, 7, 12, and 13.

359. This certainly was so in the case of stelae nrs. 22, and 24-26 which were dedicated to Any by various of his associates and subordinates.

360. The šby.w-collars do not appear worn on only one of the group of stelae nrs. 20-30, namely nr. 24. This has been included, however, because of the presentation of the bovine to Any, an act which is paralleled in several of the tomb scenes which narrate the events immediately after the collars have been bestowed, see Davies, The Rock Tombs of el Amarna VI, pl. 20, idem. The Tomb of Nefer-Hotep pl.17, and compare idem. The Rock Tombs of el Amarna II, pl. 37.

361. See above, n. 228, for references.

362. For the restoration of the name, see Davies, The Rock Tombs of el Amarna V, 10. For the name see PN I, 140, 6.

363. For the name, see ibid.

364. See Davies, op. cit. 6 and pl. 8, and compare Bouriant, op. cit. 49.

365. See Bouriant, loc. cit. He mentioned, ibid. n. 2, that a

fifth stela had been found, but that he was unable to locate it in the Cairo Museum.

366. See Davies, loc. cit. 7.

367. Ibid. 8 and pls. 8-10, 20. Pls. 8 and 20 show the statue in in the shrine. Only in the scene reproduced in pl. 9 is the offering table preserved.

368. Davies, loc. cit. pl. 10 and earlier, though in a less accurate copy, Bouriant, loc. cit. 56 fig. 21.

369. See Davies, loc. cit. pl. 9.

370. What is preserved on the wall here is   which certainly is to be restored "(His wife), the lady of the h[ouse] Aa---". Davies assumed that she had survived Any because of her speech:

"She says: '----- son ----- you arrive -----. He (i.e. the king) commanded for you your place of eternity'".

However, on the basis of the speech of the servitor Meryre' who offers Any a libation in the same scene (see below), it is more likely that the figure of Any is not that of the deceased Any at a funerary banquet in the Afterworld, but rather the living Any who is celebrating at a banquet after having been rewarded by the king.

371. Sḏm-ꜥš and rwḏ. For the former, see now E.S. Bogoslovsky, "Servants" of Pharaohs, Gods, and Private Persons (on the Social History of Egypt XVI-XIVth Century B.C. (Moscow: 1979, in Russian). For the latter, see Gardiner, Ancient Egyptian Onomastica I, 32* A102 and idem. "Some Reflections on the Nauri Decree", JEA 38 (1952) 28.

372. I take ir.tw as a perfective sḏm.f with future reference,

see Gardiner, <u>Egyptian Grammar</u> par. 450, 3, and ibid. par. 448 for the spelling. If ꜣin is rendered as it normally is as the preposition introducing the agent "by", the resulting sentence, with its arbitrary mixture of the pronouns .k and .f, is quite awkward. Such awkwardness disappears if we understand in as a parenthetic phrase meaning "says", see Gardiner, op. cit. 433 and pars. 436-437.

373. This rendering of wdꜣi is a bit free, but the sense is clear enough.

374. Literally: "the mountain (dw) of Akhetaton" which can hardly be anything other than the cliffside where the tombs of the Amarna nobles were located.

375. There is just enough room in the lacuna at the bottom of the line to restore m st. This is virtually assured by the following nhh at the beginning of the next line, for while st m3ʿt is the more usual term for a cemetery, what else could the st nhh have been?

376. I cannot explain this spelling of k3 with the prothetic reed-leaf.

377. What is preserved is ꜣink(?) m dd.k(?) followed by the titles of Meryreʿ, sdm-ʿš and rwd, written corruptly with the foreleg rather than the bowstring, n sš nswt. I have no suggestion for the corrupt portion preceding the titles.

378. For this anticipatory use of m3ʿ-hrw, see above, n. 297, and the references cited there.

379. See Davies, op. cit. pl. 9.

380. Compare the hieroglyph 𓀢 (Gardiner, op. cit. Signlist A 26) which is used as the determinative in such words as nꜣis "summon", "call", dwꜣi "call", or the vocative interjection ꜣi "O".

381. Although only the foot and lower part of the jar are preserved, it can hardly be anything else.

382. See Sandman-Holmberg, <u>Texts from the Time of Akhenaton</u> 41-42.

383. The parallels in the tomb of Huya, ibid. 41, have n ḏdw nswt for which there is just enough room in the lacuna here, with space for the preposition n at the beginning of the next line.

384. There is a lacuna approximately three-quarters of a square high at the beginning of the line, the upper part of which undoubtedly contained the preposition n, if it was was written with the water zigzag. However, if the preposition was written with the Red Crown, this would have filled the entire lacuna. Beneath this is a clearly written imy-r below which, at the left, are three tiny, unevenly spaced, vertical strokes. In view of Any's title "steward", attested on five of the six stelae (nrs. 22, 25, 26, Cairo CG 34.179 and Cairo CG 34.181) as well as elsewhere in the tomb, the restoration which immediately comes to mind is that of the same title. It must be admitted, however, that pr ⊓ does not really fit the preserved traces. They do suit the writing ⋒ which could easily have come from a confusion of the hieratic writings of ⋔ and ⋔ .

385. In his drawing, Davies, loc. cit. shows, with a question mark, what may have been a horizontal sign, curving downward at the left and thickened with a perceptible blob at its right end. Sandman-Holmberg's handcopy here, loc. cit. does not include these traces. If my restoration of the preceding title as "steward" (see preceding note) is correct and since

Any was the steward of the temple-estate of Amūnhotpe II (n
pr ꜥ3-ḫprw-rꜥ, see Davies, loc. cit. pl. 20), it is not impossible that this questionable, slightly-curved, horizontal
sign was the poorly-rendered curved top of a cartouche. This
obviously would have contained the prenomen of Amūnhotpe II
which is also present in the scene as part of the text identifying Any:

> "The scribe of the king, the one whom [his] lord loves,
> [the scribe of the offering table of] the Aton, the
> scribe of the altar, he who s[upplies (restore hn)]
> nourishment for the lord of the Two Lands in Akhet-
> aton, [the steward of the temple-estate] of ꜥAakhep-
> rureꜥ, granted life, Any, who shall be justified ----
> in peace".

With the exception of hn, which is based on the preserved
traces, all of the other restorations here were made on the
basis of Any's titles recorded by Davies, loc. cit. 7. Although imy-r ⌐pr⌐ [ꜥ3-ḫprw-rꜥ]? seems to have been written
instead of imy-pr n pr ꜥ3-ḫprw-rꜥ, the omission of n pr need
not trouble us greatly. The title and its specifications
could be expressed by a direct genetive. If this had been
the case, the artist who painted this text could easily have
made an error here.

386. I have no suggestions whatsoever for the few traces which
are recognizable here. The parallels are of no help.

387. Although nb is incorrectly written with the k-basket, it is
nevertheless certain from the parallels, see Sandman-Holmberg,
loc. cit.

388. Rwḏ, though garbled, is certain from the parallels. I have

no suggestions for the badly-preserved signs which follow at
the beginning of the next line. The parallel texts have hr
is.k "upon your tomb-chamber", but what is preserved in the
first two squares of the break is the trace of a tall vertical sign at the left, beneath this what seem to be a k3-arms
and a stroke. Davies, loc. cit. 17, restored [in the abode],
presumably having been influenced by the parallels.

389. It is most probable that the relative form of mri was written
here, although I cannot explain the writing with the hoe, beneath which was a now-lost small sign and a stroke. Davies
also recognized and translated this as a relative, but clearly had reservations about it: "which thou lovest(?)".

390. Following the translation of Davies, loc. cit. The parallel
text in the tomb of Huya reads: nis.tw d3mw nb(w) hpr.f. The
Any text reads nis, followed by a lacuna which is just big
enough for the determinative. Beneath this are the traces of
a bird's feet and tail and there is enough room for a t-loaf
in front of its breast. This line then concludes with the
walking legs for which I have no suggestions. The next line
begins with d3mw nb, beneath which is a lacuna approximately
one square high, just enough room for plural strokes and the
hpr-beetle, the phonetic complement of which starts the following line. This is followed by the 'nd-netting needle which
makes no sense and is probably to be emended to .f.

391. M h.t.k occurs in all of the parallel texts from the tomb of
Huya. There is just enough room for it, if slightly squeezed
together, in the lacuna.

392. Davies here recorded: wnn.k m s3 n illegible traces .tw [---]
htp-di-nswt. This is certainly to be restored wnn.k m s3 n

⌜ir⌝.tw [n-f] ḥtp-dỉ-nswt.

393. I really do not know what this last phrase means. Davies
translated it as I have, but questioned his translation.
There is **a lacuna** at the beginning of the line which has
enough room for the genetival n and immediately below this
the pr-sign and stroke occupy the left half of the square,
suggesting that some short, squat sign originally stood at
the right. I have no suggestion as to what this might have
have been.

394. Davies, loc. cit. translated "and [water] from thy sluice(?)"
but the lacuna is not big enough to restore the three water
zigzags, the moreso since at its lower right side is a short
vertical stroke which can only be the right hand element of
the plural strokes. This is followed by m sb3 n, an almost
imperceptible trace at the left of the beginning of the next
line, and n-k. I must admit that I have no suggestions here.
There are no parallels from the tomb of Huya.

395. See above, n. 365, for the reference.

396. See my "The Iconographic Theme: 'Opening of the Mouth' on
Stelae", JARCE 21 (1984) 175-177.

397. See Davies, op. cit. 6-7.

398. See above, nn. 230-233.

399. The moreso since their tombs are not, to my knowlege, preserved.

Chapter 3: Afterthoughts

It is not my intention to recapitulate here the various
and immediate conclusions which have been arrived at in the preceding two chapters. These, I believe, are evident and need no
further amplification. Nevertheless, a few additional remarks and
afterthoughts may be in order.

Along with the scarab, the ushebty, the sarcophagus, and
the statue, the stela is one of the most familiar objects which
has survived from Ancient Egypt. However, only one of its types,
the commemorative/historical royal is studied for and within its
intrinsic context as an historical document. The others, the
private stelae, particularly those votive and funerary types,
which clearly constitute the vast majority of the monuments of
this category, are studied for their artistic content, for their
religious context, for the philological and onomastic information
provided by their texts, when such are present, and, on occasion
for the socio-economic data which can be gleaned from them. Only
rarely are they studied as purely historical documents. Yet every
object which is preserved from Pharaonic Egypt should be considered as and is, in fact, an historical document and should also be
studied from this point of view. This is not to say that the traditional and conventional perspectives which are used to study
private stelae should be discarded. Rather they should be approached with new questions and new perceptions as I have attempted
to do with the stelae which were investigated in Chapters 1 and 2
and in two earlier studies.[400]

The main group of stelae examined in Chapter 2 clearly illustrate an actual event, the private, or rather, individual, personal public ceremony in which a faithful servant of the king was

rewarded with gold, particularly with gold šby.w-collars, and
with its aftermath when the servant so-rewarded returned home
from the ceremony, proudly wearing these very same collars. The
importance of this event in the life and career of the individual
recipients of the reward is underscored by its relatively frequent appearance in the narrative biographical scenes occupying the
public portion of their tombs. Indeed, in the tomb of Any at Amarna, although the ceremony and its aftermath do not figure in
the preserved decoration inside the tomb, stelae which illustrate
various aspects of its immediate aftermath filled a series of
niches cut in the rock passage immediately outside the tomb entrance. The representations of Any inside the tomb in what are con-
ventionally described as funerary scenes likewise show him wearing
these same collars. The very fact, however, that the collar is
worn in such scenes in the tomb or in their analogues on stelae
or even on statues would seem to confirm their importance and
their significance to the individuals pictured with them. This,
in turn, would seem to reiterate that when they appear, their very
appearance recalls the ceremony at which they were awarded.

In Chapter 1, the scene which every stela examined shares
in common is one picturing the king in the act of slaying an enemy
or group of enemies in the presence of a god, a scene and motif
usually interpreted as symbolizing the timeless triumph and invincible power of the royal persona.[401] Yet, while this is undoubtedly correct, I have attempted to show that this stereotyped, symbolic, conventional theme is nevertheless rooted in an actual
event, the ritual execution of a captured enemy ruler during the
ceremonial thanksgiving offered by the pharaoh to the god(s) at
the conclusion of a successful military campaign. Certainly there

is reason to assume that the king's performance in such a ceremony
would have been viewed by all those who were spectators to it,—
for clearly this ritual slaughter was public, one part of a public
spectacle—, as the most tangible demonstration of the awesome
might and power of the king, concrete testimonial of his inevitable triumph over his foes and of his omnipotence in all matters.
Inasmuch as any achievement of the king automatically became part
of the royal myth and became integrated into the king's persona,[402]
it is easy to see how this very real event could then be metamor-
phasized into a symbolic concept and how its depiction then entered the iconographic repertoire of the Egyptian artist as a conventional stereotype which visually conveyed this concept.

It is not only in the act of smiting an enemy that the
king appears on private stelae. Often he is shown making some
kind of offering to one or another of the gods[403] and on analogy
with the real ceremony underlaying the smiting scene, I submit
that in these cases as well, a specific event in time, the king's
participation in some specific religious ceremony at which the in-
stigators of the stelae in question were also present is likewise
being commemorated. Although it is outside the parameters of the
present study to attempt to determine exactly which religious rituals might have been involved, it might be pointed out that at
least one, illustrated on stela Cairo JE 45548 and which pictures
the king offering to several processional barks, those of Amūn,
Mūt, and Khonsu,[404] must be connected with a ceremony inside the
temple in either a so-called hall of barks, i.e. the depository
within the temple where the processional barks were stored when
not in use, or else in one of the chapels where these portable
boat-shrines which contained a cult statue of the god were kept.

Such ceremonies are often depicted on the walls of the appropriate room of the temple where they took place.[405]

If such private stelae do, in fact, even though incidentally, commemorate a real ceremony in which the king participated,
we may wonder if the scenes of those private stelae on which the
king does not appear and which, after all, form the vast majority
of the preserved corpus of these monuments (and not only from the
New Kingdom), are likewise rooted in an actual event which took
place at a point fixed in time? An examination of the stelae discussed in Chapter 2 suggests that this was the case, that incidents which had an especial meaning and significance for the owner
or dedicator of the stelae, the two not necessarily being the
same person, could and did figure in their scenes. This is demonstrated just as vividly by the group of stelae whose scenes picture the processional bark of a god delivering an oracle to the
dedicator of the stela[406] or by those showing the funerary rite
of Opening-of-the-Mouth being performed.[407] In each of these instances, there is no question but that an actual incident is being
portrayed. This, in turn, suggests that those stelae scenes which
show either the deceased alone or with members of his family making an offering to the gods, or those showing a member or members
of his family making offerings to the deceased might also picture
actual events rather than conventional stereotypes. In two of my
recent studies on the Egyptian iconography of the Asiatic god Reshep, I attempted to show that the representations of the deity
on New Kingdom stelae were not symbolic abstracts of the god himself, but rather, like the pictures of Ramesses-Montuemtowe on
the Qantir stelae or those of the Sphinx on the Giza stelae, were
concrete depictions of specific, individual cult statues of the

god.[408] There is no reason not to suppose, then,that on those
monuments where the dedicator is pictured making an offering this
was also the case, that what actually was being portrayed was an
act of worship at a specific point of time in a specific temple
or shrine. In short, the stela's owner was making offerings to
the cult statue(s) of the divinity or divinities involved. Likewise, when it is the deceased to whom offerings are being made by
various members of his family, we should understand that it was
not so much his spirit, his ka in the Afterworld, which is being
shown, but his tomb statue in the tomb during a funerary banquet.
This latter, in fact, may have been the inspiration for that
large group of stelae whose texts identify the deceased as an 3ḫ
ikr n Rʿ "a spirit who is effective for Reʿ" and whose pictures
show the deceased sitting, standing, or kneeling and holding a
lotus.[409] These could very well have been depicting, not the deceased, but his tomb statue.

In each of these cases, however, it should not be assumed
that, in addition to picturing real events in real locations at
real points in time, such scenes did not also have a timeless
symbolism, that they did not simultaneously convey the notion
that the actual event, whatever it might have been and wherever
it might have taken place, was continually and unendingly being
repeated forever for the duration of Eternity. This, after all,
is one of the basic motivations underlaying virtually all Egyptian
mortuary and monumental art: the infinite, timeless repetition of
whatever was being pictured so that it lived, continued, and was
repeated forever. Whether this desire for eternal repetition,
everlasting continuation, or whether this symbolic interpretation
was both the original and primary motivation for the appearance

of the scenes found on the private stelae of the New Kingdom and probably of the earlier periods of Ehyptian history as well, is a moot question, one which is only incidental to this study. It seems clear enough to me that such scenes did have a real context, did portray actual events, that they did have a historicity. With this understanding in mind, then they certainly provide us with a new and hitherto untapped source of historical documents, though it is true not so much for political history as for social and/or religious history.

Footnotes:

400. In both my "A Memphite Stela..." and my "The Iconographic
Theme..." To the stelae which I have discussed in the first
of these, add now stela Hannover 1935.200.442, published by
Munro, "Untersuchungen zur altägyptischen Bildmetrik" 41
fig. 44.

401. See above, n. 8, for references.

402. See above, n. 129 and the literature cited there.

403. E.g. stelae Cairo JE 20395 (published by R. El-Sayed, "Stèles
des particuliers relatives au culte rendu aux statues royales
de la XVIIIe a la XXe Dynastie", BIFAO 79 (1979) pl. 46),
Cairo 14/10/69/1 (published by Gaballa, "Some Nineteenth Dynasty Monuments in the Cairo Museum", ibid. 71 (1972) pl. 22),
Boston 25.635 (published by D. Dunham, "Four New Kingdom Monuments in the Museum of Fine Arts, Boston", JEA 21 (1935) pl.
17 nr. 2), passim.

404. See my "A Memphite Stela..." 98 n.39, 109 pl.2, and the references cited there

405. See D. Arnold, Wandrelief und Raumfunktion in ägyptischen
Tempeln des Neuen Reiches (Berlin: 1962) 34 n. 21b, A.R.
David, Religious Ritual at Abydos (c. 1300) (Warminister:
1973) 80-81.

406. See my "A Memphite Stela..." 96 n. 34, 97 n. 36, and the references cited there.

407. For this particular aspect of the funeral ceremony, see E.
Otto, Das ägyptische Mundöffnungsritual (Wiesbaden: 1960)
and G. Goyon, Rituels funéraires de l'ancienne Égypte (Paris:
1972) 87-120.

408. See my "The Winged Reshep" 73 and my "Reshep Times Two" 164-

166. For the cult statues of Ramesses-Montuemtowe on the Qantir stelae and those from Giza which picture the Sphinx, see my "The Winged Reshep" 82 nn. 34-38.

409. For the ꜣḫ ỉkr n Rꜥ and the stelae picturing them, see now the impressive study of R. Demarée, The ꜣḫ ỉkr n Rꜥ-Stelae: On Ancestor Worship in Ancient Egypt (Leiden: 1983) and, earlier, Bruyère, Rapport sur les fouilles de Deir el Médineh (1934-1935): troisieme parte (Cairo: 1939) 151-167: "Le culte du Khou Aker ".

Appendix

Four rock-cut stelae were deliberately omitted from my e-
numeration in Chapter 1: the stela set up at Kasr Ibrim in the
reign of Seti I by the viceroy of Kush, Amenemope, a stela set up
at Aswan in year 2, month 3 of Shomu, day 26 of Ramesses II, and
two of the lesser stelae, nrs. 12 and 13, at Abu Simbel. Of these
the Aswan stela could very well have been included in Chapter 1.
It was excluded because of the length of its text, although it
conforms perfectly with the other stelae of this chapter in every
other respect. The two Abu Simbel stelae, save for the wretched
remnants of their texts, have never been published. My own photographs of them are poor and reveal virtually nothing. The late
Labib Habachi kindly looked at them for me, but with little better
result:

> "Nothing visible more than what can be seen in the upper
> register: Ramesses II smiting a prisoner with Amenre of-
> fering him the scimetar, and followed by a hawk-headed
> god, most probably Harakhti. Nothing shows if in the
> lower register was the representation of ... people".[410]

Consequently, since I have not really been able to study these
two monuments and since I am unwilling to make any judgements a-
bout them on the basis of the extremely-sketchily published des-
criptions,[411] other than noting their existence below, they have
been omitted from any further consideration. The stela which the
viceroy Amenemope commissioned at Kasr Ibrim differs in two part-
ticulars from the other stelae which has the triumphal scene. Instead of being clubbed to death, the victim is being slain by a
spearthrust, and the action, at first glance, appears to be taking place on the battlefield rather than inside a temple. The

presence of an empty chariot and its attendant horse-team next to
the king would seem to imply that he had just dismounted from he
vehicle in order to dispatch his enemy.[412] I will return to these
apparent incongruities after I have described the stelae.

31. Rock-cut stela on the east bank of the Nile, not far up-
stream from the shrines of Kasr Ibrim. Bibliography: R.A. Caminos, The Shrines and Rock-Inscriptions of Ibrim (London: 1968) 83-
90 and pls. 39-40, F. Hintze, "Die Felsenstele Sethos I bei Qasr
Ibrim", ZÄeS 87 (1962) 31-40 and pl. 3, KRI I, 98-99. For earlier publications, see Caminos, op. cit. 83 and PM VII, 94. (Fig.
33).

Only the lower part of the scene, framed by a vertical
border line and set off from the text below by a thickish ground
line, is preserved. At the extreme left a god stands on a rectangular pedestal.[413] His body from the waist down and a bit of
his clenched left hand and the w3s-staff which it holds are still
visible. There are neither traces nor room for his right hand to
hang down straight at his side. It is probable that the missing
arm, as Caminos observed, must have been extended to offer the
king a sword.[414] As all that is preserved of the god's dress is
his short kilt and the animal tail attached to the rear of his
belt, his identity is in question. The sacrificial prisoner, a
Nubian, kneels in front of the god. He has thick lips and wide,
flaring nostrils. His dress includes a massive earring, a short
bag-wig, a broad collar, a short kilt of stiffened material,[415]
and the sporran worn by Nubians affixed to his belt in front.[416]
His right knee rests on the ground line, its leg stretching back-
wards so that the foot projects in front of the god's pedestal.
His right arm flails upwards wildly. His left hand clutches his

kneecap. The king vigourously strides forward towards towards him.
With one hand and arm, neither of which are preserved, he stabs
the struggling captive with a fatal thrust through the abdomen.
Such is the violence of the deathblow that the speartip has completely passed through the victim's body and juts out of the small
of his back. With his other arm the king grasps the Nubian's hair
firmly to steady the body for the death thrust. The king wears
the archaic-patterned kilt, a wide belt, and the lion's tail. His
right foot covers and obscures the left foot of the prisoner. To
the right an undulating line line slopes up diagonally from the
ground over to the right border. On this the king's waiting chariot and its team of caparisoned horses stands. Of the two weapon
cases attached to its side, that for the spears or javelins is
empty. The wavy line certainly indicates the uneven flat desert
terrain. Part of the chariot's wheel is covered by the king's
left calf and the pawing forelegs of the horses project beyond
the frame of the scene.

Underneath this violent tableau is a hieroglyphic text of
twelve lines pertaining directly to it and three vertical lines
which identify the a male figure in the lower left corner as the
dedicator of the stela. Holding his symbols of office and elabor-
altely dressed, he has around his neck a thick, bulging, choker-
like necklace around his neck, undoubtedly a šby.w-collar.[417] The
main text reads:[418]

"Long live the Horus, the Mighty Bull who appears in Thebes,
who causes the Two Lands to live, the Embodiment of the Two
Ladies, who repeats births, powerful of sword, who repels
the Nine Bows, the Horus of Gold who repeats appearances,
rich of bows in all lands, the king of Upper and Lower Egy-

pt, Menmare'-Tutre', the Son of Re', Seti-merneptah,
granted life forever and ever, the good god who smites
the Nine Bows, rich of heart, who overthrows his enemies,[419]
who slaughters Kush, who tramples down the Tnw-folk,[420]
who carries off their chiefs[421] as prisoners, the Horus,
the Mighty Bull, firm of heart like the Son of Nūt, the
valiant king who makes his border at any place he desires,
he[422] spends the seasons of ploughing in Tomery and the
seasons of his harvests[423] among the knnw-folk,[424] dest-
roying their farms,[425] hacking up[426] their cities. His
horses are sated with grain and his soldiers are intoxi-
cated with wine through the victories of his sword. To
him come the foreigners of the South, bowing down, and
the Northerners, making obeisance to his power. That
which Re' the Father encompasses is beneath his counsel
and they obey, their hearts like one, without their being
rebellious.[427] They tag after his feet like hounds do,[428]
in quest of his giving[429] the breath of life to them.
O victorious king who protects Egypt, who tramples down
the hillmen, who repels the flatlands in their places,[430]
the rulers of their foreign lands who did not acknowledge
Egypt, who were rebellious against his majesty (l.p.h.),[431]
your valiant strength has carried them off,[432] your power
has trampled them down, the dread of you has encircled[433]
their lands, and your plans have baffled them, O goodly
ruler who slays his enemies,[434] who has destroyed [435]
the land of the Nehesi with his sword, whose southern
frontier (reaches) as far as the wind (does), while the
northern one penetrates to the end of the Great Green

Sea,[436] the king of Upper and Lower Egypt, Menmare'-Tutre',
the Son of Re', Seti-merneptah, the Beloved of Amūnre' king
of the gods, granted life forever and ever".

This text, of course, is not a descriptive narrative to
the scene above, but is rather a speech, a panygeric addressed to
the king by the viceroy Amenemope. The three vertical lines of
text which precede and identify him contain an additional speech:

"The king's son of Kush, Amenemope, he says: 'Your Father,
Amūnre', protects[437] (you) with all life, stability, and
good fortune. He gives[438] to you the South like the North.
All countries bow down to your power. All lands are united
beneath your sandals'."[439]

32. Rock-cut stela dated to regnal year 2 of Ramesses II
at Aswan. Bibiliography: De Morgan, Catalogue des monuments I,
6; LD III, pl. 175g; KRI II, 344-345. For additional bibliography, see PM V, 245 (Fig. 34).

The text of this stela has been published on several occasions, but its scene has been reproduced only in the line drawing
of De Morgan. The curve of the stela's top is formed by the winged sundisk. The tableau beneath this is comprised of two similar
scenes. In the center, facing outward, are respectively Khnūm and
Amūn, each offering a sword with his right hand to the king. Khnūm
holds a w3s-staff in his left hand, Amūn an ʿnḥ. In front of and
over the head of each is a speech. That of Amūn reads: "Words
spoken by Amūn: 'I have given your sword to you'". The speech of
Khnūm reads: "Words spoken by Khnūm, lord of Samut:[440] '(I have
given to][441] you every (---]'". In front of each god the figure of
the "lord of the Two Lands, Wosimare'-setepenre', the lord of Diadems, Ramesses-mi'amūn, granted life like Re'"[442] slays a pros-

trate enemy. Each figure of the king, wearing the Double Crown,
wields the maceaxe with his left hand and holds a bow in the same
hand with which he grasps the hair of the foe whom he is about to
kill. The victim in the right hand scene kneels on both knees
toward Khnūm, but has swivelled his torso toward the king to whom
he raises both hands in a futile gesture of supplication. The
prisoner being slain before Amūn kneels on one knee toward the
god, but has also turned his upper body to the king, raising both
hands to him to beg for mercy. This captive wears a capotelike
upper garment, a tight-fitting skullcap(?) and an ankle-length
kilt. The other has a hairdo reaching down to his shoulder and
likewise wears a sleeved upper garment. Unfortunately De Morgan's
drawing does not allow any real conclusions to be made about the
ethnicity of the victims. Behind the upraised arm of each Ramesses
is the statement: "trampling the chiefs of the land of Nubia",[443]
from which we may assume that the victims are Nubians representing two different tribes or regions.[444] Underneath and separated
from the double scene is a hieroglyphic text of eleven horizontal
lines. The text reads as follows:

> "Year 2, month 3 of Shomu, day 26, under the majesty of
> the Horus, the Mighty Bull, the Beloved of Maʿat, the
> Embodiment of the Two Ladies who protects Egypt, who cap-
> tures the foreign lands, the Horus of Gold, rich of years,
> great of victory, the king of Upper and Lower Egypt, the
> ruler of the Nine Bows who overthrows the rebellious ones,
> the lord of the sword, the lord of the Two Lands, Wosimareʿ-
> setepenreʿ, the Son of Reʿ, of his body, his beloved, the
> lord of Diadems, Ramesses-miʿamūn, the Beloved of Amūnreʿ
> the king of the gods, and of Khnūm the lord of Samut.

"Long live the good god, the Montu of millions, the one
strong like the Son of Nūt, the fighter on the battlefield, the lion, powerful of heart,[445] he has overthrown
hundreds of thousands in the completion of an instant,
the great wall of his army on the day of battle, the fear
of whom has penetrated all lands,[446] Tomeri (i.e. Egypt)
rejoices when the ruler is in it, for he has extended its
borders forever. The Asiatics are destroyed and their
towns are looted.[447] He has trampled down the foreigners
of the North, the Tjemehu are overthrown on account of
[their] fear of him, and the Asiatics are desirous of the
breath (of life) from him,[448] the one who, by means of
his campaigns, causes that Egypt lives,[449] that their
their hearts are filled with his plans, that they sit
(peacefully) because of the shadow of his sword, and that
they do not fear any foreign land.[450] He has destroyed
the[451] fighting men of the Great Green Sea, the great
water of the Northland.[452] While they lay asleep, the
king is wakeful. Precise of counsel, not a thing which
he says fails,[453] and the foreigners come to him carrying their children in order to beg the breath of life
from him. His battlecry is powerful throughout the land
of Nubia, his strength drives back the Nine Bows. Babylon,
Hatti, and Yey[---][454] bow down to his power, the king
of Upper and Lower Egypt, the lord of the Two Lands,
Wosimareʿ-setepenreʿ, the Son of Reʿ, of his body, the
lord of the sword, Ramesses-miʾamūn, [the beloved of]
Amūnreʿ, Khnūm, Satis, and ʿAnuket".

Beneath this long text is an additional set of scenes and texts, of which those on the left are virtually completely destroyed,[455] but which undoubtedly duplicated those on the right.[456] At the extreme right a man, wearing a shoulder-length wig and an ankle-length kilt, kneels and raises both hands in the gesture of adoration. In front of him are six vertical lines of text which is continued in two additional short vertical groups over his arms and in front of his face. A third group is in the field behind his head. This inscription reads as follows:

"Giving praise to the lion, the lord of [---],[457] kissing the ground to the lord of the Two Lands, that he may give [-----][458] the prophet of the Primeval God,[459] his beloved, [-----][460] his majesty upon all his victories [----][461] every [----], the overseer of the fortress(?)[462] [-----]."[463]

33a-b. Rock-cut stelae nrs. 12 and 13, at Abu Simbel, south of the great temple of Ramesses II. Bibliography: KRI II, 771-772, PM VII, 118. (Not illustrated).

The scenes of this pair of stelae have not been published and their texts are mostly lost. The description given in PM simply notes "the King smites captives before Amūn". That given by Kitchen for nr. 13 expands this slightly: "king strikes foe with mace before Amun and Horus", while that sent to me by Habachi[464] adds the fact that Amūn is offering the king a sword. The preserved portion of the text of nr. 12 contains the nomen, prenomen, and two epithets of Ramesses II,[465] and that of nr. 13 but little more:

"Long live the Horus, the Mighty Bull, the Beloved of Maʿat, the Embodiment of the Two Ladies, [--- --- --- ----] lands, the Horus of Gold, rich of years, great of victories, the king of Upper and Lower Egypt, the

lord of the Two Lands, Wosi(ma)reʿ-[setepenreʿ, the Son of
Reʿ], Ra(messes-miʿ)amūn [------]. The good god, the Son
of Amūn, great [------] who slaughters the chiefs and the
[great one]s[466] of every [foreign land --- --- ---] heaven
[-------]".

While it is probable that these two stelae are to be considered as
privately-commissioned monuments, as are the other rock-cut stelae
at Abu Simbel, there is no way of determining who commissioned
them, under what circumstances they were commissioned, or what,
specifically, they may commemorate. Consequently, other than having noted their existence here, they have been excluded from consideration in my discussion and analysis of the stelae surveyed
in Chapter 1. This is not the case, however, with stelae nrs. 31
and 32. The former has been dealt with here, rather than in Chapter 1, mainly because its scene differs from the usual iconography
of the death of the enemy. Here the action seems to be taking
place on the battlefield rather than in the temple courtyard and
the prisoner is being slain with a spearthrust rather than being
clubbed to death. However, it is difficult to disassociate the
Kasr Ibrim rock-stela from the other rock-stelae commissioned by
the viceroy Amenemope at Aswan.[467] These almost certainly commemorated the victorious conclusion of a campaign of Seti I in
Nubia, probably in his year 8.[468] Now, since the death of the
captive is taking place in front of the statue of the god, who is
also simultaneously offering the sword to the king, it is not unlikely that we have here a conflation of several scenes which include the victory on the battlefield and the subsequent sacrifice
of the captured chief in the temple.[469] It has been suggested that
the motivation for Amenemope's commissioning this and the Aswan

texts was, simultaneously, to commemorate the victory, his participation in it, and his installation as viceroy. Since, in the
Kasr Ibrim scene, he seems to be wearing the gold šby.w-collars,
it is, in the light of Chapter 2, tempting to further assume that
they possibly were awarded to him because of some deed of valour
of his in the course of the war and that he was also, albeit in-
directly, commemorating the award as well, but this can only be
pure speculation.

Although the Aswan inscription is dated to a specific
point in time in the reign of Ramesses II, it should not, as it
usually is, be reckoned as a <u>royal</u> inscription,[470] nor should it
it be assumed that it was the king himself who was responsible
for it. In spite of its beginning with a date and the king's
titulary, the text is not a narrative. It is a panygeric addressed to the king, although unlike that contained in the Kasr Ibrim
stela, he is not addressed in the second person. Moreover, this
text is probably not to be disassociated from that of the dedicator pictured beneath it. Although broken and somewhat incomprehensible, it continues to describe the exploits of the king. Insofar as it seems to correspond completely in its iconographic
and schematic details with the stelae studied in Chapter 1, like
them it should be scrutinized for whatever historical implicati-
ons it may possess. Its pictorial element implies that the victory which it commemorates was over Nubians, but the text claims
victory over Libyans, Asiatics,[471] "the fighting men of the Great
Green Sea", i.e. a Sea People, and even Hatti and Babylon are
represented as making overtures of submission. But these triumphs, or rather claimed triumphs in year 2 can hardly be reconcil-
ed with the dated wars of Ramesses II. His major confrontation

with the Hittites at Kadesh took place in regnal year 5, three
years after the date of the Aswan stela. His inscription of year
4 at the Nahr el-Kelb near Beirut, two years after the Aswan
text's date suggests that his campaigning in Syria-Palestine did
not take place much before then,[472] and I have attempted, elsewhere, to show that most of his undated Asiatic wars, if not all
of them, probably took place between years 10 and 18.[473] Only the
war against the Sherden (= "the fighting men of the Great Green
Sea") and possibly a Libyan war take place in year 2. While there
there are a number of references to military activity on the part
of Ramesses in Nubia, none of these, other than that implied by
the scene of the Aswan stela can be associated with a specific
date[475] and, as has been suggested above, it is not unlikely that
this war was the same as that which, though without any date, is
depicted on the walls of the Beit el-Wali temple of Ramesses
which actually took place during the period when he was coregent
with his father.[476] If this is correct, then the other triumphs
alluded to in the Aswan inscription, over the Libyans, the Asiatics, the Sherden, even the submissive gestures of the Hittites
and the Babylonians, could very well refer to the foreign wars
of Seti I in which Ramesses II could have participated as a
prince royal, crown prince, or coregent.[477]

Footnotes:

410. Personal communication from Cairo, dated 24 August 1981.

411. See below, stelae nrs. 33a-b.

412. For similar scenes where the king has dismounted from his chariot to fight on foot, see, e.g. Wreszinski, _Atlas_ II, pls. 34, 116, 140, 146, and 154.

413. Caminos, op. cit. 84, calls this a "short platform" which would mean that the god was standing on a raised flooring or stage. This, in turn, suggests that it was the god, himself, incarnate, who stood there. A pedestal, on the other hand, indicates that it was a statue of the god before whom the prisoner was being killed. This would be highly improbable if the action was taking place on the battlefield, for ther is no evidence that the Egyptians carried divine statues into battle. It is not impossible that there is a conflation of two scenes and two ideas here: victory on the battlefield, followed immediately by the ceremonial execution of the captive enemy chief in the nearest temple.

414. Loc. cit. n. 7.

415. Ibid.

416. On this particular item of dress, see H.G. Fischer, "The Nubian Mercenaries of Gebelein", _Kush_ 9 (1956) 56.

417. Although the internal detail of the individual biconical gold beads has not been indicated, the bulge of the collar above the line of Amenemope's shoulder can hardly be anything else but the curved profile of the last visible bead, see above, Chapter 2, Section A, nn. 226-228.

418. Essentially I have followed the translation of Caminos, op. cit. 85-86, though with some slight modifications. These are indicated in the following notes.

419. For rkw "rebel", "enemy", see <u>Wb</u>. II, 456, 13-20.

420. Caminos, op. cit. 86, the comment to line 3, takes Tnw as an otherwise unattested ethnogeographic designation. It must be admitted, however, that the possibility of its being a corrupt writing for Rtnw "Retjenu", i.e. the Syro-Palestinian area, is a tempting one, see Caminos, loc. cit. for references. If so, then Kush, mentioned in the preceding line is balanced by Rtnw here. However, a spelling of Rtnw with the foreign people determinative, rather than that of the foreign land is not recognized by <u>Wb</u>. II, 460, 10-15. On the other hand, see Gauthier, <u>Dictionaire des noms géographiques</u> III, 141, where a writing is noted.

421. For the unusal spelling of wr.w with the man smiting with a stick rather than the man holding a staff, see Caminos, loc. cit. n. 5.

422. Emphasis supplied. The antecedent of "he" is, of course, Horus in line 1, followed by the long stream of qualifying praises and then resumed by .f of irr.f.

423. Following Caminos, op. cit. 87 n. 4.

424. Again I have followed Caminos, ibid. 88, the comment to line 5, and rendered this as an otherwise unattested ethnogeographic designation. Again, the suggestion that this is also a faulty transcription of Rtnw (above, n. 420) is tempting, the moreso since these people seem to have both farms and towns. While the Nubians undoubtedly engaged in farming, to my knowledge, there is no evidence that they possessed urban centers large enough or sophisticated enough to warrant their being called by the Egyptian term niwt "city". On this point, see my "The Nubian War of Akhenaton" nn. 66 and 123.

425. Caminos, op. cit. 88, renders mnw as "plantations", but under the influence of the term as used in the Antebellum South the nuance which "plantation" conveys to me is somewhat distorted. Consequently I have opted for the more neutral "farms".

426. For some graphic illustrations of ḥb3 "to hack up" which led to its use as a technical term to describe attacks against walled areas, cities, see my "Siege Warfare in Pharaonic Egypt", Natural History 78 (March 1964) 13-14.

427. I prefer to understand bšt as either a noun or an infinitive and take nn bšt.sn "their rebellion/rebelling does not exist" as a virtual relative clause parallel to and complementing the preceding ib.sn mi w⸳ "their hearts like one". Caminos, loc. cit. prefers to see nn bst.sn as a gnomic statement "and (they) will not rebel".

428. Caminos' picture of hounds crawling behind their master, loc. cit. 85, is illchosen because neither hounds nor any other canines crawl. They do run alongside of or tag behind their masters. Ḥnḥn, Wb. III, 384, 8-13, which is even attested with a canine determinative, means "to follow after", "to accompany" which quite suits the translation I have proposed.

429. For this more literal rendering of sb.tw rdit.f, see Caminos, ibid. 89.

430. Compare Caminos, loc. cit.

431. I interpret everything after "O victorious king" at the end of line 8 and the beginning of line 9 until "in their place" in the middle of line 9 as a series of specifications which qualify "O victorious kings", all of them antecedents in

anticipatory apposition to the subject of the next four sentences: "<u>your</u> ... strength", "<u>your</u> power", "<u>your</u> dread", "<u>your</u> plans".

432. Likewise, I have taken everything following "rulers" in the middle of line 9 until "(l.p.h.)" near the beginning of line 10 in the same way, only here "rulers" and the qualifying specifications are the antecedents to the objects of the verbs in these sentences: "<u>them</u>", "<u>them</u>", "<u>their</u> lands", and "<u>them</u>".

433. For the spelling of p$\d{h}$r, see the comments of Caminos, loc. cit.

434. See Caminos, ibid. the comment to line 11.

435. Caminos, ibid. translates sk.n.k as written "you have destroyed" and then emends the suffix .f of $\d{h}$pš.f to .k in order to be consistent with sk.n.k. Hintze, op. cit. 39, however, preferred to see sk as a participle, emending n to the strong arm determinative, with the k-basket as the phonetic complement. Since an emendation seems necessary either way, I prefer that of Hintze, and take sk t3 N$\d{h}$siw as a participal phrase parallel to the preceding 3b km(3)tyw.f.

436. To translate w3$\underline{d}$ wr as "ocean" is almost pleonastic. Those bodies of water which we today describe as "oceans" were probably beyond the ken of the Ramesside Egyptians. The "Great Green Sea" here was undoubtedly the Mediterranean.

437. Caminos, op. cit. 90, translates hw it.k as a wish "May your Father protect", but there is no reason not to understand it as an affirmative sentence.

438. Since di.f is a s$\underline{d}$m.f and not a s$\underline{d}$m.n.f, to translate by the Present tense seems preferable.

439. See Caminos, loc. cit.

440. According to Gauthier, <u>Dictionnaire</u> V, 32, a locality in Upper Egypt, possibly the island of Bigeh. Breasted, <u>ARE</u> III,
205 par. 479, translated, simply, "the cataract region".

441. Following the restoration of Kitchen, op. cit. 344.

442. Mì Rꜥ only in the text of the right hand scene.

443. In each instance this phrase is preceded by another. That
of the left hand scene reads: ⸜⸝⸞⸟, that of the right
hand scene ⸜⸝⸞. These were undoubtedly epithets descri-
bing the king, in the light of which it is probably better
to translate ptpt as a participle: "the one who tramples".

444. On this point see my "The Nubian War of Akhenaton" nn.78-80.

445. The text has mꜣì sḫm-ìb. Breasted's rendering, loc. cit. as
"strong-hearted lion" presumes that sḫm-ìb is used adjectiv-
ally here. While this, of course, is possible, it is equally possible to take it as an independent epithet.

446. Literally: "his fear has penetrated" (or: "penetrates", the
verb is a sḏm.f with noun subject.

447. By "Asiatics" (Stìyw) presumably are meant the inhabitants
of Syria-Palestine.

448. The text has t̲ꜣw.f, literally: "his breath", which can only
refer to t̲ꜣw n 'nh "the breath of life".

449. Written ⸜⸝⸞⸟ where the seated god (seated king according to Lepsius, loc. cit.) is surely not to be taken as the
1st person singular suffix pronoun .ì, but as the determinative of the participle dìw. For the instrumental use of the
preposition m, see Gardiner, <u>Egyptian Grammar</u> par. 162, 7.
Breasted, loc. cit. apparently did not fully understand this
portion of the text which he translated "who sends Egypt on

campaigns".

450. Bn snd.sn n ḫ3s.t nb.t "literally: "Their fear does not exist (or: They do not fear) on account of any foreign land".
Ḥ3s.t, in spite of the plural strokes, should be understood
as a singular.

451. For the writing of n3 just with n, see Erman, Neuägyptische
Grammatik par. 174.

452. Š ꜥ3, literally "Great Lake", "Great Pool", here certainly
the Mediterranean.

453. Literally: "There does not fail that which he has said,
everything".

454. Only the beginning of this toponym is preserved, thus: 〔glyphs〕.
Kitchen, loc. cit. would restore: 〔glyphs〕. Breasted, loc.
cit. note d, suggested: "probably Arvad or Isy-Cyprus".

455. Only the first two words of the text are preserved: "Giving
praise [--------]".

456. These were recorded only by De Morgan, loc. cit. His copy
was repeated by Kitchen, op. cit. 345, without, however, being collated either with the original or with a photograph
of the original.

457. Restore ḫꜥ.w "Diadems", ḫpš "the sword", or the like if the
lacuna was, as Kitchen, loc. cit. implies, only a single
square. However, it is not certain that only a single square
was lost. Where such vertical columns of text are accompanied by the kneeling figure of the speaker, those columns of
text farthest from the figure usually fill the full height
of the register, growing shorter only when they have to accomodate the figure. De Morgan's drawing shows no cross-hatching indicative of lacunae at the bottoms of any of these

lines, but De Morgan was not the most accurate of copyists, and certainly there were such lacunae. That following the preserved nb, assuming that the text continued down to the ground line, was a little more than two and one half squares high.

458. Kitchen, op. cit. 345 n. 9d, "Loss (if any) unknown" is misleading. The lacuna following di.f (see preceding note) is almost two squares high.

459. Written: ⌐⌐⌐ , where the stroke is certainly to be restored hm-ntr. Since this is a title, we would expect it to have been followed by either a personal name or a specification. Mri.f "his beloved" which follows the group ⌐⌐⌐ suggests the latter. The group is either understood as a garbled writing of tpy or of p3w.ty, Wb. I, 496, 14, "the one belonging to the primeval time", "the primeval god". I prefer the latter, but it is not found with this spellling.

460. I have no suggestions for this line which reads ⌐⌐⌐ and which ends in a lacuna a little more than one square high.

461. After "all his victories" there is a lacuna about one square + high. The text immediately following, and which ends in a similar lacuna, is completely unintelligible to me. It seems to read: ⌐⌐⌐.

462. Following the emendation of Kitchen, loc. cit. n. 10b, that the group before the man's face is to be read imy-r htm.

463. From its position in De Morgan's drawing, where the topmost sign preserved is on a level below the crown of the adorant's head, we may assume that something originally stood above the group, certainly part of a title, and that the man's

name is also lost.

464. Above and behind the king's head is: "Wosi[ma]re⁽-[Setep]en-[re⁽] Ra[messes]-mi⁽amūn, granted life, the Horus, Powerful-of-arm, the Lord of the sword". All that is legible of the main text is the beginning of the second line: "the king of Upper and Lower Egypt, Ra[messes-mi⁽amūn -------]".

465. See above, n. 410.

466. Following the restoration of Kitchen, op. cit. 772.

467. See above, n. 143.

468. Ibid. and also n. 160, above.

469. See above, n. 413.

470. E.g. Kitchen has included it in vol. II of KRI: Ramesses II, Royal Inscriptions, rather than KRI III: Ramesses II, his Contemporaries. Breasted, loc. cit. has included it among the royal inscriptions, as does J. Schmidt, Ramesses II: A Chronological Structure for His Reign (Baltimore: 1973) 25, where he wishes to redate it to year 10.

471. I.e. Syro-Palestinians.

472. For the Hittite war, see Faulkner, "Egypt from the Inception of the Nineteenth Dynasty..." 221.

473. See above, n. 141, for references.

474. For the Sherden war of year 2, see J.Yoyotte, "Les stèles de Ramses II á Tanis. Ier partie ", Kemi 10 (1949) 60-74. For the possibility of a Libyan war in the same year, see Faulkner, op. cit. 230, nn. 4-5.

475. For the Nubian wars of Ramesses II, see Faulkner, ibid.

476. See above, n. 143.

477. For the most recent study of Seti I's foreign wars, see now W.J. Murnane, The Road to Kadesh. Slightly earlier, but still

of the greatest importance is the trenchant study of Spalinger, "The Northern Wars of Seti I: An Integrative Study",
<u>JARCE</u> 16 (1979) 29-47. See also Faulkner, op. cit. 218-224
and idem. "The Wars of Sethos I", <u>JEA</u> 33 (1947) 34-39.

Addenda

For some inexplicable reasons, the material contained in the two addenda which follow was omitted from the main text.

1. The following rock-cut stela should be listed and described in the Appendix immediately after stela nr. 31. Although it has the catalogue number 31a, it should be noted that its footnotes start with number 478.

31a. Rock-cut stela, west side of the ancient road between Aswan and Philae. Bibliography: De Morgan, loc. cit. nr. 123; Habachi, loc. cit. 26; KRI I, 302; for other publications see PM V, 247. (Fig. 35).

The king, wearing the Blue Crown, has dismounted from his chariot. In the hand with which he grasps a kneeling enemy by the hair he also holds what is probably a bow.[478] His other hand, hanging at his side, has thrust a shafted weapon into the body of the foeman.[479] A groom steadies the prancing chariot-horse. Behind the captive, another elaborately dressed man kneels with both hands raised in salutation to the king who is identified by a pair of vertical cartouches as "the good god, Menmareʿ, the Son of Reʿ, Seti-merneptah". The kneeling adorant is named in a caption of four vertical lines. These also contain a brief invocation to the king:

"Giving praises to your ka, O victorious king, O Horus who causes the Two Lands to live![480] Made by the first charioteer of his majesty, the king's son, Amenemope, the son of the king's son, (Pa)ser".

One last point to be noted here is the nationality of the sacrificial victim. Although, like all the other rock-cut stelae commissioned by Amenemope at Aswan (see above, stelae nrs. 15-17) no internal details of any of the figures are indicated in the

various publications, the outline of the captive's hairdo, his
short, pointed, beard, and his seemingly-sleeved garment not only
argue against his having been a Nubian (as he is on the other
three rock stelae of Amenemope at Aswan as well as that at Kasr
Ibrim), but rather suggest that he was a Libyan.[481] Virtually
every scholar who has dealt with these particular stelae have
taken them as referring to the same event.[482] If this is correct
and if the identification just given for the nationality of the
victim of Aswan rock inscription nr. 123 is also correct, then
it would appear that there is a contradiction here. This, however,
is probably not the case or, if it is, it can be easily resolved.
We might start by noting that, in strictu sensu, the tableau of
Aswan nr. 123 does not not actually show the king smiting the enemy,
though, as was the case on the Kasr Ibrim monument, there can be
no doubt that is about to, or has transfixed his prisoner with
the spear which he holds. Like the Kasr Ibrim scene, the action
here also seems to be taking place on the battlefield, with the
king having just dismounted from his chariot. The Nubian war and
victory which the other rock stelae commemorate seems to have
taken place in Seti's regnal year 8?.[483] On the Kasr Ibrim stela,
however, the text of which is much,much,longer than those of the
other monuments, it would appear that, unless it is mere rhetorical hyperbole, Seti is claiming victories in the North against
various foes, and while Libyans are not explicitly named here,
it is clear from his Karnak battle scenes that he fought a war
against the Libyans.[484] If such a victory had been won, there is
mo reason why it could not have been depicted in a rock stelae on
the Nubian marches, the moreso since there is good evidence that
captives were transported from one part of Egypt's empire to another where they were executed and their corpses put on public

display.[485]

Footnotes:

478. The apparent curve of the lower edge of what seems to be a
knife is actually a lock of the victim's hair which splays
out from the king's fist. When this is removed from consideration as part of a weapon, what is left can only be a bow,
compare Figs. 1, 3, 8, 10, 12, 18, and 34.

479. I take this to be a thrusting weapon such as the king also
wields in the Kasr Ibrim scene (see Fig. 33). Not only does
the weapon lack any visible head which might identify it as
a smiting weapon, a mace, maceaxe, or the like, its "business
end" seems clearly to be buried in the prisoner, even though
the attitude of the king as he stabs with it is rather sere-
ne and lacks the violent agitation inherent in the action of
smiting or stabbing so clearly portrayed on the Kasr Ibrim
stela. The analogy with the latter scene, save for this detail of the king's pose, is otherwise unchallengable. The
two scenes are in exact harmony, for the fact that no god is
shown here is of no consequence, as is clear from stela nr. 6.

480. Following the restoration of Kitchen, loc. cit.

481. For this Libyan hairdo, beard, and dress, see Bates, op. cit.
figs. 10, 12, 23, 35, 48, and pls. 1-3; Pritchard, ANEP figs.
1-2, 7-8, and compare stela nr. 7.

482. See above for references. Interestingly enough, no one seems
to have commented on the Libyan ethnicity of the victim of
Aswan nr. 123.

483. See above, n. 160.

484. See the Epigraphic Survey, The Battle Reliefs of King Sety
I, 87-107 and pls. 27-32.

485. See above, nn. 121-123.

2. The following works which have been cited in the footnotes
    should also be included in the Bibliography:

    Bates, O. The Eastern Libyans (London: 1914).

    Bogoslovsky, E.S. "Servants" of Pharaohs, Gods, and Private
       Persons (on the Social History of Egypt XVI-XIVth Cen-
       tury B.C. (Moscow: 1979, in Russian).

    Murnane, W.J. The Road to Kadesh: A Historical Interpretat-
       ation of the Battle Reliefs of King Sety I at Karnak
       (Chicago: 1985).

3. On page 66 the last sentence of footnote 14 should be changed
    to read: The Munich PhD dissertation of S. Schoske, Die Sieg-
    reiche König. Bildquellen zur altägyptischen Feindsymbolik
    will be published, I believe by Harrasowitz in Wiesbaden. It
    should be entered in the appropriate section of the Bibliogra-
    phy.

4. On page 137 the Bibliography of Catalogue nr. 29 should be
    now expanded to include:

    Scott, G.D. Ancient Egyptian Art at Yale (New Haven: 1986)
       126-127, 201.

    Likewise the General Bibliography should be altered to include
    it.

Fig. 1   Stela Brussels E 4499

Fig. 2   Stela *Riqqeh and Memphis VI*, nr. 12

Fig. 3   Stela Hannover 1935.200.230

Fig. 4   Stela Chicago Art Institute 1893.75

Fig. 5   Stela Metropolitan Museum of Art 64.285

Fig. 6   Stela Louvre E16373

Fig. 7   Stela Florence 2587

Fig. 8   Stela Cairo JE 88879

Fig. 9   Stela Hannover 1935.200.229

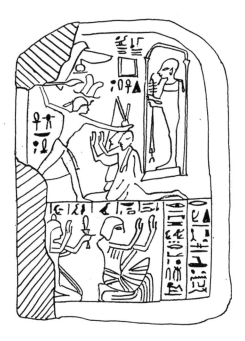

Fig. 10   Stela Hannover 1935.200.204

Fig. 11   Stela Brussels E 2386

Fig. 12   Stela Berlin (DDR) 20912

Fig. 13   Stela London (V.A.) 423.1908

Fig. 14   Stela Newark (New Jersey) 29.1788

Fig. 15   Rock Stela Aswan 124

Fig. 16   Rock Stela Aswan 5

Fig. 17   Rock Stela Aswan 12

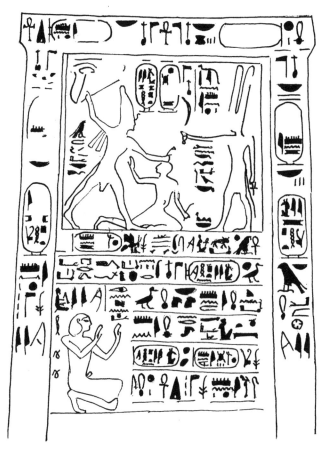

Fig. 19   Rock Stela Abu Simbel 22

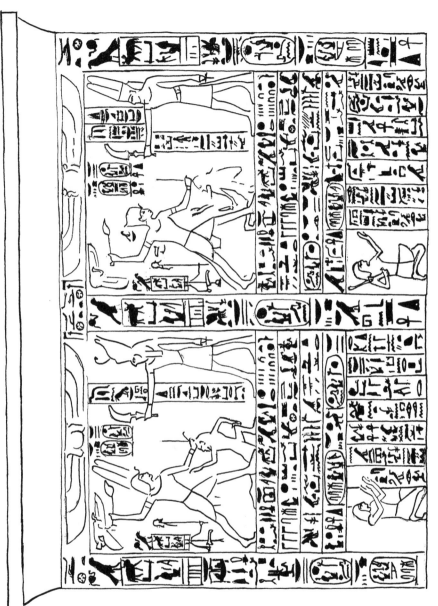

Fig. 18   Rock Stela Abu Simbel 24

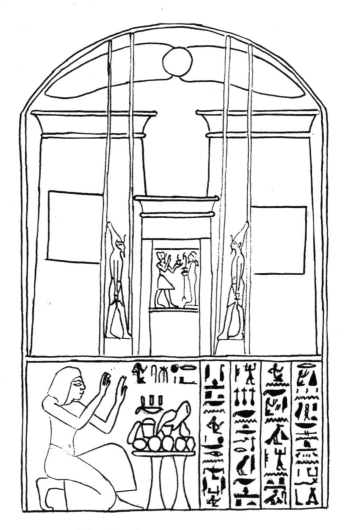

Fig. 20   Stela Cairo 16/3/35/2

Fig. 21   Stela Berlin 23077

Fig. 22   Stela Louvre C 213

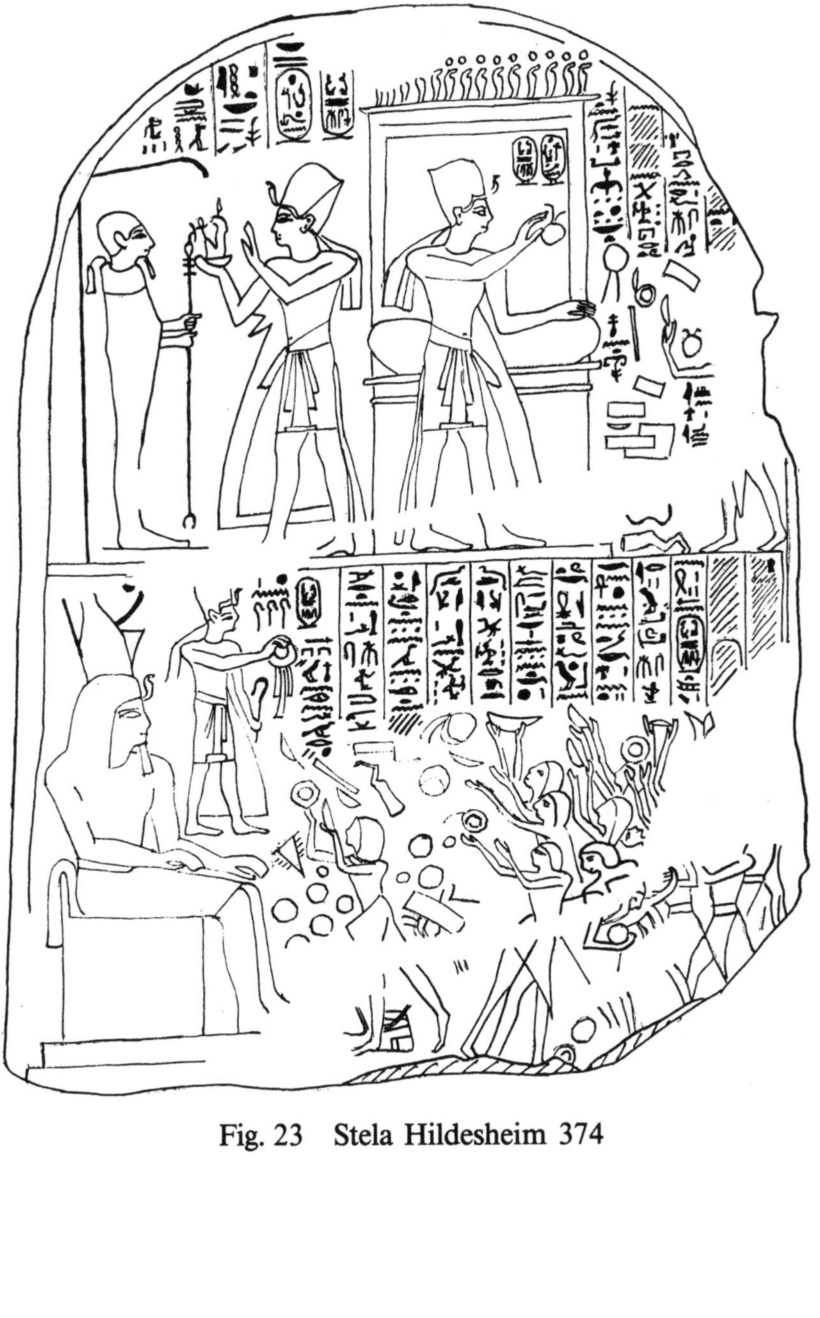

Fig. 23   Stela Hildesheim 374

Fig. 24   Stela Cairo CG 34.177

Fig. 25   Unnumbered Giza Stela

Fig. 26   Stela Cairo CG 34.176

Fig. 27   Stela Cairo CG 34.178

Fig. 28   Stela Cairo CG 34.180

Fig. 29   Stela Ny Carlsberg 897

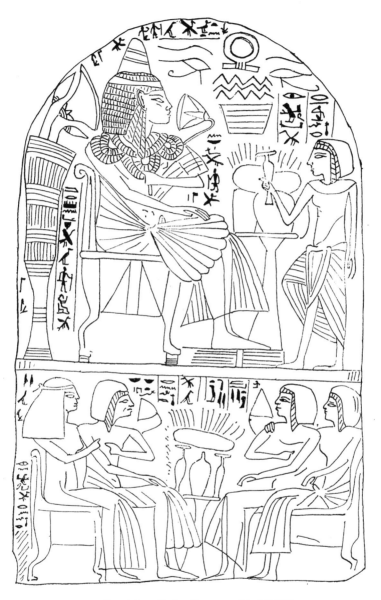

Fig. 30   Stela Louvre E 14275

Fig. 31 Stela Yale Art Gallery 28.58

Fig. 32   Stela Vatican City 253

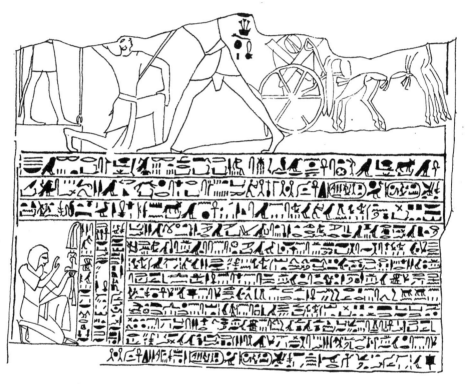

Fig. 33   Rock Stela of Amenemope at Kasr Ibrim

Fig. 34   Aswan Rock Stela of Ramesses II

Fig. 35   Rock Stela Aswan 123

Pl. 1 Stela Hannover 1935.200.230. Photograph courtesy of the Kestner
Museum, Hannover.

Pl. 2   Stela Chicago Art Institute 1893.75.   Photograph courtesy of the
Oriental Institute of the University of Chicago.

Pl. 3 Stela Metropolitan Museum of Art 64.285. Photograph courtesy of
the Metropolitan Museum of Art, New York.

Pl. 4   Stela Brussels E 2386.   Photograph courtesy of the Musees Royaux d'Art et d'Histoire, Brussels.

Pl. 5   Stela Berlin (DDR) 20912.   Photograph courtesy of the Egyptian
Museum, Berlin, German Democratic Republic.

Pl. 6 Stela Newark 29.1788. Photograph courtesy of the Newark Museum, Newark, New Jersey.

ORBIS BIBLICUS ET ORIENTALIS

Bd. 18   HEINRICH VALENTIN: *Aaron.* Eine Studie zur vor-priesterschriftlichen Aaron-Überlieferung. VIII–441 Seiten. 1978.

Bd. 19   MASSÉO CALOZ: *Etude sur la LXX origénienne du Psautier.* Les relations entre les leçons des Psaumes du Manuscrit Coislin 44, les Fragments des Hexaples et le texte du Psautier Gallican. 480 pages. 1978.

Bd. 20   RAPHAEL GIVEON: *The Impact of Egypt on Canaan.* Iconographical and Related Studies. 156 Seiten, 73 Abbildungen. 1978.

Bd. 21   DOMINIQUE BARTHÉLEMY: *Etudes d'histoire du texte de l'Ancien Testament.* XXV–419 pages. 1978.

Bd. 22/1   CESLAS SPICQ: *Notes de Lexicographie néo-testamentaire.* Tome I: p. 1–524. 1978. Epuisé.

Bd. 22/2   CESLAS SPICQ: *Notes de Lexicographie néo-testamentaire.* Tome II: p. 525–980. 1978. Epuisé.

Bd. 22/3   CESLAS SPICQ: *Notes de Lexicographie néo-testamentaire.* Supplément. 698 pages. 1982.

Bd. 23   BRIAN M. NOLAN: *The royal Son of God.* The Christology of Matthew 1–2 in the Setting of the Gospel. 282 Seiten. 1979.

Bd. 24   KLAUS KIESOW: *Exodustexte im Jesajabuch.* Literarkritische und motivgeschichtliche Analysen. 221 Seiten. 1979.

Bd. 25/1   MICHAEL LATTKE: *Die Oden Salomos in ihrer Bedeutung für Neues Testament und Gnosis.* Band I. Ausführliche Handschriftenbeschreibung. Edition mit deutscher Parallel-Übersetzung. Hermeneutischer Anhang zur gnostischen Interpretation der Oden Salomos in der Pistis Sophia. XI–237 Seiten. 1979.

Bd. 25/1a MICHAEL LATTKE: *Die Oden Salomos in ihrer Bedeutung für Neues Testament und Gnosis.* Band Ia. Der syrische Text der Edition in Estrangela Faksimile des griechischen Papyrus Bodmer XI. 68 Seiten. 1980.

Bd. 25/2   MICHAEL LATTKE: *Die Oden Salomos in ihrer Bedeutung für Neues Testament und Gnosis.* Band II. Vollständige Wortkonkordanz zur handschriftlichen, griechischen, koptischen, lateinischen und syrischen Überlieferung der Oden Salomos. Mit einem Faksimile des Kodex N. XVI–201 Seiten. 1979.

Bd. 25/3   MICHAEL LATTKE: *Die Oden Salomos in ihrer Bedeutung für Neues Testament und Gnosis.* Band III. XXXIV–478 Seiten. 1986.

Bd. 26   MAX KÜCHLER: *Frühjüdische Weisheitstraditionen.* Zum Fortgang weisheitlichen Denkens im Bereich des frühjüdischen Jahweglaubens. 703 Seiten. 1979.

Bd. 27   JOSEF M. OESCH: *Petucha und Setuma.* Untersuchungen zu einer überlieferten Gliederung im hebräischen Text des Alten Testaments. XX–392–37* Seiten. 1979.

Bd. 28   ERIK HORNUNG / OTHMAR KEEL (Herausgeber): *Studien zu altägyptischen Lebenslehren.* 394 Seiten. 1979.

Bd. 29   HERMANN ALEXANDER SCHLÖGL: *Der Gott Tatenen.* Nach Texten und Bildern des Neuen Reiches. 216 Seiten, 14 Abbildungen. 1980.

Bd. 30   JOHANN JAKOB STAMM: *Beiträge zur Hebräischen und Altorientalischen Namenkunde.* XVI–264 Seiten. 1980.

Bd. 31   HELMUT UTZSCHNEIDER: *Hosea – Prophet vor dem Ende.* Zum Verhältnis von Geschichte und Institution in der alttestamentlichen Prophetie. 260 Seiten. 1980.

Bd. 32   PETER WEIMAR: *Die Berufung des Mose*. Literaturwissenschaftliche Analyse von Exodus 2, 23–5, 5. 402 Seiten. 1980.

Bd. 33   OTHMAR KEEL: *Das Böcklein in der Milch seiner Mutter und Verwandtes*. Im Lichte eines altorientalischen Bildmotivs. 163 Seiten, 141 Abbildungen. 1980.

Bd. 34   PIERRE AUFFRET: *Hymnes d'Egypte et d'Israël*. Etudes de structures littéraires. 316 pages, 1 illustration. 1981.

Bd. 35   ARIE VAN DER KOOIJ: *Die alten Textzeugen des Jesajabuches*. Ein Beitrag zur Textgeschichte des Alten Testaments. 388 Seiten. 1981.

Bd. 36   CARMEL McCARTHY: *The Tiqqune Sopherim and Other Theological Corrections in the Masoretic Text of the Old Testament*. 280 Seiten. 1981.

Bd. 37   BARBARA L. BEGELSBACHER-FISCHER: *Untersuchungen zur Götterwelt des Alten Reiches im Spiegel der Privatgräber der IV. und V. Dynastie*. 336 Seiten. 1981.

Bd. 38   MÉLANGES DOMINIQUE BARTHÉLEMY. Etudes bibliques offertes à l'occasion de son 60e anniversaire. Edités par Pierre Casetti, Othmar Keel et Adrian Schenker. 724 pages, 31 illustrations. 1981.

Bd. 39   ANDRÉ LEMAIRE: *Les écoles et la formation de la Bible dans l'ancien Israël*. 142 pages, 14 illustrations. 1981.

Bd. 40   JOSEPH HENNINGER: *Arabica Sacra*. Aufsätze zur Religionsgeschichte Arabiens und seiner Randgebiete. Contributions à l'histoire religieuse de l'Arabie et de ses régions limitrophes. 347 Seiten. 1981.

Bd. 41   DANIEL VON ALLMEN: *La famille de Dieu*. La symbolique familiale dans le paulinisme. LXVII–330 pages, 27 planches. 1981.

Bd. 42   ADRIAN SCHENKER: *Der Mächtige im Schmelzofen des Mitleids*. Eine Interpretation von 2 Sam 24. 92 Seiten. 1982.

Bd. 43   PAUL DESELAERS: *Das Buch Tobit*. Studien zu seiner Entstehung, Komposition und Theologie. 532 Seiten + Übersetzung 16 Seiten. 1982.

Bd. 44   PIERRE CASETTI: *Gibt es ein Leben vor dem Tod?* Eine Auslegung von Psalm 49. 315 Seiten. 1982.

Bd. 45   FRANK-LOTHAR HOSSFELD: *Der Dekalog*. Seine späten Fassungen, die originale Komposition und seine Vorstufen. 308 Seiten. 1982. Vergriffen.

Bd. 46   ERIK HORNUNG: *Der ägyptische Mythos von der Himmelskuh*. Eine Ätiologie des Unvollkommenen. Unter Mitarbeit von Andreas Brodbeck, Hermann Schlögl und Elisabeth Staehelin und mit einem Beitrag von Gerhard Fecht. XII–129 Seiten, 10 Abbildungen. 1982.

Bd. 47   PIERRE CHERIX: *Le Concept de Notre Grande Puissance (CG VI, 4)*. Texte, remarques philologiques, traduction et notes. XIV–95 pages. 1982.

Bd. 48   JAN ASSMANN/WALTER BURKERT/FRITZ STOLZ: *Funktionen und Leistungen des Mythos*. Drei altorientalische Beispiele. 118 Seiten, 17 Abbildungen. 1982.

Bd. 49   PIERRE AUFFRET: *La sagesse a bâti sa maison*. Etudes de structures littéraires dans l'Ancien Testament et spécialement dans les psaumes. 580 pages. 1982.

Bd. 50/1   DOMINIQUE BARTHÉLEMY: *Critique textuelle de l'Ancien Testament*. 1. Josué, Juges, Ruth, Samuel, Rois, Chroniques, Esdras, Néhémie, Esther. Rapport final du Comité pour l'analyse textuelle de l'Ancien Testament hébreu institué par l'Alliance Biblique Universelle, établi en coopération avec Alexander R. Hulst †, Norbert Lohfink, William D. McHardy, H. Peter Rüger, coéditeur, James A. Sanders, coéditeur. 812 pages. 1982.

Bd. 50/2 DOMINIQUE BARTHÉLEMY: *Critique textuelle de l'Ancien Testament*. 2. Isaïe, Jérémie, Lamentations. Rapport final du Comité pour l'analyse textuelle de l'Ancien Testament hébreu institué par l'Alliance Biblique Universelle, établi en coopération avec Alexander R. Hulst †, Norbert Lohfink, William D. McHardy, H. Peter Rüger, coéditeur, James A. Sanders, coéditeur. 1112 pages. 1986.

Bd. 51 JAN ASSMANN: *Re und Amun*. Die Krise des polytheistischen Weltbilds im Ägypten der 18.–20. Dynastie. XII–309 Seiten. 1983.

Bd. 52 MIRIAM LICHTHEIM: *Late Egyptian Wisdom Literature in the International Context*. A Study of Demotic Instructions. X–240 Seiten. 1983.

Bd. 53 URS WINTER: *Frau und Göttin*. Exegetische und ikonographische Studien zum weiblichen Gottesbild im Alten Israel und in dessen Umwelt. XVIII–928 Seiten, 520 Abbildungen. 1983.

Bd. 54 PAUL MAIBERGER: *Topographische und historische Untersuchungen zum Sinaiproblem*. Worauf beruht die Identifizierung des Ǧabal Mūsā mit dem Sinai? 189 Seiten, 13 Tafeln. 1984.

Bd. 55 PETER FREI/KLAUS KOCH: *Reichsidee und Reichsorganisation im Perserreich*. 119 Seiten, 17 Abbildungen. 1984. Vergriffen.

Bd. 56 HANS-PETER MÜLLER: *Vergleich und Metapher im Hohenlied*. 59 Seiten. 1984.

Bd. 57 STEPHEN PISANO: *Additions or Omissions in the Books of Samuel*. The Significant Pluses and Minuses in the Massoretic, LXX and Qumran Texts. XIV–295 Seiten. 1984.

Bd. 58 ODO CAMPONOVO: *Königtum, Königsherrschaft und Reich Gottes in den Frühjüdischen Schriften*. XVI–492 Seiten. 1984.

Bd. 59 JAMES KARL HOFFMEIER: *Sacred in the Vocabulary of Ancient Egypt*. The Term *DSR*, with Special Reference to Dynasties I–XX. XXIV–281 Seiten, 24 Figuren. 1985.

Bd. 60 CHRISTIAN HERRMANN: *Formen für ägyptische Fayencen*. Katalog der Sammlung des Biblischen Instituts der Universität Freiburg Schweiz und einer Privatsammlung. XXVIII-199 Seiten. 1985.

Bd. 61 HELMUT ENGEL: *Die Susanna-Erzählung*. Einleitung, Übersetzung und Kommentar zum Septuaginta-Text und zur Theodition-Bearbeitung. 205 Seiten + Anhang 11 Seiten. 1985.

Bd. 62 ERNST KUTSCH: *Die chronologischen Daten des Ezechielbuches*. 82 Seiten. 1985.

Bd. 63 MANFRED HUTTER: *Altorientalische Vorstellungen von der Unterwelt*. Literar- und religionsgeschichtliche Überlegungen zu «Nergal und Ereškigal». VIII–187 Seiten. 1985.

Bd. 64 HELGA WEIPPERT/KLAUS SEYBOLD/MANFRED WEIPPERT: *Beiträge zur prophetischen Bildsprache in Israel und Assyrien*. IX–93 Seiten. 1985.

Bd. 65 ABDEL-AZIZ FAHMY SADEK: *Contribution à l'étude de l'Amdouat*. Les variantes tardives du Livre de l'Amdouat dans les papyrus du Musée du Caire. XVI–400 pages, 175 illustrations. 1985.